Where Christ Is Present

Where Christ Is Present

A Theology for All Seasons on the
500th Anniversary of the Reformation

EDITED BY
John Warwick Montgomery

AND
Gene Edward Veith

BOOKS

An imprint of 1517.the Legacy Project

Where Christ Is Present:
A Theology for All Seasons on the Eve of the 500th Anniversary of the Reformation

© 2015 John Warwick Montgomery

Published by:
New Reformation Publications
PO Box 54032
Irvine, CA 92619-4032

Printed in the United States of America

All Scripture quotations are from the English Standard Version.
Copyright © 2001 by Crossway. Used by permission. All rights reserved.

Library of Congress Cataloging-in-Publication Data

Library of Congress Control Number: 2015937517

ISBN:978- 1-945500-03-9 Hard Cover

ISBN:978- 1-945500-09-1 Soft Cover

ISBN:978-1-945500-13-8 E-Book

NRP Books is committed to packaging and promoting the finest content for fueling a new Lutheran Reformation. We promote the defense of the Christian faith, confessional Lutheran theology, vocation and civil courage.

For
Dr. Howard Hoffman
Kurt and Debra Winrich
Dr. Robert Meyer
Steve Bryant, Esq.
Lay Lutherans Worthy of the Reformer

Contents

CHAPTER 1

Introduction

You Are Looking for a Church Home— or Perhaps You Aren't?

John Warwick Montgomery

The five hundredth anniversary of the heroic Protestant Reformation is upon us. But many people today haven't a clue as to why this event is so important. The purpose of this book is to make it impossible to ignore what occurred on the Eve of All Saints Day, 1517—and its tremendous significance for every one of us. In picking up this book, you are either (1) searching for a more satisfactory church home or (2) wondering why anyone would want a church home in the first place. Since this book is oriented to those readers in the first category, let me begin by saying a few words to those in the second.

If your life is just fine—no special problems other than an ingrown toenail or a few sudden bills to pay that you didn't expect— you see no point in disturbing Sunday recreation by way of attendance at a church service. But consider the following: life is remarkably precarious. In a French existentialist short story, a character receives a slight puncture wound and it proves fatal. Even if you live to the age of one hundred, eternity is considerably longer.

Moreover, there is the common human experience of boredom. Events display remarkable similarity. Those seeking satisfaction in life tire of what they are doing, whatever the activity. Relations with one partner become tiresome (thus the modern phenomenon of "serial monogamy"), but the next connection soon parallels the first (cf. the celebrated adage, "All cats are grey at night"). Those who think the answer is money never have enough; more is always better. Education? "Of the making of books there is no end, and study is a weariness of the flesh"—a remark by the author of Ecclesiastes when the number of books was immensely less than it is today.

If you don't have a transcendent center to your life, you are forced to become a demigod to yourself. In a nineteenth-century Russian novel, one of the characters—an atheistic nihilist—invites friends to his dacha; everything is tightly scheduled and organized with military precision. A guest asks, "As an atheist, why do you bother?" The answer: "It is *because* I am an atheist that I must live this way."

Oscar Hammerstein II and Jerome Kern captured the *Angst* of this world in their famous *Show Boat* libretto, "Ol' Man River": "Ah gits weary An' sick of tryin'/ Ah'm tired of livin' An' skeered of dyin.'"[1]

Why are we "skeered of dyin'"? Because in our moments of the "dark night of the soul," we are well aware of our imperfection and our radical self-centeredness—how much we have hurt others during our mortal pilgrimage. We also intuitively know that God is perfect and that "whosoever shall keep the whole law, and yet offend in one point, he is guilty of all" (James 2:10). Thus we are "without excuse" (Rom. 1:20) and fear that day when we shall stand before the Almighty Judge. What we need is a Savior—Christ as our "advocate" (1 Jn. 2:1).

The only satisfying answer to the human dilemma is, therefore, to "let God be God" (to quote the felicitous book title on Luther's theology by Philip Watson) rather than trying to play God.

But why the Christian God? Because, in short, the gods of all the other religions lack testability. Only the Christian God comes to earth and displays himself—and that "by many infallible proofs" (Acts 1:3). The longest biographical article in the greatest scholarly edition (the 11th) of the *Encyclopedia Britannica* is devoted to Jesus Christ. His historicity is solidly established, and the primary sources—by eyewitnesses and close associates of eyewitnesses—present him not as a Jewish boy scout helping little old ladies across the Sea of Galilee but as one who fulfils a vast number of highly specific Old Testament prophecies, performs miracle after miracle, dies on a Cross to take away the sins of the world, conquers death by his resurrection, and ascends to heaven with the promise to return to transform our messy world into its original paradisal state. To oppose this powerful case, one would have to throw away historical scholarship in general.[2]

So, in short, even if you pick up this book not caring much about eternity, the transcendent, or religion, you need to move up to a serious consideration of these issues. As humans, we are contaminated with self-centeredness, and it destroys our personal and societal relationships. Christianity is the only demonstrable solution for this misery: "If any person is in Christ, he is a new creature; old things are passed away, all things become new" (2 Cor. 5:17). Testimonies to the truth of this fact abound across the centuries, from St. Augustine to Billy Graham—and include, it should go without saying, Martin Luther. So why not move from religious indifference to a search for an ideal church home? We all need Jesus Christ and we need an environment in which that relationship is nourished. "Faith comes by hearing," we are told, "and hearing by the Word of God" (Rom. 10:17).

So we start upon a quest for the ideal church home. No one should expect that the search will produce a perfect religious atmosphere; we are imbedded in a sinful world, and perfection must wait for Our Lord's return in glory "to judge both the quick and the dead." But even in our messy world, there is a considerable difference in the quality of ecclesiastical institutions. As the old Negro spiritual nicely puts it, "Everybody talkin' 'bout heaven ain't goin' there."[3] And even if they *are* going to heaven, some churches make the trip immensely more difficult than it should be. Let's consider some major examples, ending with the Lutheran option—since we see this as the best solution (or the lesser of evils, if you insist).

The Mormon Church. It looks like a church, its services appear to be those of a church, and its leaders use the language associated with the Protestant evangelical movement. However, be very careful. As has been shown by detailed examination of the beliefs of the Latter Day Saints, Mormonism is not a Christian denomination at all. It is a sectarian movement of polytheistic or henotheistic character that denies the Holy Trinity and places the Book of Mormon on a level above that of the Bible, such that the Scriptures are superseded by and must therefore be reinterpreted in conformity with Mormon doctrine.[4]

But let us consider the major options within the Christian tradition—those theologies committed to the so-called ecumenical creeds of the church, the Apostles', the Nicene, and the Athanasian Creeds.

Roman Catholicism. In the nineteenth century, John Henry Newman's move to Rome occasioned a considerable stir in Protestant circles. Sadly, shortly thereafter, in 1870, the (first) Vatican Council—to Newman's great frustration—declared the pope infallible when speaking officially (*ex cathedra*) on matters of faith and morals. Today, there have been numerous Protestant—especially Anglican—clergy who have left Protestantism for the Roman Catholic Church. My former student Frank Beckwith, though not theologically trained, did so—without letting me know ahead of time that he was making the move; theological conversation, however, would have made little difference, since Frank's decision, as is evident from his autobiography, was really not a truth issue for him but a move primarily motivated by an inner conviction of divine leading and the desire to return to his familial roots.[5]

One can appreciate the pull of Rome. The Roman Catholic Church has universality and a powerful political and social presence, owing to the nation-state of the Vatican and the hierarchical structure of its ecclesiastical organization. Though deeply penetrated by theological liberalism, ever since the nineteenth-century modernist movement (Loisy and company),[6] it displays the façade of unwavering conservatism—as contrasted with the vagueness and secularity of much of mainline Protestantism. Roman Catholic opposition to abortion has attracted many Protestants whose churches have not taken a stand in behalf of the rights of unborn persons.[7]

However, there are overwhelming reasons not to buy a one-way ticket to Rome. We shall discuss just a few of them.

The Church justifies itself on the basis of the so-called Petrine theory passage in the New Testament: Jesus's response to Peter's confession that Christ is the Messiah: "Thou art Peter and upon this rock I shall build my church" (Matt. 16:18). However, the use of a word for "rock" (*petra*, a foundation) that is not the name of Peter (*petros*, a little stone) strongly suggests that our Lord was not identifying the foundation of the church with the Apostle himself but was actually referring to Peter's *confession* of Christ or to Christ himself—an interpretation that far better accords with the unqualified assertion later in the New Testament that "no other foundation can anyone lay than that which is laid, Jesus Christ" (1 Cor. 3:11)—a passage, incidentally, that clearly contradicts the Roman Catholic notion that Mary or other "saints" can mediate between God and man.[8]

Technically, no tradition in the Roman Catholic Church can be true unless it is grounded in some sense in the Holy Scriptures (including, by the way, the so-called Old Testament Apocrypha, which were not part of the Old Testament Scriptures Jesus used and which became authoritative by way of Jerome's inclusion of them in his Latin translation of the Bible). But it has required an amazing level of contorted hermeneutics to find any possible biblical basis for such teachings as purgatory or the assumption of the Virgin Mary into heaven (i.e., her ascension to heaven without experiencing death).

Moreover, the fundamental notion in Roman Catholic theology that the church is necessary to interpret Scripture suffers from gigantic circularity. If the Petrine theory passage needs the church to define its meaning in order for it to be the *locus classicus* justifying that church's superiority, did the passage have no clear meaning when Jesus originally spoke it and the earthly church (which began at Pentecost) was not yet in existence? And if the Bible is not clear without the church, how are the words of the church (its interpretation of the Bible) clear without a second-level interpreter? Does not the refusal to accept the Bible as self-interpreting destroy the idea that the church's pronouncements can be self-interpreting, thus leading to an infinite regress of theological claims, none of which can then be regarded as meaningful per se?

Furthermore, as the Reformers were at pains to point out, the notion that God's grace is mediated by the church and granted in accord with its canonical regulations (indulgences, penances, etc.)[9] leads directly to works-righteousness and a reduction of the impact of Christ's saving work on the Cross. The church inevitably slips from Christocentrism into anthropocentrism—in tragic contrast with the apostolic, New Testament stress on salvation by grace alone through faith alone, "the article on which the church stands or falls."

And because Roman Catholic theology has never really understood the central biblical doctrine of forensic justification (we are *declared*—not made empirically—righteous as a result of what Christ has done for us on the Cross), it maintains that righteousness is actually *infused* into the believer. To say that this substitutes an unrealistic emphasis on personal holiness for the correct biblical understanding of fallen man as having nothing for which to boast and being in perpetual need to return daily to the Cross for forgiveness and grace is to put it mildly. We shall observe later the very same failing in Protestant Arminianism and holiness theologies.

The results of Roman Catholicism's focus on the church itself rather than the Scriptures have been exceedingly unfortunate. Thus clerical celibacy (nowhere required of clergy in the Bible) has been one of the chief factors in the disastrous spate of sex scandals involving the priesthood across the globe. Ironically, there has been more stress in Roman Catholic circles on condemning so-called unnatural (i.e., mechanical) methods of birth control—which are nowhere reproved in Holy Scripture—than on condemning unnatural sexual activities, which Scripture categorically refuses to tolerate.

To be sure, if the only denominational choices were between nondoctrinal, secular, mainline liberal Protestantism and Roman Catholic traditionalism, one would doubtless be better off choosing the latter. But as the present book surely makes clear, these are not the only available options when one embarks on the quest for an ideal church.

Churches with Multiple Criteria of Theological Truth: Eastern Orthodoxy and Anglicanism. Eastern Orthodoxy claims that it is the preeminent historical church—going back to apostolic time—even before the organization of the Roman Church within the Western Roman Empire. Not recognizing the authority of the Roman pope, the Eastern Orthodox churches maintain a multiple standard of theological truth: Scripture, tradition, and reason. The result, however, is a theology that often seems as hospitable to unbiblical notions found equally in the Roman Catholic west: the dormition (i.e., assumption) of the Virgin Mary, purgatory, and so on. To be sure, the degree of emphasis on tradition over Scripture varies widely from one Eastern church to another; the Romanian Orthodox Church, for example, is far more scriptural in its theological approach than are the Greek Orthodox or the Russian Orthodox.[10]

Anglicanism likewise employs the threefold criterion of truth— Scripture, tradition, and reason—but, having been deeply influenced by the Protestant Reformation, displays an ecclesiastical style much more Protestant than Roman Catholic.[11] In point of fact, however, within the Anglican Communion, one finds three major subgroups: (1) the low church (emphasis on the Bible), (2) the high church (emphasis on tradition), and (3) the broad church (emphasis on "reason"). Unity is continually lauded: one must not consider those of another subgroup as unworthy of the church. The result is that an evangelical (low-church) Archbishop of Canterbury (George Carey) was followed by an archbishop who was a kind of crossbreed of broad-church liberal and high-church traditionalist (Rowan Williams). In the United States, the Episcopal Church ordains women bishops and has no problems with practicing homosexual and lesbian clergy—in clear defiance of biblical standards. And the conservative Episcopalians who have left the major denomination over this nonetheless insist on retaining a commitment to tradition alongside their belief in scriptural authority.

Another severe Anglican problem lies with its insistence on "apostolic succession" as a mark of the true church. The idea (derived from Roman Catholic dogma) is that proper ordination to the holy ministry must occur through the offices of a bishop in the succession from the original apostles. The problems with such a notion are legion. First, Scripture nowhere sets forth such a requirement; indeed, no single "church order" (Episcopal, Presbyterian, etc.) can be identified in the New Testament—the terms *episcopos, presbyter,* and the like appear to have been often used as synonyms for the pastoral office in general. Second, it is exceedingly difficult, if not impossible, to establish historically a continuous line of bishops from the apostles to the present day. Third—and most important—church officialdom has frequently manifested heretical ideas and false doctrine (think of the late medieval and Renaissance popes). The Lutheran position is far more biblical and satisfactory: the church requires not a *successio personarum* (a succession of persons) but a genuine *successio doctrinae* (a solid succession of biblical teaching).

Why should one not choose these multisource denominational routes, even though they often feature wonderful ceremony and glorious liturgical treasures?[12] For one thing, because of a logical difficulty with grave consequences. If one operates with multiple criteria of truth, one must refer to a higher standard when they disagree—and this higher standard becomes the *actual*, though unstated, criterion of judgment. As I have put it in my *Tractatus Logico-Theologicus*, "For example, one must determine whether a combination of two sources (A, B; B, C; A, C) always takes precedence over the third source in case of disagreement, or whether and under what conditions A, B, or C is to be followed even when opposed by a combination of the other two sources."[13] Concretely, since Anglicans never agree on a single, higher criterion to solve such difficulties, some Anglican communions support women's ordination and homosexual practices (on the basis of "reason") and others deny it (on the basis of Scripture and/ or tradition).

Combined with this severe logical difficulty is the related—and highly dangerous—Anglican approach to doctrinal subscription. Lutherans (Calvinists, too) insist on *quia* subscription to doctrinal statements; that is, one subscribes *because* ("quia") the statement accords with Holy Scripture. But Anglicans traditionally subscribe *quatenus*—"in so far as" the doctrinal statement accords with Scripture. This of course means that the individual subscriber can personally disregard aspects of the doctrinal statement and still subscribe to it. The result is a church in which the doctrinal beliefs of one person (or one clergy person) may be wildly different from and inconsistent with those of another. So even though we praise God for such fine Anglicans as Phillips Brooks (author of "O Little Town of Bethlehem") and C. S. Lewis, we cannot recommend the Anglican alternative.

Calvinism. I grew up in the small, western New York town of Warsaw (though no Poles apparently ever lived there). My parents were members of the Presbyterian Church, which, sadly, had united with the town's Congregational Church to form the United Church of Warsaw. My background was therefore Calvinist—but the local church had long since ceased to be much more than the ecclesiastical equivalent of a social club. After conversion to historical, biblical Christianity through the good offices of an engineering student and the Inter-Varsity Christian Fellowship at Cornell University, I began checking out the doctrinal positions of the major denominations in my search for a church home. Naturally, the Calvinist tradition (Presbyterianism, the Reformed churches) was a leading contender. Why did I not take that route?

Interestingly, a little book, *The Plan of Salvation*, by distinguished Calvinist theologian B. B. Warfield, finished off the Calvinist alternative for me. In that volume, Warfield argues for "double predestination"—that is, God's determination, in eternity, of the ultimate status of both the saved and the lost. Now Scripture definitely teaches that those who are saved must attribute their salvation entirely to the work of God the Holy Spirit; God has elected them from the foundation of the world and they have in no way saved themselves by an act of human will (Jn. 1:13; Eph. 2:8–9). However, the Bible makes equally clear that God would "have all people to be saved and to come unto the knowledge of the truth" (1 Tim. 2:4), and Jesus weeps over Jerusalem, for the inhabitants "would not" be saved (Matt. 23:37). In other words, as Luther put it, members of a fallen race have enough free will to choose damnation but not enough to pull themselves up to heaven by their own bootstraps. True, in Romans 9, God declares, "*What if* I choose vessels for destruction?"—to make crystal clear his sovereignty—but he does not say that in fact he *does* choose people to be damned. Were he to have done that, it would contradict the nature of God as love as taught repeatedly throughout divine revelation. The personal result was that I did not buy the Calvinist understanding of "the plan of salvation."

What is the source of the Calvinist error here? It is a desperate desire (shared by Arminians) to present a logically consistent theology—even when such a laudable endeavor bruises the clear teaching of Scripture. We don't know how the divine election of the saved and the human responsibility for the lost can be reconciled, but we must not draw inferences from either of these scriptural truths that would deny the other truth. As Lutheran theology states it, one must never infer from one biblical teaching a doctrine in contradiction with another clear biblical teaching.

Later I discovered that this chimerical quest for a more "rational" theology infects the Calvinist system in general. So the Calvinist will not agree to the real presence of Christ—body and spirit—in the Lord's Supper, even though Christ in instituting the Eucharist states unequivocally, "This is my body," and Paul says that some are sick and others have died as a result of taking holy communion "without discerning the Lord's body" (1 Cor. 11:27–30). Why? Because a body (the Calvinist declares) can't be in two places at once. To retain

the sacramental character of the Eucharist, the Calvinist either constructs a special meaning of the liturgical phrase *sursum corda* ("lift
up your hearts") so that our spirits are raised to heaven to commune
with Christ there—he is apparently glued to a position on the right
hand of the Father—or communes with Him "spiritually" in a special
way here on earth during the Communion. I found all such rational-
ization unnecessary at best and spurious at worst. With Luther, who,
in the great Marburg colloquy against Zwingli, just kept writing on
the table with chalk, "*Hoc est corpus meum*," I prefer to believe that
God can be wherever He wishes, body as well as spirit. Odd that
this poses a problem for twenty-first century people, when we have
known for a century that matter and energy are interconvertible.

Finally, I found most Calvinist church services unutterably dull
and didactic. The Calvinist stress on Law and on the Old Testament
colors their worship in general. One is reminded of Calvin's Genevan
rite of 1542, which is so condemnatory and legalistic that even Calvinists almost never use it.[14] True, Presbyterians and the Reformed
churches have in recent years learned much from the stronger liturgical traditions, but they still have a long way to go. The three-hour
sermons of Puritan divines are now but history, but the Calvinist
preacher has a real problem being concise. I rather like the humor-
ous Lutheran adage, "No one is saved after the first twenty minutes."[15]

**Evangelicalism (Often with Arminian, Holiness, and Charis-
matic Twists).** The dynamism of evangelical congregations is often a
powerful force in drawing one to their church life—especially if one
has experienced the misery of liberal churches, where the secular is
elevated to ultimate significance and where the thrills are minimal as
one wraps bundles for the Red Cross or participates in anticapitalist
and environmentalist rallies.

But once one has heard the evangelistic message and responded
to it, what then? The pastor is often without a solid theological education, with so little knowledge of Greek and Hebrew that he could
not even order a hamburger at a McDonald's in Athens or Jerusalem. The preaching tends to follow the (limited) spiritual experience of the preacher instead of drawing on the in-depth resources
of the church through the centuries. One hears trivial melodies and
poverty-stricken repetitions ("I'm so happy") instead of the glories of Bach and Mendelssohn; the marimba, not the organ. Indeed,

personal experience seems to substitute for Scripture; spiritual fads seem more important than doctrinal truth. If indeed "faith comes by hearing and hearing by the word of God," there is little opportunity for spiritual growth, since the Word is subordinated to religious experientialism.

Many (but by no means all) evangelical churches are Arminian in theology—whether they would recognize the term or not. The stress is placed on man's decision making: "decisions for Christ." And because there is no real understanding of God's election and our inability to save ourselves, the congregation is never really sure of its salvation. Thus parishioners "go down the aisle" and return to "the sinner's bench" repeatedly. Instead of God being glorified for His saving work, sinners are made the center of everything through their decision making.

As in Roman Catholicism, where such a theology prevails, at stage center, sanctification/holiness replaces justification. The stress is not on Christ's perfect work for a fallen race but on the sinner's "growth in grace" and increase in "personal holiness." John Wesley's notion of "Christian perfection" gains ground—against all empirical evidence.[16] This of course makes effective evangelism more and more difficult, since those outside the church have no difficulty in identifying "hypocrites in the church" and staying clear of them.

From the Methodist holiness churches to the charismatic movement is a short step. Evidence of holiness and "second blessings" is manifested by miraculous gifts of the spirit (healings, speaking in tongues). The problems here are overwhelming: as linguists have emphasized, language must have some recognizable structure, which is conspicuously absent in charismatic utterances;[17] and divine healing, though a reality, cannot be programmed by the likes of television evangelists. We restrain ourselves from ringing the changes on the unbiblical aberrations of the so-called Word of Faith Movement (being "slain in the spirit"), the heretical preaching that with sufficient faith one will no longer suffer illness or financial difficulty, and so on. Again, those outside the church are often quicker to identify ecclesiastical nonsense than those within. The real tragedy, to be sure, is that in such contexts, the lost, instead of being drawn to the gospel and new lives, are driven in exactly the opposite direction.

Lutheranism. My examination of the confessional standards of the major church traditions following my conversion had a remarkable result. On *all*—not just some or the majority—of the disputed issues, the Lutheran position came out miles ahead of the others. Why was that? I would later come to see that the fundamental reason was that the Lutheran theology—from the time of Luther to the present—has insisted on taking Scripture *exactly as it is* rather than molding it to fit preconceived notions of what theology should be saying (whether it in fact says that or not).

Infant baptism gave me a bit of a problem. (I think of my dear, late friend Walter R. Martin, whose theology was fully Lutheran—except for his refusal to go along with infant baptism.) There is the hilarious Baptist tract titled "What the Bible Has to Say about Infant Baptism"—you open it, and it is entirely blank!

But in fact the Bible *does* speak to this issue. We are told that "without faith it is impossible to please God" (Heb. 11:6), that "faith is the gift of God" (Eph. 2:8–9), and that "faith comes by hearing and hearing by the word of God" (Rom. 10:13–17). But persons who have not yet arrived at the age of accountability (infants) cannot understand the preached word, so for them the word of salvation has to reach them in another way. That way is indicated when the New Testament speaks of "the washing of water by the word" (Eph. 5:26) and that "baptism doth now save us" (1 Pet. 3:21). Thus Jesus's Great Commission is to "go baptize all nations" (Matt. 28:19)—citizenship under the Roman law consisting, as today, of all those (including infants) born within the country or naturalized. It follows that infants should indeed be baptized—giving them the gift of Holy Spirit through the word. They (sadly) may depart from their baptism later in life,[18] but they can always return, like the prodigal son, to their father's house, for He gave Himself for them even before they could act in their own behalf.[19]

Seeing the superiority of Lutheran confessional theology over its rivals was more than a little awkward for me personally. I had never participated in liturgical worship. When the Lutheran congregation stood up, I was sitting down; when I stood up, they were sitting down. It took me a good while to discover that the services relied on millennia-old worship and benefited from the spiritual experience not just of the pastor but of a multitude of generations of believers. I discovered that the liturgy, the ecclesiastical paraments, and the clerical vestments represent and can convey the central gospel message and therefore serve as a source of preaching in themselves. So even if the preacher has a bad hair day, the gospel and central biblical truths are proclaimed. It was impossible not to go away blessed and on a level of genuine depth—what has been called not mere "happiness" but "joy."

And the church services were not mere social occasions; they were "vertically," not "horizontally," oriented. They were not rituals; they were sacramental. The Lord's Supper was not a time for lady-fingers and lemonade. As Jesus said, in the Eucharist, He is specially present—the whole Christ, body and spirit—"for the forgiveness of sins," a foretaste of that heavenly kingdom where those who have relied on Him alone for salvation will be in His presence forever. Moreover, as against the atmosphere of legalistic "religion" (root meaning: "binding") manifested in very many church settings, I found in Lutheranism not the prohibitory, negative teaching that one's activities should be limited to what is commanded in the Bible but rather the liberating viewpoint that one can do whatever is not prohibited in the Bible. So learning, science, literature, film, art, music—the entire world of God's creation was open to the believer, whose responsibility and privilege it is to conquer it for Christ. No longer was one constantly questioning whether it was "sinful" to engage in this activity or the other; instead, one began to experience what Luther called "Christian liberty"—the freedom to use all creation to serve others: "A Christian is a perfectly free lord of all, subject to none; A Christian is a perfectly dutiful servant, subject to all."[20]

So read the chapters of this book with care and see if you don't agree that, though no church is perfect, there is one ecclesiastical option whose theology, worldview, and perspective on life in this sinful world warrants your closest attention—and perhaps even commitment.

Notes

1. Jerome Kern and Oscar Hammerstein II, "Ol' Man River," from *Showboat* (1927). Quoted from International Lyrics Playground, http://lyricsplayground.com/alpha/songs/o/olmanriver.shtml.

2. I have made this point *in extenso* in my apologetics writings (see http://www.ciltpp.com and New Reformation Press, http://www.1517legacy.com). See especially my books *History, Law and Christianity* (Calgary, AB:

Canadian Institute for Law, Theology, and Public Policy, 2002); *Where Is History Going?* (Minneapolis, MN: Bethany, 1972); *Faith Founded on Fact* (Nashville, TN: Thomas Nelson, 1978); *Tractatus Logico-Philosophicus* (Eugene, OR: Wipf & Stock, 2013); *Christ as Centre and Circumference* (Eugene, OR: Wipf & Stock, 2012).

3. Quoted from LyricsMania, http://www.lyricsmania.com/everybody _talkin_bout_heaven_lyrics_acappella.html.

4. See, in particular, the publications of Walter R. Martin, such as *The Maze of Mormonism* (Grand Rapids, MI: Zondervan, 1962).

5. Francis J. Beckwith, *Return to Rome: Confessions of an Evangelical Catholic* (Grand Rapids, MI: Brazos Press, 2008).

6. Cf. John Warwick Montgomery, *Ecumenicity, Evangelicals, and Rome* (Grand Rapids, MI: Zondervan, 1969); Montgomery, "The Approach of New Shape Roman Catholicism to Scriptural Inerrancy: A Case Study," in *God's Inerrant Word: An International Symposium on the Trustworthiness of Scripture* (Minneapolis, MN: Bethany, 1974), 263–81.

7. Significantly, the Lutheran Church–Missouri Synod and the Wisconsin Evangelical Lutheran Synod, among major Protestant denominations, have consistently maintained theological opposition to abortion as being contrary to the will of God.

8. The argument that in Aramaic (spoken by Jesus) the distinction between *petra* and *petros* doesn't exist is irrelevant. What Jesus said is known only by way of Matthew's Greek account of it, and he makes the distinction. Thus Jesus must have made the distinction—even though he would not have done so by employing the equivalent of the Greek vocabulary. See Montgomery, "The Petrine Theory Evaluated by Philology and Logic," in *The Shape of the Past: An Introduction to Philosophical Historiography*, 2nd ed. (Minneapolis, MN: Bethany, 1975), 351–57.

9. Indulgences, by the way, are still very much a part of Roman Catholic Church life. See Thomas Schirrmacher, *Indulgences: A History of Theology and Reality of Indulgences and Purgatory: A Protestant Evaluation* (Bonn, Germany: Verlag fuer Kultur und Wissenschaft, 2011).

10. When I spent two weeks in Bucharest, receiving the Patriarch's medal of the Romanian Orthodox Church for my successful case against the Moldovan government in behalf of the Bessarabian Orthodox Church (under the Romanian patriarchate), I was amused to listen to severe criticism of the Patriarch of Constantinople (the primus inter pares) of Eastern Orthodoxy.

11. The Anglican Reformation in its first generation was deeply colored by Lutheran theology; see Henry Eyster Jacobs, *The Lutheran Movement in England* (Philadelphia: G. W. Frederick, 1890); Neelak S. Tjernagel, *Henry VIII and the Lutherans: A Study in Anglo-Lutheran Relations from 1521 to 1547* (St. Louis, MO: Concordia, 1965). By the second generation, Calvinist

influence became predominant. The Elizabethan settlement entailed the creation of a church that would "comprehend" (i.e., cover) the entire nation, regardless of doctrinal differences. Thus, the Thirty-Nine Articles can be subscribed to by those in the low-church, the high-church, and (with a fair number of mental reservations!) the broad-church contingent.

12. While living for a decade in England, my wife and I often attended Anglican services. (Finding a good Lutheran church there is not easy, especially because most Lutherans living in England are of Scandinavian origin.) The diocese of London is generally conservative and churches serving the legal community (the Temple Church, Lincoln's Inn Chapel) have a tradition of serious biblical preaching and theological solidity.

13. Montgomery, *Tractatus Logico-Theologicus*, 5th ed. (Bonn, Germany: Verlag fuer Kultur und Wissenschaft, 2012), proposition 2.1621.

14. See Montgomery, "The Celebration of the Lord's Supper according to Calvin," in *Christ as Centre and Circumference* (Bonn, Germany: Verlag fuer Kultur and Wissenschaft, 2012), 298–313.

15. Having said all of this, I wish to acknowledge fine Calvinist friends such as Dr. Michael Horton and express genuine appreciation for such solid evangelical church bodies as the Presbyterian Church in America (PCA).

16. Fortunately, few of the classic hymns by John and Charles Wesley are contaminated by notions of hypersanctification and hyperperfectionism.

17. See Montgomery, "Prophecy, Eschatology, and Apologetics," in *Looking into the Future*, ed. David W. Baker (Grand Rapids, MI: Baker Academic, 2001), 362–70; also Montgomery, *Christ Our Advocate* (Bonn, Germany: Verlag fuer Kultur und Wissenschaft, 2002), 255–65.

18. Contra Calvinist theology, the saved individual can subsequently fall away, since God's grace is resistible (Acts 7:51; 1 Thess. 5:19; Heb. 6:4–6). Once the child reaches the age of accountability—that age of course varying from person to person—he/she must "confirm" by personal acceptance what was received in baptism through entering into a conscious personal relationship with Christ (thus the place of Confirmation in the public life of the church).

19. We do not know the state of unbaptized infants who die before reaching the age of accountability—though we know that God is love and does not want anyone to perish (1 Tim. 2:4). But we *do* know that baptized infants are saved—so a Christian parent should surely want that gift of grace for his/her child.

20. Luther, "The Freedom of a Christian," in *Martin Luther: Selections from His Writings*, ed. John Dillenberger (New York: Anchor Books, 1962), 53.

CHAPTER 2

The Religious Landscape in the Twenty-First Century

Gene Edward Veith

Five hundred years ago, the church of Jesus Christ underwent a Reformation. The fallout from Luther's posting of his ninety-five theses on indulgences was not simply the birth of Protestantism. The Roman Catholic Church also recast itself in response to Luther's call for reforms. Had there been no Reformation, there would have been no Counter-Reformation correcting some of the abuses highlighted by Luther (e.g., the charging of money for indulgences and church offices) and promoting the kind of personal piety—as opposed to medieval formalism—associated with Catholicism today (such as praying the rosary and other devotional exercises).[1] Luther did not, as is often said, "start a new church," much less "start his own church"; rather, he was trying to reform the church that already existed by reemphasizing its essence—namely, the "good news" (the gospel) that Christ saves sinners.

The unity of the church was broken when the pope rejected the calls for reform and excommunicated Luther, starting a chain of events that did lead to the institutional fracturing of Christendom and to a plethora of alternative Christian theologies. But five hundred years ago, as almost everyone—including conservative Catholics—now admits, the church did in fact need reforming. Today, the church—including its Protestant branches—also needs reforming. Some of the issues in contemporary Christianity are very similar to those in the late Middle Ages, though others are new. But if Luther's theology can be blamed, however unfairly, for fragmenting Christianity, perhaps today it can help us recover the wholeness of Christianity.

This chapter will survey the current religious climate in the twenty-first century, an era that is simultaneously highly religious and highly secularized, a time of extraordinary spiritual and theological diversity. In the course of the discussion and in the spirit of the anniversary we are observing, I will propose some theses—not ninety-five, only four—on the kind of Christianity that is best suited for the twenty-first century.

The remedies I am offering are available by way of the same theology that was the catalyst for reforming the church five hundred years ago—Lutheranism—the case for which will be made more fully in the other chapters of this book.

Christianity and Secularism

Contrary to the expectations of nineteenth-century progressives, twentieth-century modernists, and twenty-first-century New Atheists, Christianity has not died out; rather, Christianity is flourishing and growing around the world.[2] Far from making Christianity unthinkable, modernity seems to be a factor in Christianity's growing acceptance.[3] Postmodernity too, with its reaction against Enlightenment-style materialism, has also created a climate that is open to supernaturalist worldviews, including that of Christianity.[4]

Most of the exponential growth of Christianity today is taking place in China, Africa, South America, and other areas that used to be called the "mission field." "Over the last century," says the groundbreaking researcher Philip Jenkins, "the center of gravity in the Christian world has shifted inexorably away from Europe, southward, to Africa and Latin America, and eastward, toward Asia. Today, the largest Christian communities on the planet are to be found in those regions."[5]

It should be noted that this growth has been and often is occurring in the teeth of intense persecution. Many Christians in these regions are being imprisoned and killed, their churches burned and their homes vandalized.[6] These Christian believers are suffering for their faith, as did the early Christians in the Roman Empire—a sign of authentic church growth, the blood of the martyrs being (as the adage correctly puts it) the seed of the church.

There is, however, an important exception to the triumph of Christianity over secularism throughout the world. That exception is Western Europe, historically the cultural center of the Christian faith and the source of the original evangelization of those "mission fields." The distinguished sociologist Peter Berger (a Lutheran) has opined that the fact of Western Europe's becoming increasingly secular while the rest of the world is growing increasingly religious is "one of the most interesting questions in the sociology of religion today."[7]

Part of the explanation for this is the phenomenon of the state church, which by its nature favors cultural conformity and thus liberal theology. The tax-supported state churches of northern Europe (including, sadly, nominally Lutheran ones) have in the modern era rejected the authority of Scripture and downplayed a supernatural worldview in favor of left-wing political causes. They have also used their privileged legal position to restrict and marginalize competing and more orthodox religious groups. In Germany and Scandinavia, this has included confessional Lutherans.

Predominantly Roman Catholic countries, such as Ireland, Italy, and Poland, are far less secularized, with the exception of those having a strong leftist anticlerical tradition, such as Spain and France.[8] Thus European churches have been secularizing themselves, and their influence has been to secularize their societies.[9]

The story of the United States is mixed. While former European colonies such as Canada and Australia are highly secular, with very low church attendance, the United States is, at least on the surface, very religious and very Christian. According to a recent Pew-Templeton study, 78.3 percent of Americans identify themselves as Christians.[10] Around 40 percent say that they attend church services every week.[11] Thus the nation that has most defined modernity and postmodernity is nevertheless highly religious.

At the same time, the mainline Protestant churches, for the most part, have followed their European counterparts in embracing culturally conformist, quasi-secularist theologies. And quite understandably, like the European state churches, mainline Protestant church bodies in the United States have been dwindling in membership.

Those mainline Protestant denominations—the Episcopalian, Methodist, Congregationalist, Presbyterian, and even Lutheran church bodies—that had immense influence on the American value system during her developing years (the sixteenth through the eighteenth centuries) but that in the nineteenth and twentieth centuries embraced biblical criticism and liberal theology now account for less than 18 percent of the population.[12]

Instead, churches that have resisted secularism in favor of a supernaturalist worldview have been growing. Evangelicals now constitute the largest Christian category in America, accounting for 26.3 percent of Americans. Roman Catholics are next at 23.9 percent.[13]

Yet, despite their success, evangelicals—defined roughly as those Protestant Christians who believe in the "gospel" (*evangel*) and who have a high view of the authority of Scripture (the Pew studies classify us confessional Lutherans in this group)—have also felt the pull of secularism and the temptation to cultural conformity. There are still evangelicals—those who prefer the label "fundamentalist"—who believe in separating themselves from the world, refusing to listen to secular music or to mix socially with non-Christians, and, in general, disengaging themselves from "worldly affairs." During the first half of the twentieth century, this was a common perspective among many very conservative Protestants. Christians not only retreated from the public square, diminishing the very possibility of Christian influence; they created a subculture of their own. Such a viewpoint still can be found, but most conservative Protestants now speak of engaging, influencing, and even taking over the culture.

This has entailed a political turnaround. Since the nineteenth century, mainstream Protestants have promoted the "social gospel," displacing the promises of spiritual transformation and eternal life from the individual to the collective. Salvation, for them, moved from an individual concern to a focus on programs to change society as a whole by way of social transformation and the creation of this-worldly utopias. In practice, this has meant a focus on political activism. Since the latter part of the twentieth century, the mainline Protestant churches have pursued a social gospel of the left. It has been said that one of the best ways to determine the agenda of the leftist wing of the Democratic Party is to read the pronouncements of the National Council of Churches or the resolutions from the annual conventions of mainline Protestant denominations.[14]

But in an odd mirror image of the liberal churches, in recent decades many evangelicals have been pursuing a social gospel of the right. The "Christian right" has become a political force, to the point that what was said about the mainline Protestants and their alliance with liberal Democrats can now be said about evangelicals and conservative Republicans. Certainly, political involvement on the part of Christians, as with all citizens, is a good thing, and an individual's Christianity can inform social activism in many ways. But for a church to become caught up in the power games of partisan politics weakens its transcendent focus and confuses its message to outsiders. Many Americans now associate evangelical Christianity with right-wing politics instead of with the good news of Jesus Christ.

Ironically, now that right-wing conservatism has somewhat fallen out of favor, many evangelicals, in their quest to identify with the prevailing culture, are turning toward the left. The so-called progressive evangelicals are championing environmentalism, civil rights, and antiwar messages, similar to the mainline Protestant agenda. Again, some of these causes can be commendable, but when a church adopts a political agenda, whether from the right or from the left, it tends to be at the expense of its transcendent spiritual identity and message.

Thesis 1. The church of the twenty-first century must solve its cultural problem; that is, it must embrace a theology of culture that shows how it can avoid worldliness while also equipping Christians to be engaged positively in their societies—being "in the world" without being "of the world." This solution can be found in the Lutheran doctrines of vocation and the Two Kingdoms.

Pop Christianity

Evangelicals, in their success, are also pursuing another accommodation to secularist culture. In their zeal to grow in numbers, evangelicals have in large part adopted the "church growth movement," which employs sociological research to attract new members by changing the church in order to make it more attractive to the target culture. To make themselves more appealing to the unchurched, congregations are taught to eliminate "obstacles" ranging from the lack of parking to an overemphasis on theological doctrines and to meet the target audience's "felt needs"—for friendship, self-esteem, material well-being, help with personal problems, and the like.[15]

Congregations are urged to be "seeker-sensitive"—that is, to tailor their preaching, worship, and programming to the desires of the unchurched. Sermons should be upbeat, therapeutic, and practical. Worship should eliminate traditional elements that are likely to be unfamiliar to the unchurched, such as classic hymns and liturgies. Instead, worship should employ contemporary music, replacing the organ with guitars and drums, emulating the styles and melodies of pop music. Sanctuaries are redesigned as concert auditoriums, with a huge video screen to project film clips, song lyrics, or images of the preacher. Some church growth congregations employ "entertainment evangelism," with professional vocalists instead of congregational singing, dramatic performances, and the pastor acting as the master of ceremonies. After all, it is argued, people today are entertainment oriented. They spend their time watching television, movies, or their computer screens. So, to be relevant culturally, churches also need to be entertaining and to project just about everything onto a screen.

Such religious consumerism accords well with today's market-driven economic culture. Many church growth congregations self-consciously embrace the model of consumerism, targeting "church shoppers" with sophisticated marketing campaigns and catering to their every demand. Many congregations have modeled their buildings so that they resemble shopping malls surrounded by vast parking lots. Some local churches incorporate actual shops into their facilities, including not only bookstores that sell church-branded merchandise but also Starbucks coffee, just like any secular mall.

Some very popular preachers—particularly those who have taken the next step of becoming television stars—have gone so far as to develop what is surely a different gospel—not the biblical gospel of salvation through Christ, and not the "social gospel" of either the left or the right. Rather, they preach the "prosperity gospel," teaching that if you only have faith, God will solve your financial problems and give you an affluent lifestyle. This has become a major

movement in twenty-first-century religion and is especially prominent in independent Pentecostal congregations, African American
churches, suburban megachurches, religious television, and global
third-world Christianity.[16]

Such tactics of the church growth movement have been successful in creating large congregations, producing megachurches with
attendances in the thousands (not that all have "members," since
membership suggests a level of commitment that has been identified
as an obstacle to mega-attendance).

It is noteworthy that most of those who attend megachurches
come not from the ranks of the unchurched but from smaller Christian congregations. A recent study found that only 2 percent of those
in attendance said that they were "not committed followers of Jesus
Christ," and only 6 percent had not attended another church previously.[17] And yet the megachurches chalk up huge attendance figures
that are supposed to represent successful evangelism. Needless to say,
this comes at a cost. Continually adjusting one's message to accom-
modate the theoretical unchurched can be fatal to biblical Christianity. I had a pastor who attended a church growth seminar where
he was told that "people don't want to hear about sin anymore." Sin's
too negative, he was told. Instead, pastors should preach "positive"
messages that people want to hear. I myself attended a church service
a few weeks before Christmas where the sermon theme was "How
to Avoid Stress at Christmastime." The preacher had nothing to say
about the Divine Child who was born that day or why He came.

Even churches that have adopted church growth tactics and
that have retained their Christian identity and their evangelical message run into problems. Few members of a megachurch are personally acquainted with their pastors, and few of the pastors know more
than a few people in their flock. Almost by design, the theological
teaching in these churches, geared as it is for non-Christians, tends
to remain at a very elementary level. Christians who have reached
a certain level of spiritual maturity often complain of their church's
"shallowness." But, as Ken Myers has shown, churches that try to
emulate the pop culture—the commercialized products of the entertainment industry—*cannot* be demanding or offer complex content.
The "high culture" of the fine arts, the great ideas, and the heritage of
civilizations offer rich and challenging content. Christianity accords

well with high culture, Myers observes, having inspired a great deal of it. The "folk culture" of historic communities offers traditions, values, and community. Christianity accords well with that dimension of culture. But the pop culture, by its nature, is very different from both high culture and folk culture. At the heart of pop culture is neither excellence (high culture) nor community (folk culture) but buying and selling commodities. The commercialized artifacts of religiosity offered in the church growth movement cannot be overly demanding or represent complex content—lest they drive their customers away. Purveyors of the pop culture, whether the entertainment industry or churches, must cater to the tastes of the customers to attract their business, and their products must lack permanence, going in and out of style, so that more can be sold. Christianity does not accord well, says Myers, with that mind-set.[18]

Even among Christians who seek to be "contemporary," a reaction has begun to set in against megachurches and the church growth movement. The so-called Emergent Church craves a sense of community, best to be found in small, intimate gatherings as opposed to vast auditoriums. The Emergents want a sense of mystery, as opposed to the simplistic messages of the church growthers. They also cringe at the middle-class, suburban, consumer culture that megachurches emulate and to which they appeal. The Emergents see the church growth movement as a "modernist" phenomenon, with its pragmatism and quantitative orientation. They themselves are "postmodern," rejecting the rationalistic reductionism that characterizes the baby boomer generation in favor of the more inward, ironic skepticism of the millennial generation.

But in point of fact, the Emergent Church movement is much like the church growth movement in its desire to be contemporary and to conform to the existing culture. The only difference is what each group considers the "culture." To be sure, the Emergent critique of the megachurch mentality has much to commend it. We can appreciate the Emergent Church in its search for Christian community, meaningful worship, and an authentic spirituality. But in uncritically embracing postmodernism, the Emergent Church tends to be relativist, caring little for traditional doctrines and authoritative theologies. Ironically, though, it is the very doctrines and theology they ignore that can lead them to discover what they are missing in contemporary Christianity and that can open up to them the dimensions of worship and spirituality they crave.

In both the church growth and the Emergent church contexts, the spiritual realm is drained of its meaning and reduced to a banal ideology or commodity. The rich spiritual traditions that have been cultivated in Christianity for centuries—the acts of worship and devotion, the disciplines of prayer and Sacrament, the works of art and devotion—have been largely jettisoned as being irrelevant to today's culture. Sadly, this occurs while many people today are still yearning for a spiritual dimension to their lives.

Their search might lead them to churches where something of that spiritual tradition can still be found—to Roman Catholicism, to Eastern Orthodoxy, or (as we are recommending in this book) to Lutheranism. But many, in frustration or disappointment or both, are leaving Christianity altogether. Some are turning to Islam, Buddhism, or Hinduism, but far more Americans and Europeans are leaving all organized religion behind in an attempt to cultivate their own individualistic theologies and brands of mysticism. They say that they are "spiritual, but not religious." More than 20 percent of Americans fit this category.[19] Those who describe their religious affiliation as "none" while still professing highly personalized spiritual beliefs constitute one of the fastest-growing religious persuasions.[20]

Thesis 2. The Church of the twenty-first century must recover its spiritual heritage. This means rediscovering worship, the Sacraments, the Word of God, and a life of prayer and devotion. Lutheranism shows how this can be done.

The Article by Which the Church Stands or Falls

In sum, Christianity in the twenty-first century is still flourishing, but it is weak. Churches in the United States may be full, but they are often highly secularized or, to use the older term, worldly. Different theologies are competing against each other, and yet many Christians have no particular theology at all or make up their own. So if Christianity is to be revived and the church reformed, it would be well to understand—and return to—the essence of "the faith once delivered to the saints."

What, then, is the essential, defining teaching of Christianity, that which distinguishes it from every other religion? It is *not* belief in the existence of God, belief in life after death, spiritual experiences, or moral demands. These are common to virtually all religions, not just Christianity. What is unique to Christianity is *Jesus Christ*. The definitive Christian teaching is that God became an incarnate human being in order to save us by His life, death, and resurrection. All genuine Christians believe this. We do not save ourselves; Christ saves us.

"Christianity is not a system of man's search for God," observes Peter Kreeft, "but a story of God's search for man."[21] This is a commonplace of Christian thought that takes different forms: The other religions of the world are about what we must do for God; Christianity is about what God has done for us. We do not ascend to God; He descends to us. We are not saved by our works but by Christ's work. Christianity emphasizes God's grace—His initiative, His action, in bringing us to Himself.

Christianity is not primarily about being good or attaining moral perfection; rather, it is about receiving forgiveness. This comes through Christ, who died for our sins on the Cross and rose from the dead so that sinners could receive eternal life as a free gift. This good news of God's grace in Christ is the "gospel" (a word that simply means "good news").

Though all versions of Christianity believe in these fundamentals of the faith, theological traditions and ecclesiastical structures often obscure the central truth of the gospel. That was the key issue during the Protestant Reformation five hundred years ago. Luther nailed his theses to the Castle Church door in Wittenberg because he believed that the gospel, the good news of Christianity, was being undermined by the sale of indulgences. Then it became clear that indulgences were but the tip of the iceberg: the medieval penitential system, the accumulation of merits, purgatory, the spiritual domination of the papacy, and other gross errors in the church of the day were burying the gospel under man-made practices that placed the burden of salvation back onto ourselves.

Certainly it is possible to find the gospel within Roman Catholicism—in St. Augustine, St. Anselm, in liturgies, in art and literature (one thinks of Francis Thompson's "Hound of Heaven" and Flannery O'Connor's short stories). But Rome teaches that though we are saved by God's grace, that grace, by way of the ministrations of the Church, enables us to *become* righteous and thus to *merit* our salvation. In practice, this means that, after all, it is the works we do through this "infused righteousness" that determine our salvation—not the unmerited work of Christ on the Cross on our behalf.

Other theologies may begin with God's act of salvation for us, but they often end up with our having to contribute something to save ourselves. Eastern Orthodoxy surely stresses God's Incarnation in Christ but sees salvation in terms of *theosis*, of human beings having to "become God."

Calvinism, to its credit, strongly emphasizes God's grace as accomplishing everything for salvation. And yet, its focus on God's election—that God predestines those who will be saved and those who will be damned—can have the effect of making the Cross seem superfluous. This impression is bolstered by the Calvinist doctrine of Limited Atonement, which restricts the efficacy of Christ's death to the elect, denying that Christ died for the sins of the whole world. Calvinists are thus sometimes prone to doubting their salvation and are encouraged to prove their election by offering their good works as evidence of their spiritual status. Once again, the Christian is thrown back upon himself or herself—displacing Christ as the sole source of salvation.

The Arminianism of John Wesley and of many evangelicals fully embraces the notion that we must contribute to our own salvation through our acts of decision and our good works. Certainly Arminian evangelicals preach the gospel, including the central truth that Christ died for all so that potentially anyone can be saved. But that salvation first requires an act of the will—a choice, a decision—in order to accept Christ and what He has done. After that conversion experience, followers of Wesley believe that it is possible to live a sinless life—that Christians can attain a state of moral perfection. Again, we are back to depending on our works rather than the work of Jesus Christ.

Baptist evangelicals, who tend to combine elements of Calvinism and Arminianism, gladly embrace Christ's free gift of salvation, but they tend to think of the gospel only in terms of their conversion—when they first became a Christian. After that moment of freedom and release, however, they often fall back under the demands of God's law, with little sense of how the gospel can apply to all life. Pentecostals also stress a personal conversion as a response to the gospel, but soon the focus changes to the cultivation of other supernatural experiences—second blessings, healings, speaking in tongues, gifts of knowledge—which, again, shift the emphasis from the Cross to the believer's performance. Similarly, Mennonites stress a peaceful lifestyle, the Amish foreswear modern technology, and liberal mainline Protestants focus on improving society. But the essence of Christianity—"Christ Jesus came into the world to save sinners, of whom I am the foremost" (1 Tim. 1:15)[22]—is obscured, replaced with one variety or another of self-salvation or moralism.

By contrast, Lutheran theology throws the gospel into high relief and makes it absolutely central in every facet of its teaching and practice. Specifically, Lutherans say that "justification" is the "chief article" of the Christian Church.[23] "Justification" comprises both Christ's work and how it benefits us. Lutheran theologians speak of "objective justification," referring to Christ's atonement for the sins of the whole world on the Cross, and "subjective justification," the individual sinner's reception of Christ's atonement. That subjective justification is the product of faith alone, and the faith itself is the gift of God (Eph. 2:8–9). Our relationship to God is based not on our efforts or our works (were that the case, we would be saving ourselves) but solely on what Christ has done for us. Salvation becomes ours through faith—that is, based on trust and dependence, a state created by the Holy Spirit through the Word of God and the Sacraments of Baptism and Holy Communion.

It is vital to note that in Scripture and in Lutheran theology, believing *as such* does not save us. Faith must have an object. I have heard preachers of the prosperity gospel tell their hearers to have faith in *themselves*. Rather, the object of our faith must be Christ. Lutherans thus unpack "justification by faith" by referring to "justification by grace through faith in the work of Christ."

Lutherans say that justification is "the doctrine upon which the church stands or falls." Again, it is the "chief article," the keystone of the entire edifice of theology. This will be evident in the other chapters of this book.

Thesis 3. The church of the twenty-first century must clearly focus on the essence of Christianity—namely, God's incarnation in Jesus Christ, who died for our sins and through whom can be found the free gift of everlasting life. Lutheranism is centered upon this gospel.

The Catholicity of the Church

We may perhaps seem too critical of the variants of Christianity active today. That was not our intention. There are often good reasons new theological emphases emerge and why church bodies separate from each other. One might well see the diversity of Christian thought and practice in terms of 1 Corinthians 12, which teaches that the organs of the body—eyes, ears, hands, feet—are considerably different from each other yet constitute a unified human being. So it is with the church, the Body of Christ. Thus I am not too concerned whether the different church bodies someday reach institutional unity, for I believe that, despite appearances, the church of Jesus Christ—made up of people throughout history and throughout the world whom He has saved—is already unified in Christ.

That being the case, Christians today would do well to take their place within the universal church. Especially given the anti-Christian pressures and assaults that will increasingly characterize the twenty-first century, Christians need to know who their allies are. They will need to understand and to embrace their rich and varied heritage as Christians, which gives them answers to the secularists and a strong foundation to build upon. A vital task for the twenty-first-century church is to recover, for all its diversity, its overriding catholicity.

This was also a much-heralded goal of the twentieth-century church, but its so-called ecumenical movement mostly failed. Its goal was institutional unity, which was to be achieved by minimizing doctrinal differences. This meant, in practice, deemphasizing doctrine in general, purging Christianity of its supernatural claims, thereby leaving only a social gospel and secularized, culturally conforming churches. This is the history of the mainline Protestant denominations that spearheaded the ecumenical movement. Though a measure of institutional coming together was achieved—for example, in the "United" Protestant churches of Canada, Australia, and other countries—the accomplishments of the ecumenical movement have proven mostly superficial.

A more promising way toward catholicity would be to emphasize the teachings all Christian traditions have in common. This is the way of C. S. Lewis and his "mere Christianity." Theologically conservative Christians have followed that approach to good effect. To be sure, "mere Christianity" has little to say about the Sacraments, worship, and other elements that have proven both extremely important and highly controversial in the Christian tradition. To say that Holy Communion, for example, is not important enough to belong to "mere Christianity" is to maintain a very doubtful theological position. At some point, Christianity resists the least-common-denominator approach.

The most obvious way to be "catholic" would seem to be becoming "Roman Catholic." But that would exclude the specific insights and contributions of the various Protestant traditions. Rome now admits that Protestants can be Christians, though they are "separated brethren" who need to repent of their errors and come back under the authority of the pope. But if Protestants are Christians, their Protestantism is surely a facet of the universal church.

Eastern Orthodox Christians seek for a pure expression of the church, and they find it in the church fathers, the early Councils, and an unchanging "holy tradition." This, however, excludes not only Protestants but Roman Catholics as well. The search for catholicity—for the universality of the church—must not exclude vast belief systems within the Christian tradition.[24]

Anglicanism takes seriously the need to be, in some sense, both "Catholic" and "Protestant." Anglicans try to embody a *via media* between the two traditions. In practice, this means worshipping with a rich historical liturgy, as Catholics do, while permitting a wide range of doctrinal beliefs, as Protestants do. Some Anglicans hew to the church fathers and to Thomas Aquinas; others embrace Calvinism; others are evangelical; still others are charismatic. A common way of worship can hold together people of different beliefs—up to a point. But doctrine cannot long be avoided. *Something* will have to be taught from the pulpit and in instruction classes. Too often, trying to find a middle way between Catholicism and Protestantism means being neither fish nor fowl. The default position becomes mainstream liberal Protestantism. Some Anglicans across the world, including a new communion in the United States, are reacting against the liberal theology that has taken root in the Church of England and in the Episcopal Church of the United States. These controversies are evidence that church unity cannot long survive doctrinal divisions.

Let us consider the Lutheran way of being "catholic"—an approach embracing the best of the Christian traditions, including the various kinds of Protestantism. It can perhaps best be appreciated with the help of G. K. Chesterton, then an Anglican but soon to become a Roman Catholic, who underscored the complex character of Christianity. He found that while Christianity is attacked from all sides and for contradictory reasons, the Christianity of the Apostles' Creed by its very nature brings together elements that would seem to be in opposition. It does so not by synthesizing them into a bland compromise but by affirming both sides. "We want not an amalgam or compromise, but both things at the top of their energy; love and wrath both burning," says Chesterton. He continues, "For orthodox theology has specially insisted that Christ was not a being apart from God and man, like an elf, nor yet a being half human and half not, like a centaur, but both things at once and both things thoroughly, very man and very God."[25]

Lutheranism is known for its refusal to force Holy Scripture into neat, rationalistic categories: the Christian is simultaneously a saint and a sinner; Holy Communion is bread and wine and also the true Body and Blood of Christ. Other distinctive Lutheran teachings are similarly paradoxical: the relation between Law and Gospel, the Two Kingdoms, the Theology of the Cross over against a "theology of glory."

Lutheranism is both deeply Catholic *and* deeply Protestant. Lutheranism is *very* sacramental, insisting on Baptismal regeneration and that Christ's body and blood are actually given in Holy Communion. At the same time, Lutheranism is *very* biblical, insisting on the full authority and inerrancy of Scripture and that the Word of God also functions sacramentally, as a means of grace. Roman Catholics are sacramental, with the Bible playing a secondary role, while non-Lutheran Protestants tend to place their focus on God's Word. But Lutheranism denies the dichotomy, insisting on both Word and Sacrament. Lutherans, like Catholics, worship with the historic liturgy; like Protestants, they emphasize preaching. Lutherans, like the Orthodox, study the church fathers and, like the Catholics, study medieval theologians. They affirm and recite the ecumenical Creeds and think of themselves as being continuous with the historic church. Like Protestants, they cultivate a personal faith in Jesus Christ.

Many Lutherans, in fact, prefer to call themselves "evangelical catholics"—because they are not just "Protestants," protesting or focusing on the errors of the papacy. They are "evangelical," a word that comes from the Greek word for the gospel. Historically, the term *evangelical* was the original word for "Lutheran." Many Lutherans, especially in Europe, prefer to be known as "Evangelicals." That word is claimed by many groups in the United States, but Lutherans were at least the first evangelicals.[26] They were called that because the gospel permeates everything in Lutheran theology.

For Lutherans, the Reformation was about reforming the historical church with the gospel—not knocking down the church and trying to build something new from scratch. The Augsburg Confession, perhaps the primary Lutheran statement of faith, describes the evangelical reforms that were necessary to return the church to the gospel of Christ, and it also describes what does *not* need to be reformed in the Christian tradition. As such, it expresses Christian catholicity.

Lutheranism also affirms what is best in the various Protestant theologies that were to come. Like Calvinism, it emphasizes God's grace and that God accomplishes everything needed for our salvation. Like Arminianism, it teaches that Christ died for all and that potentially anyone can be saved. Like Baptists, Lutherans love reading the Bible and preaching the gospel. Like fundamentalists, Lutherans understand that the church must be separate from the world, though like Christian activists of all stripes, Lutherans understand that Christians must be involved in the world as a force for good. Like Pentecostals, Lutherans believe that the Holy Spirit breaks into this world with supernatural gifts that convey a spiritual experience. Those gifts, for Lutherans, are the supernatural realities that are taking place in the Sacraments.

With such comprehensive teachings, Lutherans find themselves assailed from all sides. Roman Catholics attack them for being Protestants, while Protestants attack them for being "too Catholic."

Arminians think they are too Calvinist, and Calvinists think they are too Arminian. Baptists disapprove of Lutherans for having too high a view of Baptism. Pentecostals think Lutherans are too rationalistic and not emotional enough, while the Reformed think Lutheran theology, with its refusal to subject Scripture to rationalistic categories and insistence that Scripture must be taken in its natural, literal sense, is not rational enough.

Lutherans, who have a strong polemical tradition, often find themselves fighting on all sides, taking on Roman Catholics, Calvinists, Arminians, Pentecostals—just about everybody. Chesterton comments on the church's penchant for always battling over what seems to be small points of theology: "It was only a matter of an inch; but an inch is everything when you are balancing."[27] Seen properly, Lutheran theology offers a way to resolve the conflicts by a larger synthesis, one that is grounded in the Word of God.

Thesis 4. The Church of the twenty-first century must recover its catholicity so as to present a unified front to an unbelieving world. This must include preserving and building upon the riches of the historical Church in all its diversity, including the genius of both the Catholic and the Protestant traditions. This is what Lutheranism embodies.

As it did five hundred years ago, Lutheranism offers a way to reform the existing church—not just Catholicism but also Protestantism—by building it upon the foundation of the gospel of Jesus Christ. In doing so, Lutheran theology and practice is uniquely positioned to address the spiritual issues of our day and to bring Christ to the twenty-first century.

Notes

1. See, for example, Nathan D. Mitchel, *The Mystery of the Rosary: Marian Devotion and the Reinvention of Catholicism* (New York: New York University, 2012).

2. See Rodney Stark, *The Triumph of Christianity* (New York: HarperOne, 2012), 369–75, where he discusses the "secularization thesis," that modernity

increases secularism and the decline of religious beliefs. He gives abundant evidence that this is not, in fact, the case. Most other sociologists of religion, including those who once supported the secularization thesis, now agree that it is empirically incorrect.

3. Ibid., 412. This is especially the case in Africa and, most notably, China.

4. See my book *Postmodern Times* (Wheaton, IL: Crossway Books, 1994), 209–23.

5. Philip Jenkins, *The Next Christendom: The Coming of Global Christianity* (New York: Oxford University Press, 2011), 5. This is also true of Lutheranism. The United States has some seven million Lutherans. Asia has nearly eleven million. Africa has twenty-one million. See *The Lutheran World Federation—2013 Membership Figures* (http://www.lutheranworld.org/sites/default/files/LWI-Statistics-2013-EN.pdf). These numbers, which give a total of more than seventy-two million worldwide, do not include all Lutheran church bodies, such as those in the more conservative International Lutheran Council, which does not publish membership figures.

6. See Paul Marshall, Lela Gilbert, and Nina Shea, *Persecuted: The Global Assault on Christians* (Nashville, TN: Thomas Nelson, 2013), who document the persecution coming primarily from Muslims in the Middle East and Africa but also from Communist countries (such as China, North Korea, and Cuba), post-Communist countries (nations of the former Soviet Union), and militant Hindu groups (in India and Nepal). The authors found that "Christians are the single most widely persecuted religious group in the world today" and that "75% of acts of religious intolerance are directed against Christians" (p. 4).

7. Stark, *The Triumph of Christianity*, 375.

8. According to data posted at NationMaster, an online database of global statistics, weekly Church attendance in England is 27 percent; in Sweden, it is 4 percent. In Catholic countries, attendance is 21 percent in France but 44 percent in Italy, 55 percent in Poland, and 84 percent in Ireland. The extremely high rate of weekly church attendance in the conservative Catholic countries would suggest that churches that do not conform to secularism, ironically, are the most relevant in a supposedly secularist cultural climate. See "Church Attendance (Most Recent) by Country," NationMaster.com, accessed November 18, 2013. http://www.nationmaster.com/graph/rel_chu_att-religion-church-attendance.

9. This accords with Stark's analysis, *The Triumph of Christianity*, 375–83.

10. Pew-Templeton Project, *Global Religious Futures* (2013). http://www.globalreligiousfutures.org/countries/united-states#/?affiliations_religion_id=0&affiliations_year=2010&region_name=All%20Countries&restrictions_year=2011.

11. Pew Research, *"Nones" on the Rise*, Religion & Public Life Project, October 19, 2012, http://www.pewforum.org/2012/10/09/nones-on-the-rise-religion.

12. Pew Research, *Religious Landscape Survey*, Religion & Public Life Project, 2008, http://religions.pewforum.org/reports#. For a general treatment of the subject, see John Warwick Montgomery, *The Shaping of America* (Minneapolis, MN: Bethany, 1976).

13. Ibid. These are data from 2008. Such statistics, of course, are fluid and may change from year to year.

14. For a similar comment, see Peter Berger, "The Class Struggle in American Religion," *Christian Century*, February 25, 1981, 198.

15. Readers wishing a more detailed examination and critique of the church growth movement in relation to the pastoral ministry are directed to Robert J. Koester's excellent treatment, *Law and Gospel . . . with Special Reference to the Church Growth Movement* (Milwaukee, WI: Northwestern Publishing House, 1993).

16. For a scholarly study of the Prosperity Gospel movement, see Kate Bowler, *Blessed: A History of the American Prosperity Gospel* (New York, NY: Oxford University Press, 2013). For a critique of the movement, see David W. Jones and Russell S. Woodbridge, *Health, Wealth & Happiness: Has the Prosperity Gospel Overshadowed the Gospel of Christ?* (Grand Rapids, MI: Kregel Publications, 2010).

17. Scott Thumma and Warren Bird, *Not Who You Think They Are: A Profile of the People Who Attend America's MegaChurches*, Hartford Institute for Religion Research (June 2009), http://hirr.hartsem.edu/megaChurch/megaChurch _attender_report.htm.

18. Ken Myers, *All God's Children and Blue Suede Shoes: Christians and Popular Culture* (Wheaton, IL: Crossway, 2012), 23–26.

19. See Robert C. Fuller, *Spiritual but Not Religious: Understanding UnChurched America* (New York: Oxford University Press). Fuller says that 21 percent of Americans describe themselves in this way (4).

20. See Pew Research, *"Nones" on the Rise*.

21. Peter Kreeft, "The Uniqueness of Christianity," in *Fundamentals of the Faith: Essays in Christian Apologetics* (San Francisco: Ignatius Press, 1988), 6.

22. Quotations from the Bible are taken from the *English Standard Version* (Wheaton, IL: Crossway, 2001).

23. See, for example, the Smalcald Articles, Part 2, Article 1, in *Concordia: The Lutheran Confessions* (Saint Louis, MO: Concordia Publishing House, 2005), 289. That formulation also shows how faith, in the Lutheran sense, is inextricably connected to its object—namely, Christ and His Cross.

24. The same holds true, of course, for Protestants. It is true that some evangelicals, Baptists, Pentecostals, Calvinists, and Arminians do not believe that Roman Catholics and the Orthodox are Christians. They often have doubts about each other. Lutherans too can seem sectarian in their polemics, but they

are confessionally obliged to recognize that true Christians can exist even in Church bodies that they consider heterodox.

25. G. K. Chesterton, "Orthodoxy," in *The Everyman Chesterton* (New York: Everyman's Library, 2011), 340.

26. See my book *The Spirituality of the Cross: The Way of the First Evangelicals* (St. Louis, MO: Concordia Publishing House, 2010), 18–20.

27. Chesterton, "Orthodoxy," 349.

CHAPTER 3

Martin Luther and Reformation

An Evangelical Approach—Then and Now

Cameron A. MacKenzie

The dying man was restless. For many years, he had struggled with poor health, and the last few days had been tiring. Now, shortly after supper and prayer, he was suffering from pain and tightness in his chest. Although a first attack subsided and he was able to sleep, he awoke during the night from another, more severe attack and began complaining of weakness. He also started to perspire greatly. He and those around him were now afraid that the end was near, but he had recourse to the Scriptures, quoting Psalm 31:5 (and the words of Jesus!): "Father, into Your hands I commend my spirit. You have redeemed me, O God of truth," and taking comfort in John 3:16, "For God so loved the world." He also prayed, "My heavenly Father, eternal, merciful God, You have revealed Your dear Son, our Lord Jesus Christ, to me. I have known Him; I have become familiar with Him; I love Him and I honor Him as my dear Savior and Redeemer, whom the godless persecute, revile, and abuse. Take my soul to be with You." Later, his companions asked him if he still confessed Christ, the Son of God, as Savior and Redeemer—the doctrine that he had long taught and defended—and he answered clearly, indeed, strongly, "Yes." Soon afterwards, he was dead.[1]

Martin Luther was dead, but he died as an evangelical.[2] In his final moments he offered nothing to God except his faith in Jesus Christ, his Savior. Relying on His Word alone, he committed his soul to God.

Recovering the Gospel

There were other ways to die then as now. Had Luther not been Luther, the initiator of the Protestant Reformation, he might have died as a medieval Catholic, the religion of his childhood and youth. In later years, Luther remembered it as a religion of fear, a faith that presented Christ as a demanding judge, sitting upon a rainbow and committing people to heaven or hell.[3] The Christian life, therefore, meant dedicating oneself to those activities that could ameliorate the wrath of Christ, especially by participating in the ministrations of the Church. Such activities were almost countless and ranged from the trivial (like saying a "Hail, Mary") to the more rigorous (like fasting on Fridays) to the almost impossible (like going on pilgrimage to Jerusalem).[4]

Young Luther did his best to take advantage of the system but failed to find in it the assurance of God's grace that he was looking for. He even became a monk.[5] Much to the chagrin of his hardworking father, who had sacrificed greatly to provide an education that finally brought his son to law school and the brink of prosperity, Martin threw away his material prospects along with his father's dreams by joining a monastery. He did so only after a narrow escape from death. In the midst of a thunderstorm, when a bolt of lightning threw him to the ground, he made a quick bargain with one of heaven's helpers, St. Anne (the mother of the Virgin Mary). Wishing to forestall his meeting with Christ the Judge, Luther promised her to become a monk if only she would save him. When the storm subsided and he was still alive, Luther kept his promise and joined the Augustinian Hermits in Erfurt, where he had been attending school.[6]

According to no less a theologian than Thomas Aquinas, to join a religious order was the equivalent of a second baptism, a chance to wipe the slate of sin clean and start afresh upon a life that would please God.[7] No longer distracted by secular concerns and ambitions, Luther could devote himself exclusively to the service of God—and his soul's salvation. So he did.

In the case of the Augustinians, that meant a life not only of ascetic piety but also of service to the order and to society. Luther not only disciplined his flesh—at times, dangerously so—but also studied theology and eventually taught it at the University of Wittenberg. One topic that interested him was the same that prompted his entrance into the monastery in the first place: How can a person become right with God?

He later recalled his dissatisfaction with the monastic lifestyle. He could *do* what his order required, but he could not change his heart. In fact, the harder he tried, the more he failed. And the more he failed, the angrier he became with God, who, he thought, had predestined him for failure. Years later, he recalled his horror at the notion that the One who was supposed to be so merciful had willfully abandoned men like him to damnation: "I myself was offended more than once, and brought to the very depth and abyss of despair, so that I wished I had never been created a man."[8]

By taking the obligation of works righteousness so seriously—not only outer activities but also inner attitudes—Luther realized how impossible it was ever to have confidence about one's standing before God on the basis of works. But what was the alternative? It took Luther a long time to find it—and historians differ over when and how it happened[9]—but eventually, on the basis of the Scriptures, Luther came to a new understanding of the Christian religion.[10]

Luther's development into a Protestant Reformer was a matter of years, not months or days. At the behest of his superior in the order, John Staupitz—and over Luther's protests—he began teaching theology at Wittenberg in 1512 and lectured on various books of the Bible, beginning with the Psalter and then moving into the Pauline corpus in the New Testament, Romans, Galatians, and Hebrews.[11] Through such studies, Luther came to understand that Christ was not only eschatological Judge but also suffering Savior and that salvation was not a question of man's merit but of God's grace. But how did one obtain this grace in Christ? For a long time, this was Luther's sticking point. Although Christ had done much, Luther still believed that he had to do his own part. And Paul was no help at all—that is, until Luther's "tower experience."[12]

Luther's problem was not only personal, it was also exegetical, the meaning of "the righteousness of God," as he confronted it especially in Paul's epistle to the Romans. At the outset of his letter (1:17), the apostle wrote that in the gospel, "the righteousness of God is revealed." Luther thought this referred to God's character whereby He was righteous and punished unrighteous sinners. This was simply too much for the young theologian. Vividly aware of his own sins

("I felt that I was a sinner before God with an extremely disturbed conscience") and of his failures to measure up, Luther was consumed by resentment: "As if, indeed, it is not enough, that miserable sinners, eternally lost through original sin, are crushed by every kind of calamity by the law of the Decalogue, without having God add pain to pain by the gospel and also by the gospel threatening us with his righteousness and wrath!" Where was the "good news" in the gospel? That was the question. Until at last God answered it by opening Luther's heart to the rest of the text:

> By the mercy of God . . . I gave heed to the context of the words, namely, "In it [the gospel] the righteousness of God is revealed, as it is written, 'He who through faith is righteous shall live.'" There I began to understand that the righteousness of God is that by which the righteous lives by a gift of God, namely by faith. And this is the meaning: the righteousness of God is revealed by the gospel, namely, the passive righteousness with which merciful God justifies us by faith. . . . I felt that I was altogether born again and had entered paradise itself through open gates.[13]

This then became the key to Luther's new understanding of the Christian religion—an understanding that remained with him until the day he died. First and foremost, it was about Christ and his saving work. Human beings did not have to *do* anything in order to be saved, for Christ had done it all and God offered it freely to them in His Word. All they needed to make it their own was simply to trust in God's promise. Salvation was by faith *alone*.[14]

Remaining in the Gospel

Of course, there was more to Luther and to Lutheranism than this one doctrine—but there was nothing more important and it remained the centerpiece of Luther's theology. On one occasion in the 1530s, when the Protestant leaders of Germany were considering whether to attend a church council called by the pope, Luther's prince asked him for a statement of nonnegotiables for such proceedings. Luther composed the Smalcald Articles, a statement of faith based on the Scriptures that he also offered as his personal "testimony and confession." As he said, "I have remained in this confession up to now, and by God's grace, I will remain in it."[15] These articles were later included in the *Book of Concord*, those documents that even to this day define what it means to be a Lutheran.[16]

There, in the Smalcald Articles, Luther identified the "first and chief article" of the Christian religion as justification by faith alone. Practically quoting the Bible, Luther first described the work of Christ on behalf of sinners:

> Jesus Christ, our God and Lord, died for our sins and was raised again for our justification (Romans 4:24–25).
>
> He alone is the Lamb of God who takes away the sins of the world (John 1:29), and God has laid upon Him the iniquities of us all (Isaiah 53:6).
>
> All have sinned and are justified freely, without their own works or merits, by His grace, through the redemption that is in Christ Jesus, in His blood.[17]

Just two things determine a person's relationship with God: sin and the work of Christ. Sin turns God into an angry Judge; Christ turns God into a loving Father. So how do we appropriate the work of Christ? How do we make it our own? Luther answered,

> This is necessary to believe. This cannot be otherwise acquired or grasped by any work, law, or merit. Therefore, it is clear and certain that this faith alone justifies us. As St. Paul says:
>
>> For we hold that one is justified by faith apart from works of the law. (Romans 3:28)
>>
>> That He might be just and the justifier of the one who has faith in Jesus. (Romans 3:26)[18]

Once recovered from the Scriptures, justification by faith became Luther's constant refrain. He was also adamant in his confession of classical Christian truths regarding the Trinity[19] and the person of Christ,[20] and the first Lutherans argued consistently that theirs was the faith of the early Church, indeed, the true Church of all times.[21] But it was not tradition that saved or even an orthodox confession of God but only *faith* in that God—that is, faith in Christ the Savior: "Upon this article everything that we teach and practice depends, in opposition to the pope, the devil, and the whole world."[22]

Faith and Good Works

Of course, a frequent criticism of Luther's doctrine was not that it freed man from sin but for sin.[23] After all, if God required nothing from the sinner except faith, then why should a person resist temptation and do good works? Luther consistently rejected the charge of moral indifference. In the Smalcald Articles, Luther articulated the doctrine that became basic to Lutheranism: Good works inevitably follow faith. "Through faith . . . we have a new and clean heart, and God will and does account us entirely righteous and holy for the sake of Christ, our mediator. . . . Such faith, renewal, and forgiveness of sins are followed by good works." Luther even added, "We say, besides, that if good works do not follow, the faith is false and not true."[24]

Although not published until 1537, the Smalcald Articles represent Luther's position throughout the course of the Reformation. In one of Luther's better-known treatises from the early days of his career, *The Freedom of a Christian*, he summarized the Christian religion under two headings, faith and love: "We conclude . . . that a Christian lives not in himself, but in Christ and in his neighbor. Otherwise he is not a Christian. He lives in Christ through faith, in his neighbor through love. By faith he is caught up beyond himself into God. By love he descends beneath himself into his neighbor. Yet he always remains in God and in his love."[25] For Luther, both were basic to Christian existence: trust in God alone for salvation *and* self-sacrificing love to one's neighbor. In fact, the first was the basis for the second. Citing Philippians 2:1–4 ("Let each of you look not only to his own interests, but also to the interests of others"), Luther wrote, "The Apostle has prescribed this rule for the life of Christians, namely, that we should devote all our works to the welfare of others, since each has such abundant riches in his faith that all his other works and his whole life are a surplus with which he can by voluntary benevolence serve and do good to his neighbor."[26] In this way, Luther turned the argument of his critics against them, for if I need to do works for the sake of *my own* salvation, then my approach to others is essentially selfish—the neighbor becomes a means to my goal of eternal well-being instead of simply the recipient of my love that responds to his need. Truly loving one's neighbor is impossible apart from justification by faith alone.

Luther wrote often about good works and the obligations of Christian love. A glance at the four volumes devoted to "the Christian in society" in the American Edition of *Luther's Works* reveals treatises about marriage, monastic vows, the common chest, commerce and usury, education, government, obedience to the state, Sunday observance, and warfare as well as more general treatments of good works.[27] Often these works are polemical in nature since Luther defended what he believed, the clear biblical teaching regarding works as well as the gospel. Life now as well as life eternal was an essential part of Luther's theology.

Luther's First Conflict with Fellow Evangelicals

For Luther, proclaiming God's truth necessitated confronting error no matter who was promoting it, so today's Evangelicals are often uncomfortable with the harsh attacks that Luther directed not only against Rome in defense of justification by faith alone but also against those who today are a part of the Evangelical coalition (Reformed, Baptists, Pentecostals, etc.).[28] Nevertheless, in a "postmodern" world of relative truth, some find Luther's rhetoric actually refreshing because it arose from his convictions regarding the absolute truth of the Scriptures. Luther's theology offers sure footing to contemporary Christians about what to believe and how to live. So Luther's polemical style was a consequence of his concern for the truth revealed in the Scriptures, especially when it centered on either faith or love. One must not yield God's truth for the sake of worldly peace.[29]

One such episode in Luther's career that dealt with the obligations of Christian love is especially important because it resulted in the first fissure of the sixteenth-century evangelical movement. It also helped shape Luther's thinking about the nature and pace of reform.

In April 1521, Luther made his great confession before Emperor Charles V at the Diet of Worms. Based on the Scriptures and his own commitment to the gospel, Luther refused to retract his writings or recant his teachings. It was a stirring moment but also more than a little frightening, especially when it subsequently became clear that the emperor judged Luther's answer heretical.[30] Nonetheless, the emperor remained true to his word and permitted Luther to return home. But Luther never quite made it. Instead, he was "kidnapped"— actually, taken into the protective custody of his noble patron, Frederick the Wise, one of the great princes of the German Empire.[31] With Luther safe and in hiding for the next ten months, Frederick would have time for more careful consideration of what should follow.[32] But in Wittenberg, Luther's erstwhile colleagues thought it was high time for real reform to take place.

Up until this point, the Reformation had consisted almost entirely of preaching, teaching, and publishing with Luther and his followers making the case for change but without much change actually taking place. Now things began to happen and reformers began to abolish the old ways and to institute new. The climax of these efforts occurred on Christmas Day, 1521, when Luther's university colleague, Andreas Bodenstein von Karlstadt,[33] presided over mass in the Castle Church in Wittenberg.[34] Discarding priestly vestments and wearing instead a secular gown, Karlstadt read a simplified Latin mass that omitted any reference to sacrifice. Then, at the time of the Communion, he pronounced the words of Jesus's institution in German, omitted the elevation of the host, and administered the Eucharist in both bread and wine. Instead of placing the consecrated host into the mouths of those who communed as was customary, he permitted them to take the bread as well as the cup into their own hands. It was all quite extraordinary.[35]

Besides this new way of celebrating mass, Karlstadt rejected clerical celibacy and got married himself to prove it! He also taught the people that they no longer had to go to Confession before communing, that fasting was no longer mandatory, and that images had to be removed from churches. Some responded by attacking altars and images, but others were upset by this assault upon sacred traditions and customs. The town council agreed with Karlstadt, but Elector Frederick did not. He ordered the innovations to cease.[36]

With Wittenberg in an uproar, Luther returned,[37] defying the elector but restoring peace by means of a remarkable set of sermons in the city church, one a day beginning with the first Sunday in Lent (hence, the "Invocavit" Sermons) and ending a week later.[38] Right at the outset, Luther identified the problem. The reformers were not lacking in knowledge but love. They knew what was right but did not apply what they knew in a spirit of charity: "We must also have love and through love we must do to one another as God has done to us through faith. For without love faith is nothing. . . . And here, dear friends, have you not grievously failed? I see no signs of love among you, and I observe very well that you have not been grateful to God for his rich gifts and treasures."[39]

Very carefully, Luther employed the criterion of love to one's neighbor in order to address the issues that were troubling the people. In so doing, Luther revealed a pastor's heart for simple people and a spirit of moderation perhaps surprising in one who had so recently defied pope and emperor.

Luther had argued vehemently for freedom from the rules of Rome's religion, but now he urged using that freedom for those whose understanding was limited and whose faith was weak. In some matters, Luther argued that the reformers had gone beyond what the Scriptures required. For example, was it really necessary that communicants take the consecrated bread into their own hands instead of their mouths? Luther readily acknowledged that it was no sin to do so, but he maintained that insisting upon it "was not a good work, because it caused offense everywhere." Besides, it was entirely unimportant: "It does not help you if you do it, nor harm you if you do not do it." Instead, he challenged his hearers, "Why will you not in this respect also serve those who are weak in faith and abstain from your liberty?"[40]

Luther advocated the same approach even in matters where the Scriptures were clear, such as communing in both bread and wine. While acknowledging that the Lord's institution made both kinds necessary, Luther contended that the reformers were wrong to make communing in both mandatory. In his view, compulsion reduced the sacrament "to an outward act and hypocrisy." Instead, Luther advocated patiently instructing people in the Word of God: "When the Word is given free course and is not bound to any external observance, it takes hold of one today and sinks into his heart, tomorrow it touches another, and so on. Thus quietly and soberly it does its work, and no one will know how it all came about."[41]

Luther was unyielding when he thought something was a question of faith but was quite moderate when it came to love. Luther employed a striking image to make his point: "The sun has two properties, light and heat. No king has power enough to bend or guide the light of the sun; it remains fixed in its place. But the heat may be turned and guided and yet is ever about the sun. Thus faith must always remain pure and immovable in our hearts, never wavering; but love bends and turns so that our neighbor may grasp and follow it."[42] As far as Luther was concerned, his Wittenberg parishioners had failed in the office of love in their first attempt at reformation. Under Luther's leadership, they would do better.

Luther and the Law

In an age of moral decadence like our own, Luther's appeal to "love" may not be all that appealing. Many long for moral certainty and are attracted to religions that insist upon rigorous and disciplined lifestyles. In this regard, it is important to note two things about Luther's theology that remain relevant. First of all, just as Luther maintained against Rome, it is still true that religions of the Law cannot save. On the one hand, many reduce the Law to externals—for example, precise tithing of every form of income or prayer at just the right time, in just the right posture, and with just the right words. This approach is great at making hypocrites but does nothing to put people into a right relationship with God, who demands not only absolute obedience but also absolute love for God and the neighbor. So, on the other hand, those who really grasp what the Law requires realize that they cannot obey it no matter how hard they try. The Law shows them their need for a Savior but does not supply one. Only the gospel of God's free grace in Jesus can do that.

The second point to realize about Luther's reduction of Christian ethics to love (following both Jesus[43] and Paul[44]) is that Luther's "love" had content—namely, the demands of the moral law. He did not use the term *love* as a label to slap on a situation in order to excuse immorality—for example, abortion or sodomy—as often happens today.[45] If one reads, for instance, Luther's *Small Catechism*, originally intended for the instruction of children in the essentials of the Christian religion, one finds that Luther used the Ten Commandments as the basis for presenting the moral law in all its rigor.[46] For example, he explained the prohibition against murder as a law not just against killing but also against committing any bodily injury to the neighbor *and* as a positive injunction "to help and befriend him in every bodily need."[47] Moreover, right behavior with respect to one's neighbor comes only from fearing and loving God. Since this is how Luther handled all the commandments, one could hardly charge him with moral indifference.

However, Luther's disagreement with Karlstadt, begun in the wake of the Wittenberg reforms of 1521–22, not only demonstrated Luther's commitment to love for weaker brethren as a guiding principle for reform but also showed caution in interpreting the Scriptures, especially Old Testament law. Luther's commitment to the Bible was absolute, but he did not absolutize the Mosaic law.[48]

Already in the Invocavit Sermons, Luther addressed the question of prohibiting sacred images (Exod. 20:4–5).[49] While he confessed that "it would be much better if we did not have them at all. I am not partial to them," his position was that "we are free to have them or not." Luther took this approach because of ambiguity in the commandment, which said in one verse, "You shall not make for yourself a carved image," but also said in the next, "You shall not bow down to them or serve them." So what did God actually prohibit, the making of graven images or the worship of such statues?

In view of the fact that God Himself commanded Moses to make a bronze serpent (Num. 21:9) and only when, centuries later, the people began to worship it did Hezekiah destroy it (2 Kings 18:4), the prohibition of images could not be an absolute one. God also commanded Moses to put two angels on the Ark of the Covenant (Exod. 37:7), which remained at the center of Old Testament worship for ages.[50] What Luther urged, therefore, with respect to the vice of worshiping idols in his day, was the same as he did in the case of sacramental administration—namely, that pastors *preach* against the abuse, just as Paul did on Mars Hill rather than illegally tearing down the idols (Acts 17:16, 22). Indeed, Luther pointed out that the apostle even traveled in a ship on the prow of which were images of Castor and Pollux without protesting, let alone breaking them off (Acts 28:11). Paul's purpose, Luther maintained, was once again to show that "outward things could do no harm to faith, if only the heart does not cleave to them or put its trust in them."[51]

This emphasis on locating idolatry in the heart rather than in the object was a point to which Luther returned again and again. In the *Large Catechism*, published initially as instruction to pastors in the basics of the Christian religion, Luther defined "god" as "that from which we are to expect all good and in which we take refuge in all distress"; in other words, "whatever you set your heart on and put your trust in is truly your god"—whether you call it "god" or not. Luther recognized that in the medieval Church, many made idols out of the saints: "Everyone chose his own saint, worshiped him, and called to him for help in distress" (a practice still characteristic of Orthodoxy and Roman Catholicism). But Luther also spoke against "idolatries" that characterize many in the modern world who have no regard for saints and statues: "Whoever trusts and boasts that he has great skill, prudence, power, favor, friendship, and honor also has a god. But it is not the true and only God." Luther also realized that in every age, not only his own but also ours, the most common idol is money:

> Many a person thinks that he has God and everything in abundance when he has money and possessions. He trusts in them and boasts about them with such firmness and assurance as to care for no one. Such a person has a god by the name of "Mammon" (i.e., money and possessions; [Matt. 6:24]), on which he sets all his heart.... He who has money and possessions feels secure and is joyful and undismayed.... On the other hand, he who has no money doubts and is despondent, as though he knew of no God.... This care and desire for money sticks and clings to our nature, right up to the grave.[52]

Luther's caution about applying the Law of Moses literally to Christians avoided legalism but did not lead to ethical indifference. Instead, Luther thought deeply—and biblically—about God's Law to show its relevance not just for the people of his time but for people today as well.

Luther versus Zwingli regarding the Lord's Supper

In the Invocavit Sermons of 1522, Luther's debate with Karlstadt was just beginning. It would go on for many years. Other issues would arise, among them the nature of the presence of the body and blood of Christ in the Eucharist.[53] Even more than images, the question of the Real Presence fractured the evangelical movement, and Luther articulated a position that many Protestants then and now have rejected.[54] But should they? Luther based his understanding of the Lord's Supper on the Scriptures. He also demonstrated his commitment to the gospel.

One of the most consequential episodes of the Reformation occurred in October 1529, the Marburg Colloquy[55]—a meeting of several evangelical theologians, organized by one of their most prominent political leaders, Philip of Hesse.[56] Among those in attendance were Ulrich Zwingli,[57] the great reformer of Zurich, and Martin Luther himself. By this time, the controversy over the sacrament had gone on for years, had engaged numerous theologians, and had generated many treatises. Zwingli and Luther were on opposite sides. For a variety of reasons, the former insisted upon interpreting the words of institution symbolically. Thus "This is my body" meant "This represents my body."[58]

For Luther, such an understanding was unwarranted. At a highly dramatic moment in the colloquy, Luther removed a velvet cloth from the table on which he had written those very words, "This is my body," and insisted, "Here is our Scripture passage. You have not yet wrested it away from us. . . . We have no need of another passage."[59] Of course, for Zwingli and his allies, the passage itself was not enough. It had to be understood in the entire context of Scriptures and especially in accordance with the articles of faith concerning the union of two natures, divine and human, in the one person of Christ. The debate between the two theologians over this point revealed how for Luther, the text of Scripture must constrain theological speculation.

Zwingli's position was that the humanity of Christ made Luther's position untenable, because a real human body is always limited in space.[60] Since the day Christ ascended into heaven, his body has been there, not on earth, and so not present in the Sacrament. How then should one construe the words of institution? For Zwingli, there could be but one conclusion: the bread and wine were symbols of the body and blood, not the real thing.

For Luther, the argument from the nature of a human body was beside the point. Zwingli was talking about human bodies as we experience them, not a human nature in personal union with the divine. God was not limited by time and space. In Luther's *Confession Concerning Christ's Supper*, written more than a year before the colloquy,[61] the Reformer speculated about different ways in which the body of Christ could be present: not only locally (as Zwingli conceived it), but also definitively and repletively.[62] By the one—definitively—Luther meant present in the way that angels or spirits are present in a place: really there but not measurably there (without length, breadth, width, or any other measurement). This was how Jesus passed through a closed grave on Easter morning and later came to the disciples through a closed door. He occupied no space and the door and stone yielded no space, but His body *really* passed through.[63]

By the other—repletively—Luther meant the kind of presence that is characteristic of God alone, for He is "simultaneously present in all places whole and entire and fills all places, yet without being measured or circumscribed by any place, in terms of the space which it occupies." Since in Christ God and man are one person, His human nature shares the powers of the other, and, therefore, Christ's body is present everywhere just as God is present everywhere because Christ is God. For Luther, to insist that Christ is present anywhere according to the divine nature only was the same as separating His person into two. Wherever there is one nature, he maintained, the other is there also.[64]

To be sure, Luther was not really interested in showing the precise manner by which the body and blood of Jesus were present in the bread and wine—which is just as well. For many Christians in a post-Christian world, issues like these from the sixteenth century fail to resonate: the sacramental "how Christ is present" is not nearly as important as the sacramental "that Christ is present." Luther's point was to describe ways by which the body and blood of Christ could be present in order to answer Zwingli's complaint that they could not be without destroying the human nature of Christ. For Luther, Zwingli's position was tantamount to denying the power of God:

> I do not wish to have denied by the foregoing that God may have and know still other modes whereby Christ's body can be in a given place. My only purpose was to show what crass fools our fanatics are when they concede only the first, circumscribed mode of presence to the

body of Christ although they are unable to prove that even this mode is contrary to our view. For I do not want to deny in any way that God's power is able to make a body be simultaneously in many places, even in a corporeal and circumscribed manner. For who wants to try to prove that God is unable to do that? Who has seen the limits of his power?[65]

Luther believed that if God had said it ("This is my body"), we ought to believe it. Period.

Because the debate over the sacrament centered almost exclusively on the question of whether the Lord's body and blood were really there, it might seem for Luther that that was *the* important point: the "presence" of the body and blood—the kind of thinking that led to medieval abuses like *Corpus Christi* observances and bleeding hosts.[66] This is a serious misunderstanding of the Reformer's sacramental theology, since, for Luther, the ultimate significance of the Lord's Supper was as a means of grace, a delivery vehicle for the saving work of Jesus.[67]

In 1529, just when his battle with Zwingli was heading toward Marburg, Luther summarized his theology of the sacrament in the *Small Catechism*. On the one hand, he based his explanation exclusively on the words of Jesus that established the sacrament. On the other, he argued that the purpose of the Lord's Supper was to convey the forgiveness of sins.

"What is the Sacrament?" Luther asked. "It is the true body and blood of our Lord Jesus Christ, under the bread and wine, for us Christians to eat and to drink, instituted by Christ Himself."

> Where is this written? . . . The holy Evangelists, Matthew, Mark, Luke, and St. Paul, write. . . .
>
> What is the benefit of such eating and drinking? . . . That is shown us in these words, "Given for you" and "shed for you for the forgiveness of sins." This means that in the Sacrament forgiveness of sins, life, and salvation are given us through these words. For where there is forgiveness of sins, there is also life and salvation.

At this point, one might ask whether Luther had really escaped a mechanical, works-oriented view of salvation, as if one obtained forgiveness by eating. So Luther included still another question,

"How can bodily eating and drinking do such great things?" and answered, "It is *not* the eating and drinking that does them, but the *words*, which are given here, 'Given . . . and shed for you, for the forgiveness of sins'. . . . The person who *believes* these words has what they say and express, namely, the forgiveness of sins."[68]

In no way did Luther violate the central proposition of his theology—justification by faith alone. For him, the sacrament was another way that God distributed the saving work of Jesus.[69] The communicant added nothing to what Christ had earned for sinners. Instead, he received what Christ had earned for sinners—for him—by eating and drinking *in faith* according to the Savior's words. What could be simpler?

Although Luther and Zwingli concluded the Marburg Colloquy with a common statement of faith—fifteen and two-thirds articles of agreement, one-third not—the issue of the Real Presence remained outstanding ("We have not reached an agreement as to whether the true body and blood of Christ are bodily present in the bread and wine"),[70] and two great branches of Protestantism subsequently developed: Lutheran and Reformed. Many factors account for this development, but certainly one of them was Luther's insistence on the scriptural foundation and the evangelical purpose of the Lord's Supper. Neither could be compromised.

Luther and the Anabaptists

Besides the Lord's Supper, the Protestant movement of the sixteenth century splintered over baptism, especially over the question of whether it is right to baptize babies. This time both the Lutherans and the Reformed were on the same side. Those who differed were called "Anabaptists."[71] Like the division over the Real Presence, the debate over infant baptism continues to this day, and there are Evangelicals on both sides of the question. Luther's theology, however, can resolve the debate—not by forging an agreement that both parties can live with but by appealing once more to first principles—namely, the Scriptures and the gospel. Luther's doctrine is true to both.

Once again, the *Small Catechism* provides ready access to Luther's thinking about baptism. First of all, he believed that Christ had instituted it as a real means of grace: "[Baptism] works forgiveness of sins, delivers from death and the devil, and gives eternal salvation to all who believe this, as the words and promises of God declare." As with the Lord's Supper, Luther also maintained that the power of baptism lay in God's Word and not the visible element. He asked, "How can water do such great things?" and then answered, "It is not the water indeed that does them, but the *Word of God*, which is in and with the water, and *faith*, which trusts such Word of God in the water."[72] Thus Luther's approach was not mechanical but evangelical because he based it on God's promise received by faith.[73]

But what about the baptism of infants? Although Luther never had a face-to-face debate with Anabaptist leaders the way he did with Zwingli, he nonetheless addressed the issue explicitly and answered Anabaptist arguments against baptizing babies.[74] First of all, there is the question of why anyone should be baptized, adults as well as babies. What is the basis for baptism? For Luther, it is God's commandment, specifically, Matthew 28:19: "Go therefore and make disciples of all nations, baptizing them." Faith is necessary to receive the promises attached to baptism but faith does not make the baptism valid. Only the command of Jesus does that.[75]

From this starting point, Luther concluded that even if babies could not *as babies* believe and receive the promise of baptism, their baptisms would still be valid. If faith comes later, it would grasp what God had given earlier. For Luther, the command of the Lord is enough to validate the practice of centuries, but it is also true that in those centuries, whatever Christians there were had all been baptized as babies: "It is . . . the work of God that during all the time children were being baptized, he has given great and holy gifts to many of them, enlightened and strengthened them with the Holy Spirit and understanding of the Scripture, and accomplished great things in Christendom through them." Luther went on to mention John Hus, specifically, and then "very many people in our day."[76] The fact that God has brought and still brings people to faith and confers spiritual blessings upon them—people who were baptized as children—is proof that such baptisms are valid.[77]

Luther also argued that infants can believe. On the one hand, he challenged his opponents to show that they could not believe. For Luther, the denial of infant faith was highly presumptuous in view of God's mandating the circumcision of infant Israelite boys in the Old

Testament and the Lord's portraying children as ideal Christians in the New (Matt. 19:4, "Let the little children come to me . . . for to such belongs the kingdom of heaven"). On the other hand, Luther was sure that infants could believe since baptism is God's work, not man's.[78]

Commenting on the episode of John the Baptist's leaping for joy when Mary greeted Elizabeth (Luke 1:39–45) as an example of infant faith, Luther wrote,

> We can hardly deny that the same Christ is present at baptism and in baptism, in fact is himself the baptizer, who in those days came in his mother's womb to John. In baptism he can speak as well through the mouth of the priest, as when he spoke through his mother. Since then he is present, speaks, and baptizes, why should not his Word and baptism call forth spirit and faith in the child as when it produced faith in John? He is the same who speaks and acts then and now.

While acknowledging a mystery ("I grant that we do not understand how they do believe, or how faith is created"), Luther insisted that God's Word in baptism is powerful to effect the faith that lays hold on the promises of God.[79] Far from there being Scriptural grounds for rejecting infant baptism, Luther held that the Scriptures require it. By mandate, promise, and example, the Bible presents children as fit subjects for water and the Word.

Contrary to the practice of our Lord, who loved and welcomed little children, the modern world is characterized by the opposite—legal abortion as well as routine child neglect and abuse. Evangelical Christians have responded to these commonplace horrors in a variety of ways—everything from political activism to foster care and adoption. By following Luther, they could add yet another dimension to their concerns for children, one with eternal consequences, and that is baptism.

Conclusion

To many Evangelicals, the Reformation reads like one controversy after another, and each of them has left its scar upon the Church. During his career as a reformer, Martin Luther engaged in many such battles—and not just the ones discussed here. Luther was a fighter, and his polemical writings demonstrate the intensity with which he engaged his foes. His friends recognized the harshness of his rhetoric, and in his well-known confession of faith at the Diet of Worms, he even apologized.[80]

But Luther's style was not simply a matter of personality; it was also a sign of commitment—a double commitment to the authority of the Scriptures and to its saving purpose in the gospel. This kind of commitment—even more than Luther's rhetoric—can make people today uncomfortable. We are used to *political* figures who demonize their enemies, but we are not used to *religious* figures who make absolute truth claims about God, sin, Christ, and salvation.

But simply because such truth claims resound in too few churches and too few people are in those churches anyway does not mean that they are no longer true—or necessary. They are both. Luther discovered this personally and preached it publicly. Still today, we would be wise to listen.

Notes

1. This account of Martin Luther's death is based on the eyewitness report of Justas Jonas, Luther's friend and colleague, and Michael Coelius, a local clergyman, also present at Luther's death. Jonas composed it on February 18, 1546, the very day on which Luther had died early in the morning, and sent it to Luther's prince, John Frederick, the Elector of Saxony. This and several other documents related to Luther's death are available in Christof Schubart, ed., *Die Berichte über Luthers Tod und Begräbnis: Texte und Untersuchungen* (Weimar: Hermann Böhlaus Nachfolger, 1917). For a description of the entire evening, see Martin Brecht, *Martin Luther*, 3 vols. (Philadelphia: Fortress Press, 1985–93), 3:375–77.

2. Here I am using *evangelical* in the sixteenth-century sense of the term for someone committed to justification by faith alone as the heart of the gospel over against Roman Catholic opponents who emphasized faith *and* works. See R. Ward Holder, ed., *The Westminster Handbook to Theologies of the Reformation* (Louisville, KY: Westminster John Knox Press, 2010), s.v. "Evangelical" and "Gospel"; Cameron A. MacKenzie, "The Evangelical Character of Luther's Faith," in *The Advent of Evangelicalism: Exploring Historical Continuities*, ed. Kenneth J. Stewart and Michael Haykin (Nashville, TN: B&H Academic, 2008), 171–98.

3. See, for example, from 1537, Luther's remark in a sermon on Matthew 18:11, as cited in Otto Scheel, ed., *Dokumente zu Luthers Entwicklung*

(bis 1519), 2nd ed. (Tübingen: J. C. B. Mohr [Paul Siebeck], 1929), 381, and 346, 358, and 383. The entire sermon is available in vol. 47 of the Weimar Edition of Luther's works, *D. Martin Luthers Werke: Kritische Gesamtausgabe*, 127 vols. (Weimar: Hermann Böhlaus Nachfolger, 1883–1993). The Weimar Edition (abbreviated WA) also includes Luther's correspondence (WA Br), his German Bible (WA DB), and his "table talk" (WA Tr). For Scheel's *Dokumente zu Luthers Entwicklung (bis 1519)*, see WA 47:275.33–42.

4. For a brief overview of late medieval piety, see Hans J. Hillerbrand, ed., *The Oxford Encyclopedia of the Reformation* (hereafter OER), 4 vols. (New York: Oxford University Press, 1996), s.v. "Devotional Practices." For a comprehensive (and sympathetic) description, see Eamon Duffy, *The Stripping of the Altars: Traditional Religion in England, 1400–1580* (New Haven, CT: Yale University Press, 1992), 9–376.

5. More precisely, he became a "friar," or a member of one of the mendicant orders—in Luther's case, the Augustinian Hermits. This meant that Luther joined a religious order that exercised its vocation in the world. Traditionally, monks were cloistered; in other words, they lived a life of prayer in one place, their abbey. However, Luther did use the term *monk* to describe his life ("monachus"; see, for example, WA 54:185.21), and I am exercising the same liberty here. But see also Kenneth Hagen, who discusses this in somewhat more detail, "Was Luther a 'Monk'?," *Lutheran Quarterly* 24 (2010): 183–85. Also Brecht, *Martin Luther*, 1:51–54.

6. See Brecht, *Martin Luther*, 1:46–50, 58–63.

7. Thomas Aquinas, *Summa Theologiae* II-IIae q.189 a.3 ad 3. Electronic edition, http://www.newadvent.org/summa/3189.htm.

8. LW 38:190 (WA 18:719.9–11). Unless otherwise noted, English translations of Luther's works are from Jaroslav Pelikan and Helmut T. Lehmann, eds., *Luther's Works*, 55 vols. (St. Louis, MO: Concordia Publishing House, 1955–86), and are cited with the abbreviation LW.

Luther's frustration with the monastic system, especially with his failure to find peace in sacramental confession, is treated by Brecht, *Martin Luther*, 1:67–70, 76–82, but see also E. G Schwiebert, *Luther and His Times: The Reformation from a New Perspective* (St. Louis, MO: Concordia Publishing House, 1950), 145–74.

9. For example, Brecht, *Martin Luther*, 1:225, says that the new discovery "could have been no sooner than the spring, and no later than the fall, of 1518," whereas Helmar Junghans, "Luther's Wittenberg," in *The Cambridge Companion to Martin Luther*, ed. Donald D. McKim (Cambridge: University Press, 2003), 25, contends that "there is every reason to believe that this event occurred during his first lecture series on Psalms" (1513–15). Bernhard Lohse, *Martin Luther's Theology: Its Historical and Systematic Development* (Minneapolis, MN: Fortress, 1999), 85–88, has a nice introduction to the problem. See

also the volume he edited, *Der Durchbruch der reformatorischen Erkenntnis Bei Luther: Neuere Untersuchungen* (Stuttgart: Franz Steiner Verlag, 1988).

10. This was "new" to him. Luther, of course, maintained that it was the religion of Scriptures that the enemies of the gospel, especially the papacy, had obscured over the course of centuries. See, for example, Luther's *Address to the Christian Nobility of the German Nation* (1520), in which he charged the papacy with falsely claiming to have a monopoly on Scriptural interpretation (LW 44:133–36; WA 6:411.8–417.21).

11. At that time, Hebrews was still generally considered to have been written by Paul (as did Jerome). By the time Luther translated the New Testament into German (1522), he had changed his mind and believed that a disciple of the apostles had written it rather than an apostle himself. See Luther's "Preface to the Epistle to Hebrews," LW 35:394 (WA DB 7:344.9–10). For an introduction to Luther's lectures, see Peter Kawerau, *Luther: Leben, Schriften, Denken* (Marburg: N. G. Elwert Verlag, 1969), 54–61. For the authorship of Hebrews, see Donald Guthrie, *New Testament Introduction*, rev. ed. (Downers Grove, IL: Inter-Varsity Press, 1970), 685–98.

12. This was called this because of Luther's reminiscences, recorded in his "table-talk," that it occurred in a tower of the Augustinian residence, the "Black Cloister," in Wittenberg. See LW 54:193–94 [WA Tr 3:228 (#3232c)].

13. LW 34:336–37 (WA 54:185.21–186.9).

14. For Luther and Lutherans, this doctrine of salvation—or "justification by faith," as it is often called—is the center of all theology. For a good introduction to the topic, see Lohse, *Martin Luther's Theology*, 258–66. For a more thorough presentation, see Paul Althaus, *The Theology of Martin Luther* (Philadelphia: Fortress Press, 1966), 43–63, 201–18, 224–50.

15. Quotations from the Smalcald Articles as well as the other Lutheran Confessions are from Paul Timothy McCain, ed., *Concordia: The Lutheran Confessions*, 2nd ed. (St. Louis, MO: Concordia Publishing House, 2005, 2006). The abbreviations for the individual documents are the standard ones and are listed on page vii. For the original languages, see *Die Bekenntnisschriften der evangelisch-lutherischen Kirche*, 4th ed. (Goettingen: Vandenhoeck & Ruprecht, 1959). Thus, the citation for the quotation in the text is SA Preface 3 (McCain, *Concordia*, 259). For background to the Smalcald Articles, see OER, s.v. "Schmalkald Articles," and William R. Russell, *The Schmalkald Articles: Luther's Theological Testament* (Minneapolis, MN: Fortress Press, 1995).

16. Convinced that the Scriptures teach real, objective truths, sixteenth-century Reformers expressed those truths in propositions and presented them as official (and authoritative) confessions of faith. For the nature of Reformation era confessions, see Robert Kolb, *Confessing the Faith: Reformers Define the Church, 1530-1580* (St. Louis, MO: Concordia Publishing House, 1991), 15–18; Mark A. Noll, "Introduction," in *Confessions and Catechisms of the*

Reformation (Grand Rapids, MI: Baker Book House, 1991), 11–23. For the history of the *Book of Concord* and its constituent parts, see Charles P. Arand, James A. Nestingen, and Robert Kolb, *The Lutheran Confessions: History and Theology of the* Book of Concord (Minneapolis, MN: Fortress Press, 2012). For the Smalcald Articles especially, see pp. 139–58.

17. SA 2.1.1–3 (McCain, *Concordia*, 263).

18. SA 2.1.4 (Ibid., 263).

19. SA 1.1–2 (Ibid., 262).

20. SA 1.3–4 (Ibid., 262). For Luther's affirmation of traditional Trinitarian and Christological doctrine, see Lohse, *Martin Luther's Theology*, 207–10, 219–22.

21. See, for example, AC Summary 1–5 (McCain, *Concordia*, 44) and AC Conclusion 5 (ibid., 63). Luther had great respect for the Church Fathers and believed that, in general, they supported his theology. But he also knew that they sometimes contradicted each other and that, in any case, the Scriptures were the ultimate standard for God's truth. To locate the true Church, one had to test the various claimants not by some sort of institutional continuity with the past but by the "marks" of the Church, most especially the Word of God. For Luther's mature thinking on this topic—as well as for his analysis of the first ecumenical councils—see his "On the Councils and the Church," LW 41:9–178 (WA 50:509–653). See also John M. Headley, *Luther's View of Church History* (New Haven: Yale University Press, 1963), 162–94; Lohse, *Martin Luther's Theology*, 277–85.

22. SA 2.1.5 (McCain, *Concordia*, 262–63). For Luther's doctrine of justification, see Lohse, *Martin Luther's Theology*, 258–66.

23. David N. Bagchi, *Luther's Earliest Opponents: Catholic Controversialists, 1518–1525* (Minneapolis, MN: Fortress Press, 1991), 148–49, 159–63, 168–73.

24. SA 3.13.1, 2, 4 (McCain, *Concordia*, 283). For the relationship between faith and works, see Lohse, *Martin Luther's Theology*, 264–66. For a more thorough treatment of this theme, see Paul Althaus, *The Ethics of Martin Luther* (Philadelphia: Fortress Press, 1972). Carter Lindberg, *Beyond Charity: Reformation Initiatives for the Poor* (Minneapolis, MN: Fortress Press, 1993), has explored Luther's thinking as it applied especially to an urban context and in comparison and contrast to medieval, Renaissance, and other Reformation thinkers.

25. LW 31:371 (WA 7:69.12–16).

26. LW 31:365–66 (WA 7:65.4–9).

27. LW 44–47.

28. The term *evangelical* is used in a variety of ways. Today, it often refers to Protestant Christians who emphasize the infallibility of the Bible, justification by faith alone, and personal conversion. This is how I am using it here. In this chapter, I am using lower case *e* for sixteenth-century evangelicals and

upper case *E* for the contemporary version. In the United States, Evangelicals of the latter type often understand their faith commitments as also requiring conservative positions on moral questions like abortion and sodomy. For the term itself, see John R. Hinnells, ed., *A New Dictionary of Religions*, rev. ed. (Oxford: Blackwell Publishers, 1995), s.v. "Evangelical." For the term as identifying a particular strain of American Protestantism, see Daniel G. Reid, ed., *Dictionary of Christianity in America* (Downers Grove, IL: InterVarsity Press, 1990), s.v. "Evangelicalism."

29. Heiko Oberman, *Luther: Man between God and the Devil* (New York: Image Books, Doubleday, 1989), 109, put it this way: "When taken seriously, it [Luther's lifelong barrage of crude words] reveals the task Luther saw before him: to do battle against the greatest slanderer of all times [viz., the devil]!"

30. Brecht, *Martin Luther*, 1:452–64.

31. Frederick (1463–1525) was one of the seven electors, princes of the Holy Roman Empire, who had responsibility for choosing a new emperor when the throne fell vacant. His protection of Luther in the early years of the Reformation was critically important. See OER, s.v. "Frederick III of Saxony."

32. Brecht, *Martin Luther*, 2:1–56.

33. Initially, Karlstadt (1486–1541) was Luther's close coworker in the cause of reform and in the early years of the Reformation was second only to Luther in publications on its behalf, but the two men developed different versions of what reformation actually meant and became bitter opponents. Karlstadt left Wittenberg in 1523 and finally ended up teaching at the University of Basel. See OER, s.v. "Bodenstein von Karlstadt, Andreas." Mark U. Edwards Jr. devotes a great deal of attention to Luther's disputes with Karlstadt in *Luther and the False Brethren* (Stanford, CA: Stanford University Press, 1975). See especially pp. 6–59.

34. For a description and explanation of the liturgy of the mass prior to the Reformation, see Lee Palmer Wandel, *The Eucharist in the Reformation* (Cambridge: University Press, 2006), 14–45.

35. Ronald J. Sider, *Andreas Bodenstein von Karlstadt: The Development of His Thought, 1517–1525* (Leiden: Brill, 1974), 153–60, http://web.ebscohost.com/ehost/ebookviewer/ebook/nlebk_28831_AN?sid=e682fa8b-99d7-4c47-b495-fe96972ed5b4@sessionmgr12&vid=1&format=EB&rid=1.

36. Ibid., 160–71.

37. For the circumstances of Luther's return, see Brecht, *Martin Luther*, 2:41–45.

38. For a summary of the sermons, see ibid., 2:59–64; for an analysis, see Neil R. Leroux, *Luther's Rhetoric: Strategies and Style from the Invocavit Sermons* (St. Louis, MO: Concordia Academic Press, 2002). The text of all eight sermons is in LW 51:70–100 (WA 10III:1–64).

39. LW 51:71 (WA 10III:3.5–4.2).

40. LW 51:90 (WA 10III:44.14–15, 44.17–45.2).

41. LW 51:90 (WA 10III:45.35–46.20).

42. LW 51:72 (WA 10III:7.9–8.2).

43. "You shall love the Lord your God with all your heart and with all your soul and with all your mind. This is the great and first commandment. And a second is like it: You shall love your neighbor as yourself." Matthew 22:37–39.

44. "Love is the fulfilling of the Law." Romans 13:10.

45. A viewpoint made famous by Joseph F. Fletcher, *Situation Ethics: The New Morality* (Philadelphia: Westminster Press, 1966).

46. *The Small Catechism* (SC) and its companion piece, *The Large Catechism* (LC), are also a part of the *Book of Concord*. See Arand, Nestingen, and Kolb, *The Lutheran Confessions*, 61–85. For Luther's treatment of the Decalogue, see Albrecht Peters, *Commentary on Luther's Catechisms: Ten Commandments* (St. Louis, MO: Concordia Publishing House, 2009).

47. SC 1 Fifth Commandment (McCain, *Concordia*, 321).

48. Luther did not accept even the Ten Commandments as binding in all details. They were a summary of the natural law written in man's heart but included details—for example, Sabbath observance—that were specific to ancient Israel. See Peters, *Commentary on Luther's Catechisms*, 73–87; Heinrich Bornkamm, *Luther and the Old Testament*, reprint ed. (Mifflintown, PA: Sigler Press, 1997), 121–35.

49. For Luther on idolatry and sacred images, see Peters, *Commentary on Luther's Catechisms*, 110–46; Carlos Eire, *War against the Idols: The Reformation of Worship from Erasmus to Calvin* (Cambridge: Cambridge University Press, 1986), 54–73; and Cameron A. MacKenzie, "No Alternatives to Jesus: Martin Luther's Definition of Idolatry as Evident in His *House Postils*," in *Aspects of Reforming: Theology and Practice in Sixteenth Century Europe*, ed. Michael Parsons (Crownhill, Milton Keynes, Bucks, UK: Paternoster Press, 2013), 16–32.

50. Although the ultimate fate of the ark remains unknown, it still existed when Solomon dedicated the temple (1 Kings 8:6) and, apparently, when Jeremiah predicted it being forgotten (Jer. 3:16).

51. LW 51:82–83 (WA 10III:29.14–30.1).

52. LC 1.1–2, 3, 5–9, 10, 12 (McCain, *Concordia*, 359–60).

53. See Edwards, *False Brethren*, 34–59.

54. See ibid., 82–111, 127–55. For a brief introduction, see Euan Cameron, *The European Reformation* (Oxford: Clarendon Press, 1991), 161–66. Alistair E. McGrath, *Reformation Thought: An Introduction*, 3rd ed. (Oxford: Blackwell Publishers, 1999), 169–96, devotes a chapter to the main types of sacramental theology in the sixteenth century. Thomas J. Davis, *This Is My Body: The Presence of Christ in Reformation Thought* (Grand Rapids, MI: Baker Academic, 2008), is devoted especially to Luther and Calvin.

55. For a brief introduction, see OER, s.v. "Marburg, Colloquy of." Both Luther and Zwingli biographers treat it at length—for example, Brecht, *Martin Luther*, 2:325–34; G. R. Potter, *Zwingli* (Cambridge: Cambridge University Press, 1976), 316–42. For a detailed analysis and careful reconstruction of the meeting itself, see Hermann Sasse, *This Is My Body: Luther's Contention for the Real Presence in the Sacrament of the Altar*, rev. ed. (Adelaide, Australia: Lutheran Publishing House, 1977).

56. Philip, landgrave of Hesse (1504–67), was a principal architect of the Schmalkald League, an alliance of cities and territories within the empire designed to protect the Reformation. He hoped that the colloquy would lay the theological groundwork for a political/military alliance between Lutherans and Zwinglians. See OER, s.v. "Philipp of Hesse."

57. For Zwingli's life and career, see OER, s.v. "Zwingli, Huldrych"; Bruce Gordon, *The Swiss Reformation* (Manchester, UK: Manchester University Press, 2002), 46–81, 119–35; and Potter, *Zwingli*. For Zwingli's theology specifically, see W. P. Stephens, *The Theology of Huldrych Zwingli* (Oxford: Clarendon Press, 1986), and, more briefly, Timothy George, *Theology of the Reformers* (Nashville, TN: Broadman Press, 1988), 108–62.

58. See, for example, Ulrich Zwingli, "On the Lord's Supper," in *Zwingli and Bullinger*, Library of Christian Classics, ed. G. W. Bromiley (Philadelphia: Westminster Press, 1953), 225. See also Stephens, *The Theology of Huldrych Zwingli*, 218–59.

59. LW 38:67 (WA 30III:147.17–18). Our information about what happened at Marburg comes from a wide variety of sources. Seven of them have been translated and published in LW 38. This particular account about Luther's velvet cloth comes from the report of Andreas Osiander, a participant in the colloquy and a reformer of the church in Nuremberg. See also Sasse, *This Is My Body*, 207.

60. For the Christological debate as it related to the presence of Christ in the sacrament, see George, *Theology of the Reformers*, 153–54, and Sasse, *This Is My Body*, 207–11. For Zwingli's doctrine regarding the person of Christ, see Stephens, *The Theology of Huldrych Zwingli*, 111–18; for Luther, see Althaus, *Theology*, 193–98.

61. Robert H. Fischer, "Introduction to Luther's *Confession Concerning Christ's Supper*," LW 37:155.

62. According to Lohse, *Martin Luther's Theology*, 230, Luther derived these distinctions from William of Occam and Gabriel Biel. See also Heiko A. Oberman, *The Harvest of Medieval Theology: Gabriel Biel and Late Medieval Nominalism*, 3rd ed. (Durham, NC: Labyrinth Press, 1983), 276. Oberman notes the first two of Luther's modes of presence in Gabriel Biel.

63. LW 37:215–16 (WA 26:327.16–329.1).

64. LW 37:216, 217–18, 222 (WA 26:329.8–11, 332.12–32, 335.19–28).

65. LW 37:223–24 (WA 26:336.28–35).

66. The first was a festival in honor of the Eucharist that featured plays, parades, and preaching. See Holder, *The Westminster Handbook*, s.v. "Corpus Christi." Hosts that bled and performed miracles were sometimes reported in the late medieval period, not always with approval by the authorities. See Francis Oakley, *The Western Church in the Late Middle Ages* (Ithaca, NY: Cornell University Press, 1979), 119, 240, and 311. For Eucharistic belief and practice at the end of the Middle Ages, see Miri Rubin, *Corpus Christi: The Eucharist in Late Medieval Culture* (Cambridge: University Press, 1991).

67. Lohse, *Martin Luther's Theology*, 312–13.

68. Emphasis mine; SC 6 (McCain, *Concordia*, 343).

69. In his *Confession Concerning Christ's Supper*, Luther distinguished between the "merit of Christ"—in other words, his sacrifice on the cross that won the forgiveness of sins—and the "distribution of merit" that takes place through the sacrament on account of the word of forgiveness that is there. See LW 37:192–94 (WA 26:294.23–297.26).

70. LW 38:88 (WA 30III:170.5–8).

71. *Anabaptist* is a sixteenth-century label meaning "rebaptizer," which their opponents coined for groups that practiced adult "believer's" baptism. See Holder, *The Westminster Handbook*, s.v. "Anabaptists"; and OER, s.v. "Anabaptists."

72. Emphasis mine; SC 4 (McCain, *Concordia*, 339–40).

73. See Althaus, *Theology*, 353–56.

74. The best known of these is probably "Concerning Rebaptism: A Letter of Martin Luther to Two Pastors" (1528), LW 40:229–62 (WA 26:144–74). He also included a section on infant baptism in the *Large Catechism* (LC 4.47–86). Jonathan D. Trigg, *Baptism in the Theology of Martin Luther* (Boston: Brill Academic Publishers, 2001), is an excellent treatment of Luther's baptismal doctrine in its historical development. See especially pp. 99–107 for Luther on infant baptism. Lohse, *Martin Luther's Theology*, 302–5, also summarizes Luther's rationale for the practice.

75. LW 40:245 (WA 26:158.28–37). See also LC 4.6–9.

76. In LC 4.50, Luther also mentioned Jean Gerson, a medieval scholar and churchman, and Bernard of Clairvaux.

77. LW 40:256 (WA 26:168.15–17). See also LC 4.49–53, 55, 57.

78. LW 40:242–43 (WA 26:156.8–158.27).

79. LW 40:242–43 (WA 26:156.34–157.6).

80. "With respect to my books written against individual persons, I admit that I have been sharper than was fitting for a professor and a monk"; J. B. Kidd, ed., *Documents Illustrative of the Continental Reformation* (Oxford: Clarendon Press, 1911), #42 (p. 84).

Luther's polemical style was noteworthy even in his own times. Philipp Melanchthon (1497–1560), Luther's good friend and colleague, actually mentioned it in his funeral eulogy for Luther. Brecht, *Martin Luther*, 3:380. For Melanchthon, see OER, s.v. "Melanchthon, Philipp."

Peter Matheson, *The Rhetoric of the Reformation* (Edinburgh: T&T Clark, 1998), 168–69, argues for the appropriateness of Luther's style, given the nature of his cause: "The charm of Luther's polemic is that he writes without regard to what is acceptable, digestible, communicable, expedient or safe. Paradigm shifts in thought demand a certain relentlessness, and moralising or psychologising calls for more humility may miss the point."

Nevertheless, modern readers often cringe when they read Luther's attacks on others. This has been especially true regarding some of his statements about the Jews, and certain critics have charged Luther with being a source for Hitler's anti-Semitism and totalitarianism (see, for example, William L. Shirer, *Rise and Fall of the Third Reich* [New York: Simon and Shuster, 1990], 236). Such accusations are extremely misleading since Luther's objections to the Jews and others were always theological and never racial, and, of course, Luther did *not* advocate genocide. See John Warwick Montgomery, "Shirer's Re-Hitlerizing of Luther," in *In Defense of Martin Luther* (Milwaukee: Northwestern Publishing House, 1970), 143–49, and Uwe Siemon-Netto, *The Fabricated Luther: Refuting Nazi Connections and Other Modern Myths*, 2nd ed. (St. Louis, MO: Concordia Publishing House, 2007), 24–25, 46–47, 49–52. For Luther's polemical style and crude language, see also Mark U. Edwards Jr., *Luther's Last Battles: Politics and Polemics, 1531–46* (Ithaca, NY: Cornell University Press, 1983), 3–5.

CHAPTER 4

Authority

The Holy Scriptures

A. S. Francisco

Every theological tradition that identifies itself as Christian maintains the authority of the Scriptures in some sense of the term, and
yet they all disagree on a number of issues concerning the theology
(and practice) of Christianity. This is largely due to the additional
authorities Christians have added alongside or on top of the authority of Scripture.

    Coming to terms with biblical authority is of the utmost impor-
tance. For what one identifies as authoritative when it comes to theology ultimately informs (if not determines) where one will end up
on the theological spectrum. Moreover, if theology is at its most
basic level a reassertion of God's revelation to humankind expressed
in the language of a particular culture, then it becomes all the more
important lest Christians idolatrously elevate and confuse the words
(and will) of men with the words (and will) of the Creator.

    That the Christian Church has always had, in one way or
another, a high view of the Bible should come as no surprise. After
all, God himself—in the person of Jesus—held the Hebrew Bible
of his day (the Old Testament) as the ultimate theological authority. At the beginning of his ministry when he was tempted by Satan
in the wilderness, he consistently responded by appealing directly
to the Bible, calling it the Word of God (Matt. 4:4). At the end of
his ministry while walking with the two confused men on the way

toward Emmaus, he directed them to "Moses and all the prophets" to explain the meaning of the events that had just transpired in Jerusalem. It was at this point—in the physical presence of Jesus after his crucifixion and resurrection—that those men came to see just what the prophetic message of the Old Testament really meant (Luke 24:13–35).[1]

Experiences like this are what emboldened the apostles and disciples of Jesus unwaveringly to preach the gospel despite opposition that soon escalated into persecution. As Clement of Rome (fl. 96) explained, "Being fully assured by the resurrection of our Lord Jesus Christ, and with faith confirmed by the word of God, they went forth in the assurance of the Holy Spirit preaching the good news."[2] Jesus had commissioned them to bring the message of the gospel "to the end of the earth" (Acts 1:8). To accomplish this, before his ascension, he promised to send them the Holy Spirit so they would be able to recall everything he taught them, guiding them in all truth (Jn. 14:15–31; 16:4–15). Eventually, after turning the world upside down with their preaching and persuasion—as the people from Thessalonica complained (Acts 17:6)—they inscribed those things of which they had been eyewitnesses or learned from eyewitnesses into the texts that make up the New Testament.[3]

Certainly not everything was written down. There was too much to write about (Jn. 20:30; 21:25). Nevertheless, what was written still comprised the inspired apostolic message in all its fullness. Thus after the generation of apostles, with their inspired teachings, had passed away, God's word remained, located in the two Testaments.

This at least is how the early church father Irenaeus of Lyons (d. 202) saw it in what is arguably the earliest extrabiblical source specifically addressing the issue of authority. Irenaeus wrote, "We have learned from none others the plan of salvation, than from those through whom the Gospel has come down to us, which they did at one time proclaim in public, and, at a later period, by the will of God, handed down to us in the Scriptures, to be the ground and pillar of our faith."[4] What these words by a preeminent early Church father tell us is that the texts comprising the New Testament were deemed (along with the Hebrew Bible) as the final authority for the Christian church. Irenaeus would also criticize those who placed other sources—especially oral tradition—alongside the Scriptures.

He was convinced that Scripture alone was sufficient for all matters of theology. This position was normative for Christian believers of the first three centuries of the Christian era. Tertullian (160–220) and Cyprian (d. 258), for example, advanced similar claims.

A competing view of authority, however, emerged in the fourth century. Basil of Caesarea (ca. 330–70) asserted, "Of the beliefs and practices whether generally accepted or publicly enjoined which are preserved in the Church some we possess derived from written teaching; others we have received delivered to us 'in a mystery' by the tradition of the apostles; and both of these in relation to true religion have the same force."[5] And Augustine of Hippo (354–430) suggested that "there are many things which are observed by the whole Church, and therefore are fairly held to have been enjoined by the apostles, which yet are not mentioned in their writings."[6] Elsewhere, in one of the most influential of Augustine's writings, was the assertion, "I should not believe the gospel except as moved by the authority of the Catholic Church."[7] What Augustine meant in this convoluted passage is hard to determine. Some of his medieval interpreters argued that the Church (and its traditions) carried only a practical or "instrumental authority." But Augustine was generally understood as proffering a view that asserted the "metaphysical priority" of the Church and its tradition.[8]

The result was a very different understanding of the authority of the Scriptures from that held by the very earliest Christian believers—specifically that "the Christian owes equal respect and obedience to the written *and* unwritten ecclesiastical traditions, whether they are contained in the canonical writings or in the secret oral tradition handed down by the Apostles through succession."[9] One can find the latter viewpoint along with the competing, earlier theological position in the writings of a number of medieval Christians. Eventually, however, the two-source theory elevating unwritten tradition to the status of an authority alongside Scripture came to predominate.

George Tavard has argued that the position of the Church having "her own revelation, independent of that which the Apostles recorded in their writings" was fully embraced by the fourteenth century.[10] Heiko Oberman, however, has challenged this and shown that the move toward the two-source approach as the dominant paradigm came earlier.[11] Already by the twelfth century, the views of

Basil and Augustine were written into canon law. It was then that "equal reverence for scriptural and extra-scriptural oral traditions" became the position of the Church.[12] Oberman also noted that scholastic theologians began to justify that view by assuming a certain coinherence between the Scripture and the traditions of the Church. As Henry of Ghent (1217–93) put it in his commentary on Peter Lombard's (1100–1160) *Sentences*, "The church and Holy Scripture agree in everything and testify to the same thing, namely to the truth of the faith, in which it is reasonable to believe both of them."[13] It became commonplace, then, to assume that Scripture and Church tradition, even though the latter may not be found in or even deduced from Scripture, implicitly agreed with each other.

The young Martin Luther (1483–1546) seems to have inherited this position. In his first lectures on the Psalms, he remarked, "As Christ is the Head of the church, so Scripture is also the head."[14] And in his lectures on Paul's epistle to the Romans, he expressed the viewpoint thus: "The authority of the church has been established, and to this day the Roman church still holds it."[15] Early in his career, he was intent on remaining "in agreement with the Catholic church and the teachers of the church."[16] Behind these early statements, most scholars see Luther as basically assuming that the historical church and its traditions were equal in authority "alongside Scripture."[17] Given the developments in the medieval church, this is not all that surprising.

All this would change, however, shortly after Luther drafted the *Ninety-Five Theses* in the fall of 1517. In a little more than three years, as the young theologian was forced by circumstances to examine his initial presumption of a basic coinherence of the Bible and the traditions of the Church, he would find himself driven to Scripture alone.

The impetus for this move came when Pope Leo X (1475–1521) notified Luther that he was being tried for heresy as his *Theses* had called into question the theory and practice of indulgence sales. To explain the seriousness of what Luther had done, the pope sent, along with the Bull summoning the German monk to Rome, a document explaining the Church's current view on authority. This document was written by the pope's theological adviser Sylvester Prierias (1456–1523) and titled *A Dialogue concerning the Power of the Pope*. It argued that contemporaneous teachings and practices of the Church rested upon the authority of the papacy. To challenge them was to challenge his divine authority, for "neither the Church of Rome nor the Supreme Pontiff reaching his decisions as Pontiff, that is, pronouncing out of his office, and doing what is in him in order to understand the truth can err."[18] In short, the document maintained that the teachings of the papacy were the "infallible rule of faith." What probably surprised Luther the most in reading this document, however, was its claim that "holy Scriptures derived their strength and authority" from the Church.[19]

Initially, Luther did not take Prierias's argument for the priority of the Church very seriously—at least he did not think it represented the official position of Rome.[20] But he soon found, particularly when he stood before Cardinal Cajetan at the Diet of Augsburg (1518), that the very opposite was the case. Luther therefore articulated his position in the following terms: "In matters of faith not only is a general council above the pope, but also any believer, provided he uses better authority or reason than the pope. . . . For the pope is not above but under the word of God."[21] This did not mean that the pope lacked administrative authority; Luther was simply insisting that "the truth of Scripture must come first. After that is accepted, one may determine whether the words of men can be accepted as true."[22] Cajetan's only response to Luther's arguments was baldly to assert the pope's authority *over* Scripture.[23]

Eight months later, Luther advanced similar arguments in his debate with the notorious polemicist Johann Eck at Leipzig (1519). He then publicly set forth his position in an open letter to Pope Leo X—affixed to his widely read *The Freedom of a Christian* (1520). There he explained, "I never intended to attack the Roman Curia or to raise any controversy concerning it. But when I saw all efforts to save it were hopeless, I despised it, gave it a bill of divorce."[24]

Luther referred to this "divorce" as having taken place before his debate with Eck. Thus it can be inferred that he had already arrived at his principle of authority before Leipzig.[25] Nevertheless, whenever this occurred, Luther not only rejected the view that the Church preceded the Scripture but also dissolved the presumed marriage between the two. He had, by this point, arrived "at the irrefutable certainty that there is no 'prestabilized harmony' between Scripture and church, that Scripture exists prior to and is ranked before and above the church."[26]

Luther's reply from the pope ordered him to recant in sixty days or be excommunicated from the Church. Convinced of the legitimacy of his convictions, Luther, during the morning of December 1520, stood just outside Wittenberg's east gate, with the university's faculty and students as witnesses to his public response. A bonfire was lit, and a host of papal books were symbolically tossed into the flames. Toward the end, Luther pulled the Bull of excommunication out of his academic gown and threw it into the fire as well, together with a copy of the canon law.[27]

The divorce was official. Luther explained his case in *Why the Books of the Pope and His Disciples Were Burned*. The papacy, he argued, had set itself over God's word in such a way as to be above reproof. If the papacy's authority was legitimate, "they would gladly permit themselves to be examined and tried. . . . But"— Luther continued—"the pope wants to blind everyone's eyes, let no one judge, but alone judge everyone."[28] This was demonstrable "by the fact," Luther declared, "that the pope has never once refuted with Scripture or reason anyone who has spoken, written, or acted against him, but has at all times suppressed, exiled, burned, or otherwise strangled him with force and bans."[29]

Knowing the fate he could meet (but providentially never did)— execution as a heretic—Luther continued to assert his position publicly. In the preface to *Defense and Explanation of All the Articles*, for example, he unequivocally stated his principle of authority and what became the formal principle of the so-called conservative Reformation:[30] "Scripture alone is the true lord and master of all writings and doctrine on earth."[31] This "forever established the *Sola Scriptura*"[32] for all to hear before the Imperial Diet at Worms (April 18, 1521), when he took his famous stand: "Unless I am convinced by the testimony of the Scriptures or by clear reason (for I do not trust either in the pope or in councils alone, since it is well known that they have often erred and contradicted themselves), I am bound by the Scriptures I have quoted and my conscience is captive to the Word of God."[33]

Luther had essentially, albeit amid very different circumstances, come to the principle of authority held by Irenaeus and the early Church fathers. And this cleared the way—by removing the theological innovations of the medieval centuries—for what Luther called a "reformation according to holy Scripture."[34]

It is important to note that Luther (and the other magisterial reformers) did not conceive of or carry out this Reformation as theological revisionists. The Protestant doctrine of *sola Scriptura* should not be understood as the rejection of church tradition in favor of subjective and novel interpretations of the Bible. The Lutheran reformers knew the dire consequences of Scripture being interpreted in a vacuum; such an approach was already surfacing amid the Anabaptists and left-wing radicals in the early days of the Reformation. "We do not act as fanatically as the sectarian spirits [i.e., Anabaptists]. We do not reject everything that is under the dominion of the Pope," wrote Luther in 1528—even though his excommunication was now a settled fact. He knew that the basic creedal formulations of the Church (the doctrine of the Trinity, the deity of Christ, etc.) were still confessed by the Church of Rome. Indeed, Luther conceded that it was from the papacy such sound doctrine "descended to us."[35] What the conservative Reformers meant by *sola Scriptura*, then, should be understood as "Scripture . . . is the only inspired, infallible, final, and authoritative norm of faith and practice. It is to be interpreted in and by the church; and it is to be interpreted within the hermeneutical context of the rule of faith."[36] In other words, while the Bible is the only inspired word of God and the Church and its traditions do not constitute a second, parallel source of revelation, the traditions of the Christian Church can aid and temper the potential subjectivism and possible sectarianism of the scriptural interpreter. The fundamental imperative, however, is that all theological declarations should correspond to and be constrained by the Word of God.

It was the Anabaptists and the broader radical reformers who took the doctrine of *sola Scripture* to the extreme when they rejected traditional, historical interpretations of Scripture and preferred hermeneutical novelty instead. When it came to authority, they placed "the private judgment of the individual above the corporate judgment of the Christian church concerning the interpretation of the Scripture."[37] And owing to their disdain for the historical Church, many of them would effectively go their own way, situating themselves outside the boundaries of the Church catholic.

To be sure, Rome would use such radicalism as positive proof of the heterodox nature of even the conservative Reformation. At the fourth session of the Council of Trent (1545–63), Rome accused

Lutherans of "twisting the Scriptures" by subjecting the interpretation of the Bible to private judgment. In reality, all the Lutheran Reformation had done was to remove what the medieval Church had *added* theologically and ecclesiastically in contradiction to biblical teaching. So in his *Examination of the Council of Trent*, the great Lutheran theologian Martin Chemnitz (1522–86) acknowledged the necessity of tradition as a check against innovative and subjective readings of the Bible manifest among the radical reformers and, at the same time, disavowed the authority of the medieval papacy as an authority over Scripture:

> No one should rely on his own wisdom in the interpretation of the Scripture, not even in the clear passages, for it is clearly written in 2 Peter 1:20: "The Scripture is not a matter of one's private interpretation." And whoever twists the Holy Scripture so that it is understood according to his preconceived opinions does this to his own destruction (2 Peter 3:16). The best reader of the Scripture according to Hilary [of Poitiers, 300–368], is one who does not carry the understanding of what is said to the Scripture but who carries it away from the Scripture. We also gratefully and reverently use the labors of the fathers who by their commentaries have profitably clarified many passages of the Scripture. And we confess that we are greatly confirmed by the testimonies of the ancient church in the true and sound understanding of the Scripture. Nor do we approve of it if someone invents for himself a meaning which conflicts with all antiquity, and for which there are clearly no testimonies of the church.[38]

Here we have one of the clearest illustrations of the difference between the Lutheran and Roman principles of authority. Both respect traditional interpretations of the Scripture as a check against unwarranted innovation and radical theological revisionism. But for Lutherans, Scripture is the *sole* source of revelation and the *final* authority—whereas for Rome, Scripture, though certainly *an* authority owing to its revelatory character, is subject to tradition, particularly papal tradition, for its proper understanding and interpretation. This means in practice that tradition—an extrabiblical source of doctrine—is elevated to revelational status. Heiko Oberman described the official position of Rome this way: "The Council of Trent admits that not all doctrinal truths are to be found in Holy

Scripture. Tradition is seen as a second doctrinal source which does not 'simply' unfold the content of Scripture . . . but adding its own substance complements Holy Scripture content-wise."[39]

It is important to note that not just the Lutherans but also the Calvinists held the position that the Bible alone is God's word and that it should be normatively interpreted within the creedal context of the historic Church. Calvin's *Institutes* asserts, "We willingly embrace and reverence as holy the early councils, such as Nicaea, Constantinople, Ephesus I, Chalcedon, and the like, which were concerned with refuting errors—in so far as they relate to the teaching of faith. For they contain nothing but the pure and genuine exposition of the Scripture, which the holy fathers applied with spiritual prudence to crush the enemies of religion."[40]

Where the Lutheran and Reformed disagreed was not so much in their principle of authority but in what they viewed as having priority in the systematic ordering of theology (for the Calvinists: the sovereignty of God; for Lutherans: the Incarnation and the Cross) and to what extent rational argument should inform biblical exegesis (e.g., in the understanding of the Lord's Supper—for the Lutherans: the real presence of the whole Christ, body and spirit, on the straightforward basis of Christ's declaration, "This is my body"; for the Calvinists: his spiritual presence only, since it would allegedly be irrational for Christ's body to be present other than at the right hand of God in heaven).

In the centuries that followed the Protestant Reformation, the viewpoint of the left-wing radicals that Scripture should be interpreted apart from any tradition began to coalesce into something new. During the eighteenth century, across the Atlantic in North America, the subjective and individualist interpretation of the radicals fused with Enlightenment rationalism and American populism. Keith Mathison has termed such a view of authority *solo Scriptura* ("Scripture interpreted by and for me alone")—in contradistinction to the Reformation doctrine of *sola Scriptura* ("Scripture alone").

This philosophy was rejected by the conservative Reformation, and for good reason. For while radical reformers claimed the authority of the Bible, epistemological priority (particularly when it came to interpreting the Bible) was ultimately given not to the Church, as in the case of Rome, or to the Scripture itself, as with the Lutheran Reformation, but to the individual reader of the Scriptures. Thomas

Müntzer (1488–1525), who was in many ways the *magister* of the radical reformers,[41] taught that God revealed himself directly to human beings. The illumination of the spirit then dictated how one interpreted the Bible.

It is not difficult to see how this approach in principle legitimizes any and every interpretation of the Bible. What eventually happened was a re-envisioning of historic Christianity, beginning in the sixteenth century and extending to the present day. Such an approach, stemming from unverifiable illuminations of "the spirit," was manifested by restorationists like Alexander Campbell (1788–1866), when he wrote, "I have endeavored to read the Scriptures as though no one had read them before."[42]

The consequence was and has been a proliferation of new Christian sects and heresies and eventually the nondenominational movement. Aaron B. Grosh (1800–1884), for example, could promote Universalism while calling the Bible the "one Master" that was his "only acknowledged creed book"—or Charles Beecher (1815–1900) could, on one hand, locate theological authority in the "Bible, the whole Bible, and nothing but the Bible" but, on the other, preach such novelties as the preexistence of the human soul before conception.[43]

As we said at the outset, the Christian church—even defined very broadly—has always recognized the authority of the Bible in one way or another. And for the most part Christians—even nominal ones—place it at the center of their overall understanding of authority. For the Roman Catholic Church, the Scriptures are treated as God's revealed word but a word that is not really complete; God's revelation needs the completion offered by the traditions and interpretation of the Church. Ecclesiastical traditions are viewed by Rome as a second—not secondary—source of revelation that not only adds to the biblical word of God but also determines how the Scriptures are to be understood.

Tradition, in this view, can confirm and perpetuate biblical doctrine, but it can also add elements not found in the text of the Bible. It can even, as in the case of dogmas such as the existence of purgatory or the perpetual virginity of Mary, squeeze beliefs out of the Bible that are quite foreign to a historical and grammatical analysis of its text. The same phenomenon may likewise be observed in Eastern Orthodox theology and even in the Anglican tradition.

Since the Reformation, Protestants of every stripe have reacted to this dual-source theory of authority. The most popular failing has been the initial elevation of the Bible above Christian tradition but then effectively jettisoning all or most all creedal and traditional ecclesiology, even when nowhere condemned by Scripture. This has left the Church with a Bible in isolation from the history of Christianity; from reliable, classical biblical interpretation; and from the ecumenical creeds and the historic confessions. The result: a Bible that could be interpreted in almost any imaginable way depending on the disposition, context, linguistic, and theological predilections of the interpreter. This approach can produce anything—the mystical and spiritualist type of Christianity first espoused by Thomas Müntzer in the sixteenth century, the premillennial dispensationalism of the Dallas Seminary and local church movement, or even the Muslim theology of the author of *The Bible Led Me to Islam*.

For all intents and purposes, *solo* (not *sola*) *Scriptura* is modern evangelicalism's view of authority. And a cursory survey of the broad spectrum of evangelicalism reveals that, while everyone claims to work from the same text, contradictory conclusions are the order of the day. The reason for this is that it is practically impossible to interpret the Bible objectively by a myopic look at the text as such. Interpreters of the Bible working from the principle of *solo Scriptura* may not interpret the Bible through the lens of unfortunate theological traditions, but they do interpret the Bible in accordance with their own biases. These biases can derive from contemporary culture, ideological assumptions, or anything that colors their worldview. Ultimately, what *solo Scriptura* does is to replace external tradition as a parallel source of theology alongside the Bible with a source that is internal, located within the *persona* of the interpreter.

The principle of *sola Scriptura* established by Luther not only militates against the dual-source theory of authority but at the same time mediates between it and the subjectivity of the *solo Scriptura* approach. On the one hand, any arbitrary elevation of episcopal tradition as a source of God's word and the consequent adding to the text of the Bible is rejected. On the other hand, there is the clear recognition that, while God's word is located in the Bible alone, it is necessarily received and interpreted by the historic Church.

That Church, however, being comprised of sinful people, is fallible. It is in need of continual reformation (*Ecclesia semper reformanda est*). To bring the Church's theology back into line with God's word, Luther rightly saw the Scripture and the Scripture alone as the only instrument capable of achieving the needed corrections.

The Lutheran theological tradition sees itself not as an innovation of the sixteenth century but as the continuation of the Church of Christ, founded on the apostles' teaching and preserved in spite of the corruptions of medieval and modern antibiblical doctrines and practices.

What *sola Scriptura* provides is a clear principle of authority for faith. To keep such faith grounded and constrained by the Word of God, Lutherans are willing to listen to the history of the Church. This does not mean naïvely accepting its errors; it means critiquing it where it has failed but at the same time accepting its gifts where they are consonant with biblical teaching.

Thus the Lutheran Church is a confessional body—accepting with joy the ecumenical creeds of Christendom (the Apostles', Nicene, and Athanasian Creeds) and the magnificent confessional statements of the Reformation as contained in the *Book of Concord*. The contributions of the historic Church are received with joy—but (to cite the Preface of the Formula of Concord, the last of those great Confessions) Scripture remains as the "only standard by which all teachers and writings must be judged." For this reason, the Lutheran tradition offers Christians who strive to be faithful to God's word the surest way to order both their theology and their ecclesiastical and personal lifestyle.

Notes

1. Quotations from the Bible are taken from the *English Standard Version* (Wheaton, IL: Crossway, 2001).

2. 1 Clement 42:3, in *The Apostolic Fathers*, ed. Kirsopp Lake (New York: G. P. Putnam's Sons, 1919), 1:81.

3. On this, see J. E. Komoszewski, M. J. Sawyer, and D. B. Wallace, *Reinventing Jesus: How Contemporary Skeptics Miss the Real Jesus and Mislead Popular Culture* (Grand Rapids, MI: Kregel Publications, 2006), 21–38.

4. Irenaeus, *Adversus Haeresus*, in *Ante-Nicene Fathers*, ed. Philip Schaff (Peabody, MA: Hendrickson Publishers, 1996), 1:415.

5. Basil, *De Spiritu Sancto*, in *Nicene and Post-Nicene Fathers*, ed. Philip Schaff (Peabody, MA: Hendrickson Publishers, 1996), 8:42.

6. Augustine, *On Baptism, against the Donatists*, in *Nicene and Post-Nicene Fathers*, ed. Philip Schaff (Peabody, MA: Hendrickson Publishers, 1996), 4:475.

7. Augustine, *Against the Letter of Mani*, in *Nicene and Post-Nicene Fathers*, ed. Philip Schaff (Peabody, MA: Hendrickson Publishers, 1996), 4:131.

8. Heiko A. Oberman, "*Quo Vadis Petre?* Tradition from Irenaeus to Humani Generis," in *The Dawn of the Reformation: Essays in Late Medieval and Early Reformation Thought* (Edinburgh: T&T Clark, 1992), 278.

9. Oberman, "*Quo Vadis Petre?*," 277.

10. George Tavard, *Holy Writ or Holy Church?* (New York: Burns & Oates, 1959), 36.

11. See note 8 for bibliographical details. For a full exposé on the crisis of the status of Scripture, church, and tradition, see Beryl Smalley, *The Study of the Bible in the Middle Ages* (Notre Dame: Notre Dame University Press, 1964), 215ff.

12. Oberman, "*Quo Vadis Petre?*," 277.

13. Quoted in Carl A. Volz, *The Medieval Church: From the Dawn of the Middle Ages to the Eve of the Reformation* (Nashville: Abingdon Press, 1997), 162.

14. Jaroslav Pelikan and Helmut T. Lehmann, eds., *Luther's Works*, vol. 11 (St. Louis, MO: Concordia Publishing House, 1955ff.), 517(hereafter cited as LW).

15. LW 25:415.

16. LW 31:16.

17. Bernard Lohse, *Martin Luther's Theology: Its Historical and Systematic Development*, trans. Roy A. Harrisville (Minneapolis, MN: Fortress Press, 1999), 187.

18. Sylvester Prierias, "Dialogus de potestate Papae," in *Documents Illustrative of the Continental Reformation*, ed. B. J. Kidd (Oxford: Clarendon Press, 1911), 31.

19. Prierias, "Dialogus," 32.

20. See Carter Lindberg, "Prierias and His Significance for Luther's Development," *Sixteenth Century Journal* 3 (October 1972): 50.

21. LW 31:265–66, 266–67.

22. LW 31:282.

23. H. Schüssler, "Sacred Doctrine and the Authority of Scripture in Canonistic Thought on the Eve of the Reformation," in *Reform and Authority in the Medieval and Reformation Church*, ed. Guy F. Lytle (Washington, D.C.: Catholic University of America Press, 1981), 62–64.

24. LW 31:338.

25. Lohse argues that even though Luther had not expressly stated his principle of Scripture alone by the time of his meeting with Cajetan in 1518, he was in fact working from it (Bernard Lohse, "Luther und die Autorität Roms im Jahre 1518," in *Christian Authority*, ed. G.R. Evans [Oxford: Clarendon Press, 1988], 152).

26. Lohse, *Martin Luther's Theology*, 188.

27. Cf. John Warwick Montgomery, "Luther and Canon Law," in *Christ Our Advocate* (Bonn, Germany: Verlag fuer Kultur und Wissenschaft, 2002); Montgomery, "Luther and Libraries," in *In Defense of Martin Luther* (Milwaukee: Northwestern Publishing House, 1970).

28. LW 31:395.

29. LW 31:395.

30. This is the title of C. P. Krauth's magisterial treatise, *The Conservative Reformation and Its Theology*, reprint ed. (St. Louis, MO: Concordia Publishing House, 2007).

31. LW 32:11–12.

32. M. Reu, *Luther and the Scriptures* (Columbus: Wartburg Press, 1944), 19.

33. LW 32:112.

34. LW 32:122–23.

35. Oberman, "*Quo Vadis Petre?*," 285.

36. Keith A. Mathison, "Solo Scriptura: The Difference a Vowel Makes," *Modern Reformation* 16, no. 2 (2007): 26.

37. Alister McGrath, *Reformation Thought: An Introduction* (Oxford: Basil Blackwell, 1988), 107.

38. Martin Chemnitz, *The Examination of the Council of Trent*, trans. Fred Kramer (St. Louis, MO: Concordia Publishing House, 1971), 208–9.

39. Oberman, "*Quo Vadis Petre?*," 288.

40. Quoted in Mathison, "Solo Scriptura," 27.

41. See Steven Ozment, *Mysticism and Dissent: Religious Ideology and Social Protest in the Sixteenth Century* (New Haven: Yale University Press, 1973), 61–97.

42. Quoted in Mathison, "Solo Scriptura," 27.

43. Ibid., 27

CHAPTER 5

The Way of Salvation

The Gospel

Rod Rosenbladt

Almost any church that bears the name "Christian" will say things about "the Gospel." Christians are agreed that "Christ saves sinners." But there is quite a bit of difference among Christians as to what that proposition means. This chapter will attempt to summarize those differences in understanding regarding "the Gospel." And when examined, we will find that those differences are quite substantial—hardly what anyone would call "trivial" or "secondary."

For each position, we will quickly look at the background to Christian justification: a church's position as to the extent of, the effects of, and the depth of the Fall. Why? Because our post-Fall condition is logically linked to our view of the cross of Christ, *how* His death and resurrection "save sinners." We will look in some detail as to what each church claims is the doctrine of justification: *how* the death of one particular Jew has anything to do with what C. S. Lewis calls "putting us right with God." We will see in each case that groups of Christians affirm and/or disaffirm many of the details about this Gospel "saving"—that is, the details of *how* Christianity "works."

The reader would do well to keep central in his or her mind the following questions: *Is* this version of the Gospel presenting a free gift to me as a sinner, or is it somehow earned? If it is "earned," how exactly do I have to earn it? If the Gospel's benefits are truly and genuinely gratis, truly free gifts to sinners, do those benefits just *begin* as a free gift, then turn into something else? That is, do they *continue* to be free to me, or are there things I must *do* to ensure that they remain truly mine? If they do *not* continue to be free to me, what must I do to make sure that what I was freely given at the start I do not forfeit along the way? Are there things I must *do* (or *not do*) to avoid losing the initial gift of the benefits of the Gospel? If so, what are the details of those things I must do or not do?

Such an exercise of the brain has not only theological benefits (being sure that what one has embraced is genuinely "the Gospel" and is a true representation of the Apostolic message proclaimed again and again in the book of Acts) but also *psychiatric* ramifications. Luther knew by bitter experience that the absolute worst of inward conditions was *doubt—particularly*, doubt with regard to God's attitude to him or her. Could it possibly be true that we could *know* for sure that God is gracious to us because of Christ's work in our behalf, day-by-day, hour-by-hour, sleeping or waking? If such a thing is possible, what are the exact details underlying that kind of confidence, that kind of deep and definitive inner relaxation?

Most of us know people who are deeply convinced of the truth of something that we consider unsound. And we naturally want to avoid falling into a similar position ourselves. What position with regard to "the Gospel" can solidly undergird a confidence that we are not (as Mark Twain put the matter) "believin' what you know ain't true?" On that question (the question of the "truth-value" of a given Christian church's basic propositions), the Lutheran position is magnificently covered in virtually *all* the writings of Dr. John Warwick Montgomery.

Roman Catholic: The Gospel of Justification as Sanctification

"The Gospel" of Rome was finally "put to paper" at the Council of Trent (1545–63). What is the nature of the Gospel, according to those Roman thinkers? At Trent they set forth their view of justification (what Lutherans called "the Gospel") in a series of theses and antitheses. Various canons (particularly 12, 13, and 14) made clear what they said the Gospel was *not*, and they pronounced "anathema" on this view. What the Gospel was *not* was the forensic or judicial view of how sinners are justified before God (and in particular, the view of the "heretics" of that day—that is to say, the Lutherans). Specifically condemned was the Gospel that "men are justified freely by the remission of sins and the imputation of Christ's righteousness." *White Horse Inn* host Dr. Michael Horton rightly says that "at Trent, Rome anathematized the Gospel!" And so they did.

It comes as a surprise to many non-Roman laity how often Roman thinkers freely quote the Bible on the subject of salvation by grace (Rom. 3:24, 28; 4:5; Gal. 2:16–21; Eph. 2:8–10; Titus 3:5–8). But the Roman Catholic has no trouble at all asserting that justification is an act of God's "grace!" Any move toward Christ, they acknowledge, is and has to be a result of God's "sanctifying grace." Without "prevenient" ("going-before-us") grace, we would not be inclined to Christ, not be inclined to seek justification before Him.

But man the sinner can and must cooperate with two initial "graces" (first with "actual" or "prevenient" grace, second with "sanctifying" or "cooperating" grace) in order to be justified before God. And fallen man is capable of each of these cooperations. How so? At the Fall, Adam and Eve were deprived of the "extra-added gifts of grace" (the ability to fear, love, and trust in God above all else and to love their neighbor as themselves). Adam and Eve were weakened by the Fall, were in need of "medicinal" or healing grace if they were to be justified before God. But Adam and his children most definitely are *not* "dead in sin." If we are creatures of "concupiscence" (the driving desire within for sin), it is not itself sin, *nor* should we view ourselves as "totally depraved." Adam and Eve retained after the Fall certain "natural attributes" (particularly their rationality and their freedom of will with regard to "things heavenly"—that is, matters concerning their relationship with God). Given the nature of their post-Fall condition, God could and did call for them to cooperate with His grace. He called on them to "prepare" for justification. They could not (positively) make themselves worthy of grace, but they could (negatively) make themselves "less unworthy," less "unsusceptible" of that grace. Because of the truth of the aphorism "God never refuses His grace to him who does what lies within his power," it is possible for fallen man to either resist God's grace or consent to it. As put in another aphorism, "God alone makes conversion a possibility, but man makes it a reality."

What is the nature of justification, according to Rome? What is the Gospel? We have already pointed out that they rejected the Lutheran view that it was the *favor dei propter Christum* ("the favor of God on account of Christ"). The Gospel, according to Rome, is that justification is *not* just "remission of sin" but it *includes* "renewal, the sanctification and renewal of the inner man." (The Lutherans, of course, accepted passages about the "new birth," the "new creature" [e.g., Rom. 6]—but these were [at least logically] *subsequent* to the sinner being gratuitously declared completely righteous while yet in the depth of his awful, sinful condition [justification before God while still at our moral worst (Rom. 5:8)].) This justification, the Lutherans said, was based on the Person and work of Christ *for us*, particularly His objective vicarious death *for us*, for our sin, and His righteousness imputed to us, to our accounts—reckoned by God as if really ours. It was *not* based on any prior "change" or "quality" within us. The Word of the Gospel does not just forgive (it definitely does do that); it raises from complete spiritual death those who are haters of God and *dead* in sin. Haters of God don't ever want to cooperate with God, and dead men can't.

Rome's Gospel of Justification centers on "the renewal" and is said to be a lifelong *process* rather than an instantaneous declaration. This process is approximately what non-Roman Christians call "sanctification." Justification, according to Rome, involves actually *changing* an individual unjust sinner into a genuinely just man. And since Rome's doctrine of justification *includes* such renewal, growth in Christ, renovation, transformation, and so on, it is of necessity a theology of *doubt*. If you were raised Baptist, you must kiss off what you were taught about "assurance of salvation" if and when you convert to Rome. There can be no such assurance when "your transformation or renovation is part of the deal" in justification. You will have bequeathed to you a theology that purposely prevents you from any such "assurance." The Council of Trent strongly maintained the *uncertainty* of justification. No one (including the pope or Mother Theresa) can have a certainty about their justification—unless (like the thief on the cross) God gives them a direct revelation about it! And even if He were to give you such a revelation, how would you be sure that it was what it seemed? About Scripture, there is a great case for its being written revelation, but there is no such case with regard to "personal, direct revelations!" You could not rationally trust one even if God gave it to you! A sentence like "Work out your own salvation with fear and trembling" (Phil. 2:12)[1] will necessarily take on a new and terrifying meaning for you. And in principle, you can never know whether you have done enough to qualify. This was exactly what Luther faced as a monk, and no matter which of the many counsels he received from his superiors, all of them came to naught as "answers" to his nagging doubts regarding his standing before God. And no wonder! There was always something of "him" in the so-called answers he received!

The Council of Trent maintained that the Roman Christian *could have* a degree of certainty ("moral certainty"), but it would always ebb and flow. The anxious Roman Christian was directed to the "fruit of justification": his or her good works (always "grace-empowered," of course!) as truly meritorious indicators of one's state. God was contractually obliged to grant merit to the sinner for these and most certainly would. And they were told that it was possible to do *more than was required* for one's own justification! So-called works of supererogation (works even beyond perfection) were possible—on the part of not only "the saints" but the rest of us as well! Rome's counsel of "assurance" was to look to these for the assurance you sought. Hope is found only in *real* inner change—*not* in God's declaration of the righteousness of another being instantly credited to you as if your own. "Keep on keeping on," using the grace given you in the sacramental system, and hope that you have done enough to qualify. Assurance lies in your gradual "renewal," in "becoming actually just." Any "Gospel" that centers in God's declaration of the *favor dei propter Christum* is, Rome says, a *false* "Gospel."

A Brief Bibliography pro/con the Roman Catholic Theology

The Baltimore Catechism. Various editions.

Engelder, Theodore, W. Arndt, Th. Graebner and F. E. Mayer. *Popular Symbolics: The Doctrines of the Churches of Christendom and other Religions Examined in the Light of Scripture.* St. Louis MO: Concordia, 1934. Part II (B), "The Roman Catholic Church," 147–206.

Hardon, John, S. J. *The Catholic Catechism: Contemporary Catechism of the Teachings of the Catholic Church*. New York: Doubleday, 1981.

Klotsche, E. H., *Christian Symbolics*. Burlington, IA: The Lutheran Literary Board, revised ed., 1929. Chapter 3: The Roman Catholic Church, 58–132.

Mayer, F. E. *Religious Bodies of America*. St. Louis, MO: Concordia, 1954. 4th ed. revised by Arthur Carl Piepkorn, 1961. Part II: *The Holy Catholic Apostolic Roman Church*, 25–126.

Ott, Ludwig. *Fundamentals of Catholic Dogma*. Translated by Patrick Lynch. Rockford, IL: Tan Books, 1974.

Pelikan, Jaroslav. *The Emergence of the Catholic Tradition (100–600)*. Vol. 1 (1971) in *The Christian Tradition: A History of the Development of Doctrine*. 5 vols. Chicago: University of Chicago Press, 1971–1991. See also vol. 4 (*Reformation of Church and Dogma [1300–170]*), Section 5 ("The Definition of Roman Catholic Particularity," 245–331).

Piepkorn, Arthur Carl, *Profiles in Belief*. New York: Harper and Row, 1977, vol. I, part IV (12), "The Roman Catholic Church— Theology and Doctrine," 211–38 and (13), "Nature and Function of the Church," 239–78.

Ratzinger, Joseph Cardinal. *The New Catholic Catechism*. New York: Doubleday, 1994.

The Gospel of Lutheranism: "Free for All!"

What is "the Gospel" according to Luther and his Confessional Lutheran followers? Simply put (and from the Bible), one might cite what St. Paul explicitly refers to as "the Gospel" in a few verses of 1 Corinthians 15:

> For I delivered to you as of first importance what I also received: that Christ died for our sins in accordance with the Scriptures, that he was buried, that he was raised on the third day in accordance with the Scriptures, and that he appeared to Cephas, then to the twelve. Then he appeared to more than five hundred brothers at one time, most of whom are still alive, though some have fallen asleep. Then he appeared to James, then to all the apostles. Last of all, as to one untimely born, he appeared also to me. (1 Cor. 15:3–8)

Or perhaps 2 Corinthians 5:19 ("that God was in Christ reconciling the world to Himself") or Romans 4:5 ("But to him who does not work but trusts in God who justifies wicked people, his faith is reckoned as if it were righteousness") or even the familiar John 3:16.

If one is seeking the simplest exposition from *outside* Holy Scripture, most Lutherans would reflexively think of Luther's exposition of the meaning of the Second Article of the Apostles' Creed in the *Small Catechism*:

> I believe that Jesus Christ, true God, begotten of the Father from eternity, and also true man, born of the Virgin Mary, is my Lord, who has redeemed me, a lost and condemned creature, purchased and won [delivered] me from all sins, from death, and from the power of the devil, not with gold or silver, but with His holy, precious blood and with His innocent suffering and death, in order that I may be His own, and live under Him in His kingdom, and serve Him in everlasting righteousness, innocence, and blessedness, even as He is risen from the dead, lives and reigns to all eternity. This is most certainly true.

Another source to which we can turn if our question is "What is the Gospel?" is Luther's famous preface to his greater *Commentary on St. Paul's Epistle to the Galatians*.[2] In this short preface, Luther tackles the question of what he calls "Christian righteousness" or "the righteousness of faith," as opposed to other kinds of righteousness. He argues that all the latter (political righteousness, ceremonial righteousness, the righteousness of the Law, etc.) have this in common: (1) they are all instances of what is *opposed to* Christian righteousness or the righteousness of faith, and (2) they all consist in our works, what can be achieved by us.

Luther characterizes "the righteousness of faith" as (1) a righteousness that God *imputes* to believers *without works*; (2) quite the opposite of political, ceremonial, legal, or works "righteousness"; and (3) *passive*—one that we simply receive and for which we work *nothing*, render *nothing* to God.

Luther goes on to demonstrate how, in times of terrors of conscience caused by the Law or when facing death, no man is able to look at anything but his *active* righteousness, his own works, his own worthiness measured by the Law. But the Law is no remedy. It *cannot* bring peace to the human conscience; in fact, it makes the conscience even *sadder*, drives it to despair. The *only* remedy is the promise of grace offered in Christ: "the righteousness of faith," which we do not perform but receive, which we do not *have* but accept when God grants it to us through Jesus Christ.

Luther argues that the highest art and wisdom is *not* "to know the Law" but rather to *ignore* all works, all *active* righteousnesses. He grants that works and the performance of the Law must be demanded *in this world*, as though there were no promise or grace. Why? In order that the stubborn, proud, and hardhearted "old Adam" in us might be terrified and humbled.

He then instructs his readers on the importance of dividing these two Words of God (the one about "active righteousness" and the other about "Christian or passive righteousness"). When a man is contrite, is oppressed by the Law, is terrified by his sin, and thirsts for comfort, the wise pastor removes the Law and "active righteousness" from his sight and sets before him nothing but the Gospel and "passive righteousness" (which removes Moses and the Law). "This is our theology! By it we teach a precise distinction between these two kinds of righteousness—the 'active' and the 'passive.'"[3] Luther freely admits that both Words are necessary but "must be kept within their limits." And he spells out these limits in detail (limits of "active righteousness," limits of "passive or Christian righteousness").

Luther has an opponent ask, "Then we *hear* nothing, *do* nothing and *work* nothing with regard to the Law or about works?!" Luther replies, "*Nothing at all.* Christ is our High Priest Who is interceding for us, and here one notices no sin, feels no terror or remorse of conscience" (Luther cites Rom. 4:15). Luther describes what things look like when "Christ is truly seen" (full and perfect joy in the Lord and peace of heart) and then offers a script of what the heart can declare, can confess when "Christ is truly seen."

He admits that so long as we live here on earth, both Words— the Law as well as the Gospel—remain. But neither must be allowed to cross the boundaries of its domain. Paul's *Epistle to the Galatians* was written to sustain us in knowledge of this "Christian righteousness," to encourage us to reject any "active righteousness" that would leak over into the doctrine of justification. "For if the doctrine of justification is lost, the whole of Christian doctrine is lost."

And according to Luther, there *is no middle ground* at this point. Stray from the Scriptural teaching regarding "Christian righteousness" and we will necessarily relapse/revert back into "active righteousness," and Christ will be completely lost sight of. We will fall back into a trust of our own works.

After charging the Anabaptists with being clueless regarding this distinction, Luther encourages pastors and teachers to always urge and inculcate this doctrine of faith or "Christian righteousness."[4] If they do not do this, Christ will be so obscured in teaching that no one will be correctly taught or comforted! To this end Luther encourages pastors and teachers to "exercise yourselves by study, by reading, by meditation, and by prayer" so that you will be able to instruct/rightly console your own conscience and that of others: to take yourself and them from the Law to grace, from "active righteousness" to "passive righteousness," from Moses to Christ. Luther devotes space to analysis of the devil's habit in our affliction, in times of conflict of conscience, how he first frightens us with the Law in order to drive us to despair. Then he uses passages from the Gospels wherein Christ Himself requires works from us, threatening us with damnation in the case we do not perform them. In this case, we must be skilled at distinguishing God's one Word from His other Word. If we are not adept at this, we will be convinced that we are under the Law and Christ is (for us) no longer a Savior but a lawgiver. Luther again offers his reader a script: what a believer must say to the Law under such circumstances!

Luther closes with confidence that this "Christian righteousness" will always produce earthly good works—no matter our vocation here on earth.

A second historical Lutheran gem on the subject of the sinner's justification before God is Philipp Melanchthon's *Apology of the Augsburg Confession*, Article IV. It spells out the Biblical details of the justification of sinners, *and* contrasts it with the Roman doctrine. *Apology* IV begins by claiming that the article of justification of sinners is the *main doctrine* of Christianity.

Overall, the Lutheran claim is that sinners do *not* receive forgiveness of sins because of their own merits but freely for Christ's sake and through faith in Him *apart from works*. The major points of this claim are these (in the order given in the Augsburg Confession):

1. All Holy Scripture should be divided into two chief doctrines: the Law and the Promises.

2. There does exist a "righteousness of reason," a "civic righteousness," but it is *not* to be seen as saving, as if it stood in place of Christ and His death and resurrection *for us*. It is earthly only, a gift of God to restrain sinners in the realm of the civil. And because always performed by our "flesh," these civil works are *not* meritorious before God but quite the contrary: they are sin!

3. The faith that justifies is *not* just a "historical faith" (assent to the true facts with regard to Jesus Christ, His life and death—even His resurrection!). Rather, it is a confident acceptance of God's offer promising forgiveness of sins through Christ's death and resurrection *for us*. Such saving faith is made up of three elements: (1) the promise itself, (2) the fact that this promise is free, and (3) the merits of Christ as the price and propitiation. True knowledge of God, true worship of God, is the *opposite* of merit: it is composed of accepting His blessings, receiving His mercy in the Person and work of Christ. The only true consolation for sinners when afflicted is God's free mercy and forgiveness of sins based on Christ's merit and *not* on any of our own.

4. The preaching of God's law (or of penitence on the part of the sinner) fills the heart with serious fears—fears that need true consolation. True consolation happens only when our hearts believe Christ's promise that *for His sake* we have forgiveness of sin.

5. Sinners cannot deal with the true God except by means of His (external) Word—that is, His written promises. Justification takes place *only* through God's (external) Word. To believe means to trust in Christ's merits—*not* in our (imagined) "merits." Anyone who denies that faith in Christ justifies teaches only the law and *does away with Christ* and the Gospel. Anyone who teaches that because of Christ and through faith in Him, we are truly accounted (as if) righteous and accounted acceptable before God teaches the true Gospel.

6. Sinners obtain the forgiveness of sins *only* by faith in Christ. Love to God and neighbor, good works, *will* follow such faith. But these are *never* the basis of a sinner's justification before God. Trust in any supposed "merit" of love or works is *excluded* from justification. Trusting in our own love or merits cannot stand against the wrath of God. But it is Biblically certain that sins are forgiven because of Christ the Propitiator. Such forgiveness is promised *for Christ's sake*. Because of this, it can be accepted *only* by faith (since it is the nature of a promise that it can be accepted only on faith).

7. This faith in Christ *is* the righteousness by which we are accounted righteous before God—and *not* because "faith" is some work worthy in itself. Rather, this trust in God's promise to sinners is a matter of God benevolently (gratuitously) creating within sinners (ex nihilo) the acceptance of His own promise in Christ.

8. Anyone who teaches that justifying faith justifies based on its consequent works ("faith formed by love") rejects faith in Christ and destroys the entire promise of the free forgiveness of sins and of the righteousness of Christ. Anyone who teaches that love justifies teaches only the Law. "Justification by love" is a wicked and empty trust in the sinner's own righteousness, and as such, it insults Christ. Works can never pacify the conscience but instead drive it to despair; only God's promise in Christ can pacify the troubled conscience.

The background to this understanding of the Gospel lies in the Lutherans' understanding of the depth and effects of Adam's Fall. They defended a view of our Fall that was total, "to our very core, to the very depths of what is *us*." From that fateful event described in Genesis 3, the Lutherans maintained that (with regard to "things heavenly") our intellects became utterly darkened and our wills completely bound in unbelief.[5] We make no "move" back toward our Creator (1) because not a single man, woman, or child wants to and (2) because even if we *did* want to, we could not. In Adam, each of us is both "dead in sin" *and* an active hater of God. We are completely devoid of faith in Father *or* Son, unable to exercise even "a stitch of it"—and *proud* of that fact!

With regard to the Person of Christ, Lutherans have always affirmed the contents of the "Ecumenical Creeds" regarding the true humanity and the complete deity of Jesus Christ *and* the Scriptural claim that He is *one* Person, undivided.[6] We affirm that His deity is manifested *through His body*—a "communication of attributes" but without a confusion of substance. (This is, of course, the Christological basis for the Lutherans' view of Holy Baptism [born again by water with the Word of Promise] and the Lord's Supper [reception of the benefits of His work via material elements—bread and wine]).

With regard to Christ's work, Lutherans made use of the "net" of His work as Prophet, Priest, and King in order to "catch the verses." Though our early theologians were not the first to employ this "net," they saw it as very helpful in making sense of a large number of Biblical verses on the subject of the work of Christ. (Parenthetically, our *Book of Concord* has no section labeled "The Work of Christ" but instead features Melanchthon's studies of the Biblical words associated with the cross—*how* the Bible text describes Christ's cross and blood and death saving sinners.)

In the Reformation era, Lutheran theologians stressed Christ's "Priestly" or "saving" work, because *the* question of the sixteenth century was about how God justifies sinners. And the upshot of it was this: God declares sinners as if they were righteous—*not* based on their virtues, merits, or good works, but *freely* (gratuitously) and solely *for the sake of Christ*—particularly for the sake of His vicarious and substitutionary death in our stead but also for his sinless law-obeying life lived *for us*. When a man, woman, or child believes that he or she has been received into grace *and* that his or her sins have been forgiven *for Christ's sake*, "this faith God counts for righteousness before Himself."[7]

As we see in both Luther and Melanchthon, the key elements that are central are that the justification of sinners rests on it being (1) a *judicial* act on God's part for Christ's sake (*per Christum*) and that (2) it is given/received solely through faith in Christ (*sola fide*). The first aspect is set against any sort of idea that the Gospel includes any degree of "transformation" of the sinner or of any imagined "good works." The Gospel is news of free salvation based solely on what Luther called "alien righteousness"—the righteousness of another judged as if it were true of us sinners—and that when we are at our very *worst*, completely unimproved, unchanged (Rom. 5:8). And this "declared righteousness" is perfect (it is *Christ's*, after all) and instantaneous—*never* to be confused with some "lifelong process" or "life of obedience" or "transformation."

The second point ("through faith" in Christ *alone* or *only*) is really about Christ, too (as opposed to superficial and silly analyses of the strength or weakness of the believer's inner faith). It is a proposition about the *Object* of saving faith more than about the nature of trust (*fiducia*) in the receiving subject. Faith in Christ involves a certain death within us: the death of one of our strongest, most immovable convictions—that is, that justification is finally about *us* and is based on some "virtue" or "quality" we possess (in this case, "faith"). It is *not*. In fact, any idea of our virtue or lack of it in this matter of justification demands nothing less than a wooden stake driven through its vampire heart! Justification is about the entire Gospel taking place *outside* of us (*extra nos*). One of the ways the Reformers described "sin" was *incurvitas in se*—being curved in on self, bent of spine so that the "object" of our worship is really *us*. Correlatively, through the Gospel, God straightens our spines so that we (for the first time) have our gaze directed outward, *away* from self and *toward* the Lamb of God Who takes away the sin of the world. So strong is our inner bent (no pun intended!) toward "virtue" or "transformation" being a necessary aspect of justification that Luther said the only force that can battle it is the regular preaching of Christ to us, the regular hearing of what our Baptism was and was *not*, and the regular reception of the Lord's Supper. To put it another way, the mighty force of the Gospel going into our ears, onto our heads, and into our mouths is alone enough to do battle with this inner "given" that is always active inside us, seducing us into believing that "virtue" has something to do with sinners being "justified before God." It does *not*. When Martin Chemnitz discussed what he called "the exclusive particles" in the Bible text with regard to justification, they included the positive aspects: "by imputation" and "by the remission of sins." But his list (and this is the point for us here) also included the negatives: "apart from, not" (with regard to the law) and "*not* because of our works."

The early Lutherans were also convinced by the Bible text that what American evangelicals used to talk about (the assurance of salvation) was not only *possible* but was "normal" and sane. The grounding for it was *not* in any sort of sensuous inner feelings of grace or peace (later associated with Methodism, Wesley's use of Rom. 8:16–17) but with the Gospel promises contained in the *external* Word (the Bible text). And what made such assurance possible was a Gospel that did *not* include our "sanctification" or "transformation" as basis. So long as the believer holds to the Gospel as a righteousness solely possessed by someone else—from beginning to end—then assurance is possible. What makes it impossible, unreachable, is any form or degree of our sanctification "leaking over" into the column labeled "justification." The slightest degree of this, according to Luther, meant that "all is lost!"

"So give us an example of this in action. What would that look like?" It would look like an old, uneducated Appalachian grandmother dying and talking to her pastor. She would be saying to him, "I bring nothing but sin to the Judgment, Pastor. All I will be able to say before the Lord Jesus is, 'But You died for me, died for my sin.' That's it, Pastor! That's all I have." Luther would say of that uneducated, dying grandmother that she is a true theologian—and one who is completely prepared for death!

An Essential Bibliography of Lutheran Theology

Primary Sources

Book of Concord. Various editions.
Luther, M. *The Bondage of the Will*. American Edition 33, no. 3: 15–295. Selections included in various anthologies.
———. *The Freedom of the Christian [Christian Liberty]*. American Edition 31, no. 327: 333–77. Philadelphia: Fortress Press, 1959. Included in various anthologies.
———. *Greater Galatians Lectures of 1535*. American Edition vols. 26, 27. Preface, selections included in various anthologies.
———. *The Small Catechism*. Various editions.
———. *Two Kinds of Righteousness*. American Edition 31, no. 293: 297–306. Included in various anthologies.

Secondary Sources

Althaus, Paul. *The Theology of Martin Luther*. Translated by Robert C. Schultz. Philadelphia: Fortress Press, 1966.

Arnold, W. H., and C. George Fry. *The Way, the Truth, and the Life: An Introduction to Lutheran Christianity*. Grand Rapids, MI: Baker Book House, 1982.

Chemnitz, Martin. *Justification: The Chief Article of Christian Doctrine*. Translated by J. A. O. Preus and edited by Delpha H. Preus. St. Louis, MO: Concordia, 1986.

Christian History 34 (XI, 2): Martin Luther, The Early Years.

Christian History 39 (XII, 3): Martin Luther, The Later Years.

Engelder, Theo, W. Arndt, T. Graebner, and F. E. Mayer. "The Evangelical Lutheran Church." In *Popular Symbolics: The Doctrines of the Churches of Christendom and other Religions Examined in the Light of Scripture*, 1–136. St. Louis, MO: Concordia, 1934.

Förde, Gerhard O. *Justification by Faith—A Matter of Death and Life*. Philadelphia: Fortress Press, 1983. Reprint, Sigler Press, 1991.

———. *Where God Meets Man; Luther's Down-to-Earth Approach to the Gospel*. Minneapolis: Augsburg, 1972.

Klotsche, E. H. "The Lutheran Church." In *Christian Symbolics*, 133–93. Burlington, IA: Lutheran Literary Board, 1929.

Kolb, Robert. "Lutheranism—Theology." *Encyclopedia of the Reformation*, vol. 2, 467–73.

Kolb, Robert, and D. Lumpp. "The Righteousness of the Law and the Righteousness of Christ." In *Martin Luther, Companion to the Contemporary Christian*. St. Louis, MO: Concordia, 1982.

Leaver, Robin A. *Luther on Justification*. St. Louis, MO: Concordia, 1975.

Marquart, Kurt E. "Justification: Crown Jewel of Faith." In *Light for Our World: Essays Commemorating the 150th Anniversary of Concordia Seminary, St. Louis, Missouri*, ed. John W. Klotz. St. Louis, MO: Concordia Seminary Press, 1989.

Mayer, Frederick E. "The Soteriological Approach to Christian Doctrine." In *The Religious Bodies of America*, 127–96. St. Louis, MO: Concordia, 1954. 4th ed. revised by Arthur Carl Piepkorn, 1961.

Mueller, Steven, ed. *Called to Believe, Teach and Confess*. Eugene, OR: Wipf & Stock, 2005.

Paulson, Steven. *Luther for Armchair Theologians*. Louisville, KY: Westminster John Knox, 2004.

Pelikan, Jaroslav. *Reformation of Church and Dogma (1300–1700)*, vol. 4 of *The Christian Tradition: A History of the Development of Doctrine*. 5 vols. Chicago: University of Chicago Press, 1971–91.

Piepkorn, Arthur Carl. *Profiles in Belief*. New York: Harper and Row, 1978. Vol. 2, Part 1 (2), "Lutheran Churches—Doctrine and Theology," 40–67, and (3) "Nature and Function of the Church," 68–104.

Preus, Robert D. *Justification as Taught by Post-Reformation Lutheran Theologians*. Fort Wayne, IN: Concordia Theological Seminary Press, 1982.

Rupp, E. Gordon. *The Righteousness of God*. Series: Luther Studies. London: Hodder and Stoughton, 1953.

Sasse, Hermann. *Here We Stand: The Nature and Character of the Lutheran Faith*. Translated and edited by Theodore G. Tappert. New York: Harpers, 1938.

Veith, Gene Edward. *The Spirituality of the Cross*. St. Louis, MO: Concordia, 1999.

Walther, C. F. W. "Justification." In *Essays for the Church*, vol. 1. Translated by Everette W. Meier. St. Louis, MO: Concordia, 1992.

Watson, P. *Let God Be God*. Philadelphia: Muhlenberg, 1948.

The Gospel of Calvinism: Justification as Eternally Decreed

What is "the Gospel" according to confessional, "three-forms-of-unity" Calvinism?

Happily, confessional Lutherans and confessional Calvinists have much overlap on the doctrine of justification by grace alone through faith alone based on Christ's death alone. There *are* some differences but *not* of the same magnitude we find in the case of other Christian doctrines. And this should not surprise anyone, given Calvin's high praise of Luther ("an Apostle in our midst") and his expressed gratitude to Luther for his work on the Biblical doctrine of the justification of sinners.

With regard to Adam's Fall, Calvin followed Luther's reading (primarily of Biblical texts from the pen of St. Paul) on the nature and effects of the Fall on Adam and on all his progeny. *All* men and women, from conception forward, are hostile to their/our Maker, filled with concupiscence, and *dead* in our sin. We are completely bound of will (in the case of what the Reformers called "things heavenly"), completely inclined *against* the Gospel, and completely unable to respond positively to the announcement of it.

What of the doctrine of the Person of Christ? Here confessional Lutherans and confessional Calvinists *do* have significant differences, ones that our confessions openly acknowledge. Both confessions sign on without reservation to the "Ecumenical Creeds" (Apostles', Nicene, and Athanasian). Both confessions defend both the full deity and also the full humanity of Jesus Christ and His being a single Person. Calvin, along with Luther, repudiated *both* the Eutychian/ monophysite heresy and the Nestorian heresy with regard to Christ's Person. But the two confessions divide as to how we *understand* the relationship between Christ's divine nature and His human nature. Confessional Lutherans affirm a "communion of attributes" but *not* a confusion of substances (in particular, the *genus of majesty*: that Christ evidenced His deity through His humanity, His body). Confessional Calvinists repudiate this communion or communication.

What about the doctrine of the work of Christ? Through Melanchthon's friendship with Calvin, the division of Biblical passages into the categories of (1) prophet, (2) priest, and (3) king is a part of both Lutheran and Reformed confessions—with emphasis on His saving work as "priest" (not surprising, since the whole sixteenth century centered on the theological argument as to how sinners are saved). Luther and Calvin were one in embracing the Biblical view of the atonement as primarily *forensic*. That is, the best way to understand *how* the death of Christ saves us sinners involves embracing what is often—and snidely, pejoratively—called "the forensic view." (Mainline Protestant liberals join sixteenth-century Roman polemicists in their attitude of condescension with regard to this view!) Christ's death saves sinners by fulfilling what Isaiah prophesied (chap. 53) regarding the future Messiah's saving work: it would involve terrible suffering on His part, but that suffering would all be substitutionary and would be *for* us sinners, in our stead, and "vicarious." (The key, defining preposition of substitution is "for"—Christ saves sinners by dying *for* us, in our stead.) And that righteousness of His is, Calvinists and Lutherans confess, imputed to believers as if really *theirs*.

What is, then, "the Gospel" according to Calvin? It is the amazing news about what Christ accomplished for *some* sinners in dying for them. But Reformed Calvin and his Reformed followers understand justification beneath the larger doctrine of God's sovereignty. This means many things, but one of them is that Christ died *not* for all men but only for those whom God elected from before the foundations of the world (the third point of the famous Five Points of High Calvinism). The justification of His elect people took place in eternity and then later in time. The individual comes to realize that he or she is, in Christ, justified before God *and was* from time immemorial. So understanding election or predestination is the primary way of understanding one's justification.

Regardless of the details of "supralapsarian" or "infralapsarian" views of election, this puts the Christian in a cognitive bind. If Christ died only for particular people but not for all, did Christ die for me . . . or no? And how does one solve that question? Until recently, I evidently misunderstood this. My impression was that God graciously allowed the Reformed believer to see just a bit of his or her "growth in grace" as an indicator of election. But the best Reformed theologian in the world, Dr. Michael Scott Horton, corrected me on this and told me that what I thought was "the Reformed view" of assurance was the one advocated by the Puritans. At the time, I then asked him about what was the more universally held Reformed view of assurance. He answered, "I know by my faith in Christ, Rod." When Dr. Horton tells me what "the Reformed view of X" is, I trust that he knows it more accurately than any other human being in the world! If Dr. Horton tells me that X is the Reformed view, I believe that it *is* the Reformed view!

Luther, as a faithful *Augustinian* monk, had faced the "terrors of predestination" early on in the writings of St. Augustine. He was *not* unfamiliar with the problem. When Luther agonized over the question of righteousness for years as a monk, he took each and every counsel of his superiors as completely dependable and tried them all. But he found that they all, under pressure, collapsed—particularly the "internal" or "subjective" ones. Over the succeeding years, Luther was driven to solve the question of "assurance" by fleeing to his Baptism and to the Lord's Supper—to *objective* answers as opposed to subjective ones. That meant that whenever a Christian believer was walking along the edge of the dark abyss ("Am I really included in Christ or no?"), wondering, in doubt (Luther knew the contours of this one all too well and thought that doubt was the most awful of conditions), he pointed the believer *not* to his or her faith in Christ but to God acting by Baptism to engraft him or her into Christ and all His benefits and to the Lord's Supper, where the pastor pronounces him or her *forgiven* by partaking of the true Body of Christ and the true Blood of Christ: "This is the true Body of Christ which was given into death *for your* sin. This is the true Blood of Christ which was *shed for you*, for the forgiveness of *your* sin."

A Brief Bibliography pro/con the Calvinist Theology

Primary Sources

Calvin, John. *The Institutes of the Christian Religion*. Edited by J. T. McNeill and translated by Ford Lewis Battles, Library of Christian Classics. Philadelphia: Westminster, 1960.

Calvin, John, and Bp. J. Sadoleto, *A Reformation Debate*. New York: Harper and Row, 1966.

Secondary Sources

Buchanan, James. *The Doctrine of Justification*. Grand Rapids, MI: Baker, 1955. First published in 1867.

Christian History 12 (V, 4): John Calvin.

Christian History 4 (III, 1): Ulrich Zwingli.

Engelder, Theo, W. Arndt, Theodore Graebner, and F. E. Mayer. *Popular Symbolics: The Doctrines of the Churches of Christendom and of Other Religious Bodies Examined in the Light of Scripture*. St. Louis, MO: Concordia, 1934. Part 3 (B), "Reformed Bodies," 209–28; 241–50.

Horton, Michael S. *The Christian Faith: A Systematic Theology for Pilgrims on the Way*. Grand Rapids, MI: Zondervan, 2011.

———. *Putting Amazing Back into Grace*. Nashville: Thomas Nelson, 1991.

Klotsche, E. H. "The Reformed Church." In *Christian Symbolics*, 194–254. Burlington, IA: Lutheran Literary Board, 1929.

Mayer, F. E. *Religious Bodies of America*. St. Louis, MO: Concordia, 1954. 4th ed. revised by Arthur Carl Piepkorn, 1961. Part IV: *The Reformed Bodies*, 197–282.

Muller, Richard A. *Post-Reformation Reformed Dogmatics*. Grand Rapids, MI: Baker, 1987.

Murray, John. *Redemption Accomplished and Applied*. Grand Rapids, MI: Eerdmans, 1955.

Packer, J. I. *Knowing God*. Downers Grove, IL: Inter-Varsity Press, 1993.

Pelikan, Jaroslav. *Reformation of Church and Dogma (1300–1700)*, vol. 4 (1984), Section 4 in *The Christian Tradition: A History of the Development of Doctrine*. 5 vols. Chicago: University of Chicago Press, 1971–91.

Piepkorn, Arthur Carl. *Profiles in Belief*. New York: Harper and Row, 1978. Vol. II, Part III, "Reformed and Presbyterian Churches," 261–95.

Sproul, R. C. *Essential Truths of the Christian Faith*. Wheaton, IL: Tyndale Publishers, 1992.

———. *Grace Unknown: The Heart of Reformed Theology*. Grand Rapids, MI: Baker, 1997.

———. *What Is Reformed Theology?* Grand Rapids, MI: Baker, 1997.

Warfield, Benjamin B. *Calvin and Calvinism*. New York: Oxford University Press, 1931.

———. *The Plan of Salvation*. Grand Rapids, MI: Eerdmans, 1980.

Wendel, François. *Calvin: Sources et évolution de sa pensée religieuse*. Paris, 1950. Translated by Philip Mairet as *Calvin: The Origins and Development of His Religious Thought* (New York: Harper and Row, 1953).

Wesley: The Gospel of Christian Perfection

Young John Wesley (1703–91), fifteenth child of Samuel and Susanna Wesley, fulfilled his mother's wishes, attended Christ Church Oxford and studied for the priesthood. There he mastered Greek and distinguished himself in his master's thesis defense. During his Oxford years, young Wesley was deeply influenced by the writings of William

Law—for example, *A Serious Call to a Devout and Holy Life*. Following the counsel of Law, John determined to be "totally committed to God." John and his brother Charles formed what others pejoratively called "The Holy Club" and in it labored to reproduce the "primitive Christianity" of the Book of Acts (Acts 2:42).

Following his graduation and lacking "assurance of his own salvation," Wesley thought that if there was any way to such assurance, it lay in becoming a missionary. So he did this, travelling to America hoping to preach Christ to the American Indians. He ended up serving a parish instead. On a sea voyage back to England, it seemed that a storm was going to sink the ship on which he was a passenger. He feared dying but noticed a little group (Moravians) who seemed not all that afraid to die! Wesley marveled at their lack of fear of death. Later, back in London, he fell sick and was visited by Peter Böhler, who bore in on *how* John knew that he was a Christian believer and was justified before God. Wesley answered in terms of his good works, but Böhler countered with arguments from Scripture about "faith in Christ *alone*." By Böhler's Scriptural arguments, Wesley was convinced that he lacked saving faith. The matter was resolved within Wesley when later, at a small missionary gathering at a parish in Aldersgate, he listened to the leader reading from Luther's *Preface to the Book of Romans*. Later, Wesley referred to that night as his conversion. "About a quarter before nine, while he [Luther] was describing the change which God works in the heart through faith in Christ, I felt my heart strangely warmed. I felt I did trust in Christ, Christ alone, for salvation; and an assurance was given me that he had taken away my sins, even mine, and saved me from the law of sin and death."[8]

Wesley resolved to preach what had been delivered to him that night: the saving New Testament Gospel of faith in Christ (*sola*) as understood by Luther. And preach it he did—throughout the English Isles and in America. When his own Anglican parishes shut their doors to him (charging him with "enthusiasm"—the eighteenth-century equivalent of "Pentecostalism"), Wesley did the unthinkable for a bright, sophisticated Oxford graduate: he decided to preach the Gospel *outdoors*. People thronged to hear him, so much so that some historians have gone so far as to claim that the *one factor* that prevented a repetition of the French Revolution in England was John Wesley preaching the Gospel of Christ in every little village and town!

What was the content of the Gospel Wesley preached? It was, as it developed, the Gospel understood not so much as Luther expounded it but closer to the version expounded by Arminius in Holland. What does that mean? It means an understanding of Adam's progeny being truly *fallen, guilty, and condemned* (so far, so good) but still retaining enough freedom of will (with regard to what the Reformers called "things heavenly") that fallen hearers are at least "able to accept Jesus Christ as their personal Lord and Savior" (to use the twentieth-century description). The seasoned reader will at this point note the similarity to Rome's "synergistic" (God and man cooperating) answers *and* the significant difference between Arminianism and what Luther and Calvin confessed, preached, and taught.

Say that a given person *does* accept Christ and His saving priestly work of dying *for* him or her, *for* his or her sin, and "experiences the new birth." Is that justifying, according to Wesley? Yes and no. For Wesley, the Gospel accepted actually justifies a sinner before God. (Wesley said that "justification" meant simply that his or her sin was forgiven.) About the second saving Biblical factor cited by the Reformers—the instantaneous imputation of Christ's righteousness to every believer—Wesley waffled.

It seemed to Wesley (and his many forebears on this point) that preaching the imputed righteousness of Christ (His "active obedience to the law," credited instantly to believers as if they themselves had obeyed the law) would inevitably lead to passive indifference with regard to striving after a true Christian life of personal holiness.

This leads us to consider what the Wesleyan bodies call "the second blessing": Wesley's doctrine of Christian perfection—what Wesley considered his greatest gift to the church of the West. Once one had experienced the new birth, it was incumbent on him or her to begin striving "might and main" to actually attain Christian perfection prior to dying. Wesley's reading of 1 John 3:9 ("He that is born of God doth not commit sin") and Philippians 4:13 ("I can do all things through Him [Christ] who strengthens me") and other passages convinced him that the "real" goal of the Gospel was the perfecting of the Christian believer prior to death—a radical departure (again) from the theology of the Reformers (who two hundred years prior had met the doctrine of Christian perfection in the theology of Rome). To Luther, the "goal" of the Gospel was the justification of sinners—their embrace of the sufficiency of the Person and work of Christ to have done *for them* what the law requires *of them* and a concomitant rejection of any allowance of "Christian living" to sneak over, no matter how subtly, into the column "justification." Even the slightest instance of this, Luther said, and *all is lost!*

What were the primary effects of Wesley's doctrine of Christian perfection? It caused the Christian believers' attention to be turned away from the objective Christ and His saving work in behalf of sinners ("Christ *pro nobis*") and back onto self—checking one's progress or growth in Christ ("Christ *in nobis*") as indicator of one's status before God. (Some Lutherans had fallen for this same devastating error under Spener and Arndt during the era of Pietism.) Wesley had counseled his ministers (1) to evangelize pagans and (2) to urge believers on toward Christian perfection. This meant that the diet from the pulpit was a steady diet of "Law" rather than "Gospel"—as if the Gospel had already done its converting work and was no longer needed by Christian believers. (Today's American "evangelical" diet of recipes, tips for victorious Christian living, and so on is *not* a new thing in Christian history but traces back to Wesley's doctrine of Christian perfection.)

What of "assurance?" For that, Wesley pointed his followers to Romans 8:16–17 ("The Spirit Himself bears witness with our spirit that we are the children of God")—not Baptism, not Lord's Supper, but instead an "inner testimony" of the Holy Spirit to our spirit. Literally thousands have "gone on the rocks" trying to make this system of "law-Gospel-law" actually work and finally (in the face of their continuing sin) decided to leave Christianity! And which of us, given the nature of "the Gospel" of necessary Christian perfection, could blame a single one of them?

A Brief Bibliography pro/con the Wesleyan Theology

Primary Sources

Heitzenrater, Richard, ed. *The Works of John Wesley*. Bicentennial Edition. Oxford: Clarendon Press, 1975–83.

Outler, Albert C., ed. *John Wesley*. New York: Oxford University Press, 1964.

————, ed. *Sermons* [of Wesley]. 4 vols. Nashville, TN: Kingswood Books, 1984–87.

————, ed. *The Works of John Wesley.* 26 vols. Nashville, TN: Abingdon Press, 1984.

Wesley, John. *A Plain Account of Christian Perfection.* Annotated edition. Edited by Mark T. Olson. Post Falls, ID: 2006.

Secondary Sources

Cannon, William R. *The Theology of John Wesley, with Special Reference to the Doctrine of Justification.* New York: Abingdon-Cokesbury Press, 1946.

Cell, George C. *The Rediscovery of John Wesley.* New York, NY: Henry Holt, 1935. Reprinted University Press of America, 2002.

Christian History 2 (II, 1): John Wesley.

Christian History 69 (XX, 1): The Wesleys.

Engelder, Theo, W. Arndt, Theodore Graebner, and F. E. Mayer. *Popular Symbolics: The Doctrines of the Churches of Christendom and of Other Religious Bodies Examined in the Light of Scripture.* St. Louis, MO: Concordia, 1934. "The Methodists," 282–92; "Arminianism," 228–33.

Hildebrandt, Franz. *Christianity According to the Wesleys.* London: Epworth Press, 1955. Reprinted Durham, NC: Labyrinth Press.

Klotsche, E. H., *Christian Symbolics.* Burlington, IA: Lutheran Literary Board, 1929. "Arminianism," 266–69; "The Methodists," 300–313.

Lindström, Harald G. A. *Wesley and Sanctification: A Study in the Doctrine of Salvation.* Translated by H. S. Harvey. Stockholm: Nya Bakförlags Aktiebolaget, 1946. Reprinted Zondervan Publishing, 1982.

Mayer, F. E. *Religious Bodies of America.* St. Louis, MO: Concordia, 1954. 4th ed. revised by Arthur Carl Piepkorn, 1961. Part V: *The Arminian Bodies,* 283–342.

Oden, Thomas C. *John Wesley's Scriptural Christianity.* Grand Rapids, MI: Zondervan, 1994.

Pelikan, Jaroslav. *Christian Doctrine and Modern Culture (since 1700),* vol. 5 of *The Christian Tradition: A History of the Development of Doctrine.* 5 vols. Chicago: University of Chicago Press, 1971–91.

Piepkorn, Arthur Carl, *Profiles in Belief.* New York: Harper and Row, 1978–79.

Sangster, William E. *The Path to Perfection: An Examination of John Wesley's Doctrine of Christian Perfection.* London: Hodder and Stoughton, 1943.

Schmidt, Martin. *John Wesley: A Theological Biography.* 2 vols. Nashville: Abingdon Press, 1962–73.

Eastern Orthodoxy: The Gospel of *Theosis*

The world of Eastern Orthodox Christianity seems mysterious and exotic to many—perhaps most—Western Christians. Still, it is "a way of being Christian" that is claimed by some 215 million adherents. But it is—in principle—difficult to translate Western Christian questions and thought into Eastern Orthodox answers. For this reason, background is necessary as a preliminary to asking, "What is the Gospel in Eastern Orthodoxy?"

Monasticism has been an essential feature of Eastern Orthodoxy since the time of St. Antony and the "desert fathers"[9]—so much so that Orthodox writers have said that one cannot understand Orthodoxy without understanding its monastic tradition. "If you know a little about Eastern monasticism, you know a great deal about Eastern Orthodoxy."[10] "The cell teaches us everything."[11] The monastic's main vocation is prayer, and the goal of prayer (and, indeed, all monastic life) is union with God. Such union is possible only through a life of spiritual purification and total renunciation—a self-stripping of both material possessions and intellectual projections. This is the "way of negation," or *apophatic* knowledge. "Apophatic theology is 'the fundamental characteristic of the whole theological tradition of the Eastern church.'"[12] The phrase is derived from the Greek *apophasis*, or "denial," and is the attempt to describe what God is *not*. It is defined as "the breakdown of human thought before the radical transcendence of God . . . a prostration before the living God, radically ungrasp-able, unobjectifiable, and unknowable."[13]

Contrast Protestant thought on this and similar subjects that involve mystery. Mystery calls for analysis and explanation so far as is possible. Western Christians see all fundamental truth claims as necessarily having to pass (in some sense) the bar of reason.

In Western Christianity, theology is usually understood as a form of knowledge, or even "a science." But in Orthodoxy, this incomprehensible mystery of God is a cause for praise and celebration, and theology is an extension of spirituality or worship.[14] "At the risk of exaggeration, we might say that in the West, theology is done with books in the library; in the Orthodox East, theology is done with liturgy in the sanctuary."[15] Typical of Western Christians, Augustine and Luther discovered the Gospel slowly through study of the Biblical *text*. But the Eastern Christian directs people to participation in worship (particularly the liturgy, with the aid of icons, incense, and chanting). The worshipper, hopefully, is thereby brought to the very "outskirts of heaven itself" and actually experiences the transcendent God in a way that He wills to be found. To Eastern Christians, Protestant worship—with its emphasis on pulpit/preaching—looks more like a college classroom than it does like real worship! Sergei Bulgakov describes Protestant Christianity as a "professorial" religion in which the central figure is the scholar-professor.[16] And Alexei Khomiakov says that in Protestantism, "a scholar has taken the place of the priest."[17]

It is undeniable that in Lutheran and Protestant theology, centrality is given to the word—particularly the Word of the Gospel—more than to icons/art. But in the East, icons are the most revered form of theological expression.[18] And, as one might expect, what Lutherans and Protestants call *sola Scriptura* is openly repudiated by Eastern thinkers—if it involves "private interpretation,"[19] something that both Reformation confessions would want to clarify and in some sense repudiate.[20]

How deep was the damage inflicted upon Adam, Eve, and their progeny at the Fall, according to Eastern Orthodoxy? As creatures who bore both God's Image and His likeness (which the Orthodox distinguish from each other), Adam and Eve failed to fulfill either. As a consequence, corruption—the sickness of sin (the consequence of which is death)—changed them from "the perfect modes of existence" into "the flawed mode of existence." All of Adam's offspring inherit the consequences of his sin—but *not* the guilt of it! The Augustinian understanding of original sin is *not* part of the Eastern belief system. Orthodoxy does *not* hold that all are born deserving to go to Hell. Sin is, they say, never a matter of rule breaking but rather any behavior that "misses the mark" for which we were intended (Rom. 3:23)—a failure to live up to the goal of being like God. So sin is *not* guilt so much as a pervading sickness, a failure to achieve a goal. *And* it serves as impetus to become something more than we presently are.[21]

What of the Person of Jesus Christ? From St. Athanasius (*On the Incarnation*), the West was given a wonderful gift in Christology: the East is an ardent, fluent defender of the full deity and the full humanity of Jesus Christ, including more than a little work on His being a single Person (contra Nestorianism), and even, like Lutherans, speaks of a "communion of natures" without a commingling of substance![22] However, it was more a matter of Christ's Person than His work by which human sinners are saved. Athanasius stressed that, through His assumption of our human nature, humans are (cosmically?) saved and restored.

What of the work of Christ? He assumed a human body and nature in order to, once and for all, do away with death and corruption. By His death, He destroyed death, made it possible that men and women might be "renewed according to the Image of God." This is a matter of "being enabled to 'participate in divinity'" (*theosis*)[23]—*not* a matter of what Lutherans and Protestants stress as "justification by grace alone through faith alone on the basis of Christ's death and resurrection alone." Still, in Eastern Christianity, the celebration of Easter seems to be even more important than the celebration of Christmas.

Salvation, "being saved," refers to a *process* of being delivered from death, corruption, and Hell. And it is a gift of God. There is nothing that sinners can do to "earn" these things. Still, it has to be accepted, and man is free to reject the gift of salvation.[24] In order to be saved, man must "work together with God" (*synergia*) so that man's will, effort, and actions are perfectly conformed with, and united to, the divine. What Lutherans and Protestants call "the assurance of salvation" thus becomes a false, arrogant, and ephemeral dream!

The thing that Western Christians find amazing is the almost total absence of the doctrine of justification by faith in large segments of Orthodox history *and theology!* The East never had to fight through the issues that came to a head during the sixteenth century in Western Christianity. The doctrine that Luther considered "*the* article by which the church stands or falls" was seemingly never much of an issue in the East. In the place of the hundreds of books on the subject by both Roman Catholics and Protestants, justification in the East is "played down," while our mystical union with God is emphasized instead. *Theosis* is the major subject, and justification is simply *not central.* Contrast confessional Lutheran theology *and* Reformed theology. Justification is *the Gospel!* And it involves Christ's passive obedience "for you, for me," Him setting His face like a flint to go to Jerusalem where He knew painful death (for us all) awaited Him, and also His "active obedience," His living a life totally in accord with *all* the Father's commands, without fail, "for us." These are the bases for the declaration of "not guilty" imputed to each believer as if really the case. The Christian is, as Luther said, both saint and sinner, *simul justus et peccator.* And assured of heaven based *not at all* on his empirical condition as sinner but based on what Luther called "alien righteousness"—the righteousness of someone else whose true righteousness is reckoned to us *as if* it were true of us.

A Brief Bibliography pro/con
the Theology of Eastern Orthodoxy

Arseniev, Nicholas. "Characteristic Features of the Christian Message." In *Revelation of Life Eternal.* Crestwood, NY: St. Vladimir's Seminary Press, 1982.

Benz, Ernst. *The Eastern Orthodox Church: Its Thought and Life.* New York, NY: Doubleday, 1963.

Christian History 18 (VII, 2): How Christianity Came to Russia.

Christian History 54 (XVI, 2): The Orthodox Church.

Christian History 64 (XVIII, 4): St. Antony and the Desert Fathers.

Clendenin, Daniel. *Eastern Orthodox Christianity: A Western Perspective.* Grand Rapids, MI: Baker, 1974.

Engelder, Theo, W. Arndt, Theodore Graebner, and F. E. Mayer. *Popular Symbolics: The Doctrines of the Churches of Christendom and of Other Religious Bodies Examined in the Light of Scripture.* St. Louis, MO: Concordia, 1934. Part 2 (A) "The Eastern Catholic Churches," 137–47.

Klotsche, E. "The Greek Church." In *Comparative Symbolics,* 29–57. Burlington, IA: Lutheran Literary Board, 1929.

Lossky, Vladimir. *The Mystical Theology of the Eastern Church.* Cambridge: James Clarke, 1951.

Mayer, F. E. *Religious Bodies of America*. St. Louis, MO: Concordia, 1954. 4th ed. revised by Arthur Carl Piepkorn, 1961. Part I: *The Holy Oriental Catholic and Apostolic Church*, 9–24.

McGuckin, John. *The Orthodox Church: An Introduction to Its History, Doctrine, and Spiritual Culture*. London: Blackwell, 2008.

Meyendorff, John. *Byzantine Theology*. New York: Fordham University Press, 1974.

———. *The Orthodox Church*. Crestwood, NY: St. Vladimir's Seminary Press, 1981.

Pelikan, Jaroslav. *The Christian Tradition: A History of the Development of Doctrine*, vol. 2, *The Spirit of Eastern Christendom (600–1700) (1974)* in *The Christian Tradition: A History of the Development of Doctrine*. 5 vols. Chicago: University of Chicago Press, 1971–91.

Piepkorn, Arthur Carl. *Profiles in Belief*. New York: Harper and Row, 1977. Vol. 1, Part 2 (4), "Eastern Orthodox Churches—Eastern Orthodox Theology," 38–47.

Schmemann, Alexander. *For the Life of the World: Sacraments and Orthodoxy*. Crestwood, NY: St. Vladimir's Seminary Press, 1973.

———. *The Historical Road of Eastern Orthodoxy*. Crestwood, NY: St. Vladimir's Seminary Press, 1977.

Ware, Kallistos (Timothy). *How Are We Saved? The Understanding of Salvation in the Orthodox Tradition*. Minneapolis: Light and Life, 1996.

———. *The Orthodox Church*. London: Penguin, 1993.

———. *The Orthodox Way*. Crestwood, NY: St. Vladimir's Seminary Press, 1979.

Conclusion: What's the Value of Taking the Lutheran Route?

Why should a person deciding what *kind* of Christian he or she should be choose the Confessional Lutheran option?

First, a person chooses Confessional Lutheran because he or she sees that the doctrine of justification by grace alone through faith alone based on Christ's Person and work alone is *the* defining question—so much so that this doctrine is the basic "plot line" of the whole Bible (beginning as early as Gen. 3:15). Luther and his followers openly said that this particular article "is the one by which [a] church stands or falls."

Second, a person chooses Confessional Lutheran because a person sees that the Confessional Lutherans' definition of "the Gospel" is drawn *not* from philosophy but from many verses of Scripture read in their "natural sense." No Western church has gone into the defining detail with regard to "the Gospel" that Luther and the writers of the *Book of Concord* have. All Christians of all stripes are invited to test these Confessions for Biblical accuracy and fidelity.

Third, a person chooses Confessional Lutheran because Confessional Lutheranism affirms a robust understanding of the nature and depth of our Fall in Adam—a Fall that extends to our very core and to all aspects of us. And he or she sees the Biblical connection between this deep, genuine fallenness and the finished, sufficient work of Christ's vicarious death to save sinners—and that at our very worst.

Fourth, a person chooses Confessional Lutheran because of Confessional Lutheranism's robust embrace and Confession regarding the two natures in the Person of Christ—not for philosophical reasons, but as a fuller answer to what Anselm explicated in his *Cur Deus Homo* ("Why the God-man?"). The question for Luther and the early writers of the *Book of Concord* was singular—namely, whether the death and resurrection of this God-man actually *saves* us sinners all on its own, objectively, by itself, outside of us . . . or *not*. In paragraph after paragraph, Luther and the Confessions quote particular Scriptures to affirm that His death and resurrection actually *do* this saving.

Fifth, a person chooses Confessional Lutheran because of Confessional Lutheranism's explication (again, based on particular Scripture verses) of the doctrine of the justification of sinners as *a judicial* declaration on the part of the Holy God. Sinners are declared as if truly righteous *solely* because of Christ's "alien" righteousness imputed to us and reckoned to us (as opposed to any sort of "imparted righteousness" or improvement within us). This "imputed righteousness," said Luther and the writers of the Lutheran Confessions, is instantaneous, perfect, and sufficient to save (because of Christ's perfect nature and His promises concerning His own saving work—*not* because of any imagined "quality" lying within us sinners, not even because of the strength of our inward trust in Christ to save us). *All* the predications are about Christ's Person and saving work gratuitously done in our behalf and given to us in the preaching of this Gospel into our ears, by water applied to sinners in connection with Christ's Word of promise, and by bread and wine put into sinners' mouths by a pastor who absolves individual sinners by quotation of the absolving words of Christ.

Sixth, a person chooses Confessional Lutheran because of the Biblical precision of the work done by Luther, later by Martin Chemnitz, with regard to what are called "the exclusive particles": "by God's grace," "freely," "*gratis*," "apart from/'not with regard to' the law," "not because of our works," "by imputation," "by the remission of sins," and "through faith alone (*sola*)."

Seventh, a person chooses Confessional Lutheran because of Confessional Lutheranism's explication of "the assurance of salvation" and the Biblical rationale for this assurance. The basis of this assurance lies not at all within us sinners; on the contrary, it is on the basis (*sola!*) of Christ's Person and promises. "*Through* faith in Christ" does *not* mean "*based on* faith in Christ." Christians' confession regarding justification is not about "their personal faith in Christ"; it is about *Christ*—particularly, His claims about Who He is and what His death would do for sinners. Put another way, a sinner's justification before God is a condition in which the sinner is completely *passive*! As Luther confessed just prior to dying, "We are beggars"—each and every one of us.

Notes

1. Quotations from the Bible are taken from the *English Standard Version* (Wheaton, IL: Crossway, 2001).

2. Jaroslav Pelikan and Helmut T. Lehmann, eds., *Luther's Works*, American Edition (Philadelphia: Fortress Press, 1958), 26, 27. The American Edition hereafter is as AE.

3. AE 26:7ff.

4. AE 26:10.

5. Luther, *The Bondage of the Will*.

6. Chemnitz, *The Two Natures in Christ*.

7. *Augsburg Confession*, Article IV.

8. John Wesley, *Journals and Diaries: The Works of John Wesley*, ed. Albert Cook Outler (Nashville: Abingdon Press, 1988), 18:249–50.

9. See *Christian History & Biography* 64.

10. John Chryssavgis, professor of theology at Holy Cross Greek Orthodox School of Theology (Brookline, MA) in his "The Spirit-Bearers," *Christian History & Biography* 54.

11. Abba Moses, quoted by ibid.

12. Eastern theologian Vladimir Lossky, quoted by ibid.

13. Daniel B. Clendenon, "What the Orthodox Believe," *Christian History & Biography* 54.

14. Ibid.

15. Ibid.

16. Ibid.

17. Ibid.

18. James Billington, cited in ibid., says, "Icons are the most revered form of theological expression in Orthodoxy, which tends to crystallize in images rather than ideas." The author also cites Puritan John Foxe: "God conducted the Reformation not by the sword, but by printing, writing, and reading."

19. Typical is Eastern Orthodox theologian John Meyendorff's evaluation: "The Christian faith and experience can in no way be compatible with the notion of *sola scriptura*." Ibid.

20. George Florovsky once called private interpretation "the sin of the Reformation"! Ibid.

21. Ibid.

22. Cf. M. Chemnitz, *The Two Natures in Christ*.

23. The reader is encouraged to see the East's own writers on what they *do* and *do not* mean by theosis and how it is distinguished from pantheism (or, say, Mormonism). See their own assertions regarding "God became man so that men may become gods." "The Son of God *descended*, became man, in order that we humans might *ascend* and become like Christ."

24. "God becomes powerless before human freedom; He cannot violate it." Vladimir Lossky, *Orthodox Theology: An Introduction*, cited by Clendenon, "What the Orthodox Believe."

Chapter 6

The Means of Grace

The Word and Sacraments

Harold Senkbeil

Bridging the Gap

All Christians agree that salvation centers in the person and work of Jesus Christ of Nazareth, by whose death and resurrection we are set free from sin and death. Where we begin to part company is when we start to talk about how we connect with Jesus and His work.

We have a space and time problem. How do you and I leap from the twenty-first century back to the first century? A favorite old gospel hymn asks the poignant question, "Were you there when they crucified my Lord?" Well, the simple answer is, "No, we weren't." So though indeed the vastness of Christ's sacrificial love may cause us to "tremble," that's about as far as it goes. We can meditate on the moving reality of what happened outside the city gates of Jerusalem one cruel Friday afternoon in the Jewish month of Nissan and, barely three days later, the dawning of that first glorious Easter morning. But how does just thinking about it help us in any way?

Of course, over the centuries, well-intended Christians have attempted to bridge this space/time gap in numerous ways. Most of these attempts turn out to be variations on a common theme: what you might call "the ladder to heaven" approach. That is, the Christian engages in a series of spiritual exercises designed to connect himself or herself with Jesus and His saving work. This might take the form of an emotionally powerful conversion experience in which the individual's life is turned over to Jesus by an act of the will, inviting Jesus to take possession of his or her heart. Or in a more liturgically oriented church, it would typically involve a long process of meditation and prayer by which the earthly and bodily is left behind and the spiritual comes to the fore. Gradually the person becomes less worldly minded and more heavenly minded, thereby achieving spiritual union with the risen and exalted Lord. But there's no certainty to be had in either method. Whether emotional or spiritual, both routes connect the individual not with Christ but with personal feelings about Christ. And you can't build your life around feelings.

This is where the means of grace come in. God Himself has bridged the gap for us. While we cannot go back in history to the source of our salvation and although our sins present an impenetrable barrier to spiritual union with God, His grace—that is, His unmerited favor—comes to us through the means He has appointed. To speak more plainly still: while you and I cannot go to God, He comes to us. Not one of us can confess "Jesus is Lord" except by the power of the Holy Spirit (1 Cor. 12:3). Thus from beginning to end, salvation is God's gift: from its planning in eternity to its execution in time to its continuing benefits, salvation is all God's free gift, earned by His beloved Son and now bestowed perpetually by His Spirit through the means of grace, His powerful Word in both oral and sacramental form. Since these means are actually the tools and instruments of the Holy Spirit in creating and sustaining faith, you might actually call them the means of the Spirit. But I digress.

Jesus Christ, the Mystery of Our Salvation

The story of God's means of grace begins a long time ago—in fact, before time began. To speak clearly and honestly about these sacred means, you have to speak mystically. "For I want you to know how great a struggle I have for you and for those at Laodicea and for all who have not seen me face to face, that their hearts may be encouraged, being knit together in love, to reach all the riches of full assurance of understanding and the knowledge of God's mystery, which is

Christ, in whom are hidden all the treasures of wisdom and knowledge" (Col. 2:1–3).[1]

What does the apostle mean when He calls Jesus Christ "God's mystery?" We have a notion that "mystery" means something is beyond our normal knowledge. And of course that's partly true. But "mystery" in the Bible means more than that. In the Colossians text, you can see that the idea of hiddenness is included in the word mystery; there's more there than meets the eye. In this case, "all the treasures of [God's] wisdom and knowledge" are hidden in Jesus. But there's even more than that: "For in Him the whole fullness of deity dwells bodily" (Col. 2:9). The real reason that God's wisdom and knowledge are hidden in Jesus is that the man Jesus is also God at the same time.

Ask me how Jesus can be true man and true God at the same time and I'll be honest: I don't know. Man and God appear to be totally incompatible. Like oil and water, they don't mix and seem incapable of combination. And this is precisely the mystery. Though the finite seems incapable of including the infinite, though humanity seems hopelessly unable to encompass divinity, in Jesus the seemingly impossible has happened: God has become man, and in this one man, Jesus, God has visited His people. Not just part of God, either. In Jesus the "whole fullness of deity" dwells, and He does so "bodily." Can you imagine that? The all-powerful majestic creator of heaven and earth confined Himself in Jesus to a fertilized egg, an embryo, within the womb of His virgin mother, to be born and suckled at her breast like any human infant. Now that's what I call mystery! And the Bible does too. In fact, then, Jesus Christ is Himself the greatest mystery beyond all mysteries.

Thus we really need to begin our discussion of the means of grace with the person of Jesus. Bear with me; this may get a little complicated. But since Jesus is no ordinary person, it stands to reason that things get a little complex when we talk about Him. According to Scripture, Jesus has two natures: God and man. This is admittedly a bit mind numbing, and it has given Christians fits trying to wrap their brains around it. In the early Christian church, controversies raged for centuries over the proper way to understand the two natures in Christ. Yet ultimately, the church summarized the scriptural teaching in the three ecumenical creeds: the Apostolic, the Nicene, and the Athanasian. Since Reformation times, Lutherans have consistently and staunchly championed the ancient orthodox confession regarding the personal union of the Son of God.[2] Namely, Jesus is not two separate persons, the eternally begotten Divine Word plus the human male born of Mary roughly two thousand years ago. Rather, "the two natures, the divine and the human, are so inseparably united in one person that there is one Christ."[3] So inseparable are these two natures that we can say that when Jesus died, God died for the sins of the world. Likewise, Lutherans contend that when you eat and drink the bread and wine of the Lord's Supper, you are eating and drinking the body and blood of Jesus given and shed for you for the forgiveness of sins.

Reformed Christians, on the other hand, have always balked at taking "this is my body" and "this is my blood"—the words of Jesus—literally. For John Calvin, the finite material "stuff" of this world (such as human flesh) could not include the infinite nature of God. Yet Lutherans take Jesus at His word. Though He is genuinely true man with human flesh and blood, He is also God at the same time—and God is present everywhere in the universe. Time and space present no barriers to Him; He created them, after all. So in the sacrament of the altar, then, you receive not merely the external elements of bread and wine but also the flesh and blood of Jesus in this earthly meal. His humanity is not confined to heaven after the ascension, for Jesus the God/Man ascended into heaven so that His humanity too (including His flesh and blood) might "fill all things" with His presence (Eph. 4:10). More about that later. For now, let's acknowledge that this is certainly a great mystery!

But "mystery" in the Bible is more than just something beyond human comprehension. It includes the idea that there is more present than meets the eye—namely, that something intangible and spiritual is hidden in an outer tangible wrapping. Jesus is Himself a mystery in that the whole fullness of the godhead is concealed unseen within His human body.

Indulge me in a little language lesson: Our English word *mystery* is remarkably similar to the original New Testament Greek word *mysterion*. But when the Bible was translated from Greek to Latin (the church's mother tongue for well over a thousand years), *mysterion* became *sacramentum*. Sound familiar? Do you see the connection? When we talk about the sacraments, we're talking mysteries. And when we talk about the mysteries of the faith, we need to begin with the central mystery: Jesus Himself, God made flesh for us and for our salvation. Jesus Christ is the great Sacrament of God—as St. Paul put it, "God's Mystery . . . in whom are hidden all the treasures of wisdom and knowledge" (Col. 2:3).

Based on this foundational definition of sacrament, every Christian church derives its understanding of sacraments. The great Western church father, St. Augustine, defined a sacrament this way: "When the Word is added to the element or the natural substance, it becomes a sacrament."[4] This definition is operative among Christians to this day.

Not all churches call these sacred acts "sacraments," however; some call them "ordinances." Lutherans would certainly agree that the sacraments have been divinely ordained, or instituted/commanded by God. Jesus certainly didn't intend that they be optional. He ordered, for example, "Go and make disciples of all nations, baptizing them" (Matt. 28:19), and regarding His holy supper, He directed, "Do this in remembrance of me" (Luke 22:19). We continue to use these sacraments, however, not merely because we want to be obedient to the commands of Jesus. We use the sacraments primarily because they are His gifts to us by which He comes personally to give Himself intimately to us here and now in our time and space. He gives us these sacraments to bridge the gap between earth and heaven, between the material and the spiritual, between mankind's predicament and God's salvation. He gives us these sacraments to bestow the forgiveness of sins He earned for us by His cross and death. Sacraments have such great power because they are more than religious symbols or divinely ordained object lessons. They are, to borrow another phrase of St. Augustine's, "a kind of visible Word."[5] The Word of God is the efficacious power behind the sacraments.

Word and Spirit

Talk about power! If you want to know about the power of the Word of God, you need look no further than the opening lines of the Bible: "In the beginning, God created the heavens and the earth. The earth was without form and void, and darkness was over the face of the deep. And the Spirit of God was hovering over the face of the waters. And God said, 'Let there be light,' and there was light"

(Gen. 1:1–3). When you and I speak, we describe things; we speak mere vocables. When God speaks, He creates things; God speaks realities. By the sheer power of God's creative Word, light sprang out of the empty darkness of the first creation. The Word of God is never mere data, but is living and active, sharper than a two-edged sword (Heb. 4:12). It is an efficacious Word. It does what it says. "For as the rain and the snow come down from heaven and do not return there but water the earth, making it bring forth and sprout, giving seed to the sower and bread to the eater, so shall my word be that goes out from my mouth; it shall not return to me empty, but it shall accomplish that which I purpose, and shall succeed in the thing for which I sent it" (Isa. 55:10–11).

The reason the Word of God is so powerful and active is that His Word is the instrument of His Spirit. The Holy Spirit of God, working by means of His Word, does miraculous things. Just as in the initial creation God created light out of darkness and life out of the inanimate creation, breathing life by His Spirit into the man He had shaped from the dust of the ground,[6] so He calls forth the new creation by Word and Spirit. Jesus describes the sounds that come from His mouth as tools and instruments of the Holy Spirit. "The words I have spoken to you are Spirit and life" (Jn. 6:63). In fact, we see in the New Testament that whenever and wherever Jesus speaks, He gives His Holy Spirit. On the first Easter night when He suddenly appeared in the midst of his disciples, Jesus, like God the Father creating Adam, breathes His Spirit into His apostles, saying, "Receive the Holy Spirit" (Jn. 20:22).

So if we want to understand the power and efficacy of the Word and sacraments, we need to remember that the operative power in the sacraments is not in their external element (water, bread, and wine) but in the Word of God, which He joins to that element. And where the Word of God is, there is the Spirit of God. Word and Spirit are always joined together; there is no Word of God in which the Spirit is not working, and there is no Spirit to be found apart from God's Word.

Lutheran Paradox

To the uninitiated, Lutheran teaching is hard to pin down. Too much gospel to be Catholic yet too sacramental to be Evangelical. In fact, it appears that Lutherans take the compromise position between the two; clinging to relics from their Catholic origins while simultaneously highlighting the saving work of Jesus on His cross. But in fact, that's not the case. Martin Luther did not intend to splinter and fragment the church but rather cleanse it from errors that had crept in over the centuries. Far from wanting to start a new church, the Lutheran confessors' intent was deliberately catholic (i.e., universal and historic). In their words, theirs was a "teaching that was well founded on the divine Scripture and briefly summarized in the time-honored, ancient Symbols (the Ecumenical Creeds); teaching that was recognized as that ancient, united consensus believed in by the universal, orthodox churches of Christ and fought for and reaffirmed against many heresies and errors."[7]

Yet at the same time, the early Lutherans' catholic faith was also distinctly evangelical (i.e., gospel-centered). "Likewise, they teach that human beings cannot be justified before God by their own powers, merits, or works. But they are justified as a gift on account of Christ through faith when they believe that they are received into grace and that their sins are forgiven on account of Christ, who by His death made satisfaction for our sins. God reckons this faith as righteousness" (Rom. 3:21–26; 4:5).[8]

Lutherans are quite at home with paradox. Where the Bible speaks clearly, Lutherans hold unflinchingly to the biblical position even when it appears to conflict with human reason. We've already seen the greatest example of that: how could a tiny embryo within His mother's womb possibly contain all the fullness of the godhead (Col. 2:9)? How can the child nursed at Mary's breast at one and the same time be the eternal Son of God by whom all things were made (Jn. 1:3) and in whom the whole created cosmos holds together (Col. 1:17)? Yes, most clearly this remains forever true: Jesus Christ is Himself the greatest mystery of all the mysteries, or sacraments.

Thus when it comes to faith and salvation, Lutherans are quite comfortable confessing what Scripture teaches even if that means teaching something counter to human reason. For example, when it comes to how faith is created in human hearts, the defining catechism of Lutheran teaching states (I'm just quoting here), "I believe that I cannot . . . believe."[9] At first, that doesn't make sense, does it? But then consider this:

The man without the Spirit does not accept the things that come from the Spirit of God, for they are foolishness to him, and he cannot understand them, because they are spiritually discerned. (1 Cor. 2:14)

No one can say, "Jesus is Lord," except by the Holy Spirit. (1 Cor. 12:3)

So faith comes from hearing, and hearing through the word of Christ. (Rom. 10:17)

Put the implacable callousness of the sinful human heart up against the grace of God and you'll see that it's only the grace of God that achieves salvation. There's nothing any human being can do to accomplish salvation; that was done for us all once and for all when Jesus Christ, God's Son, was made to be sin in our place that we might be made the righteousness of God in Him (2 Cor. 5:21).

Lutherans believe that salvation is entirely God's work, from beginning to end. It's not some sort of bargain in which God takes the initiative and does the hardest part and then expects us to respond by doing our part in return. People don't "decide" to follow Jesus or "accept" Him as their Savior; faith is always a gift of God whenever it occurs. The sobering truth is that since Adam's sin, all mankind is spiritually dead. "You were dead in the trespasses and sins in which you once walked" (Eph. 2:1–2). Yet just as God can by His divine power raise the dead, so He creates faith out of unbelief, bringing people who are spiritually dead to life (Eph. 2:4–6). Salvation is not a two-way street; God's love alone "has broken every barrier down," as an old favorite hymn puts it.[10] His is indeed a one-way love; human endeavor contributes nothing at all to our salvation.[11] Even the faith by which we receive God's gift in Jesus is itself a work of God (Eph. 2:8–9).

Human "reason or strength" just can't breach the impenetrable barrier between God and man. Only the Holy Spirit, who called a living man from lifeless clay in the initial creation, can create living faith where there is only darkness and unbelief. And that's precisely what He does—by means of the word of the gospel. In the words of the *Small Catechism*, "I believe that I cannot by my own reason or strength believe in Jesus Christ, my Lord, or come to Him; but the Holy Spirit has called me by the Gospel, enlightened me with His gifts, sanctified and kept me in the true faith."[12]

The Forgiveness of Sins

The center of God's redeeming work in Jesus His Son and the center of the Spirit's sanctifying work are the same: the forgiveness of sins. To be candid, sin doesn't get a lot of attention in our time. An increasingly jaded and decadent world considers "sin" an antiquated word, to be discarded along with men's garters and women's corsets—relics of a bygone era. Meanwhile, the contemporary Christian world is much more interested in formulas for self-improvement and success than dealing with such unpleasantries as sin and repentance. Yet though sin and forgiveness have grown unfashionable, that makes them no less important. The ugly truth is that the soul that sins shall die. I didn't make that up; God did (Ezek. 18:4). To be precise, God didn't make it up; He simply states facts: without a living faith, no human being can go on living.

That's the way it's been ever since Eden, where our first parents despised the word and command of God and cut themselves off from Him by their deliberate disobedience. As the Lord God had told them, in the day that they ate of the forbidden fruit, they would surely die (Gen. 2:17). Well, you know the rest of the story. They did eat, and they did die—and all their children ever since. In fact, in Adam, all die (1 Cor. 15:22a). That includes you and me; death is the inevitable consequence of sin for us all. Not merely biological death but eternal death is the penalty for sin. The sins we commit against God place us under His wrath and judgment; that's the grim reality of life as it is in this world after Eden. And those sins desperately need forgiveness.

But the problem isn't just the sins we commit against God and our neighbor. We also live with fallout from sins committed against us. Hatred, animosity, suspicion, envy, ambition, pride—all leave a painful trail of turmoil and emotional suffering for those on the receiving end. People readily and regularly impose pretty harsh standards and expectations on others, and it's hard to stand up under their scrutiny. When that happens, we're left holding the bag, spiritually speaking. It's a bag full of shame, and it depletes us, deflates us, and we're left feeling belittled, incompetent, empty, polluted, and, if we're honest, hurt. That of course makes us angry. And unresolved anger isn't pretty, for it often spills over in very destructive ways, leaving innocent victims in its wake.

Shame is the first cousin of guilt. It often feels the same, with this difference: in the case of guilt, we're the sinner—but in the case of shame, we're the sinnee; that is, we've been sinned against. Shame is the result of being sinned against. Because guilt and shame are so often found together, it's often difficult to sort them out—though they are distinct realities and need to be treated in distinct ways.

The remedy for guilt is in Jesus Christ our Lord, who came declaring, "Repent, and believe in the gospel" (Mark 1:15). To be healed of sin, we need to turn from sin ("repent") and trust in the forgiveness earned by Jesus. Therefore, guilt's remedy comes through contrition and repentance. First, we confess our sin; we admit before God and our neighbor that we've done what God has forbidden and omitted to do what God has commanded. Second, by faith in the gospel, we receive absolution—that is, forgiveness—so that sin is removed and guilt before God is erased by the ransoming blood of His Son. "There is therefore now no condemnation to those who are in Christ Jesus" (Rom. 8:1). To deny our sin is to live a lie: "we deceive ourselves and there is no truth in us" (1 Jn. 1:8). But "if we confess our sins, [God] is faithful and just to forgive us our sins and to cleanse us from all unrighteousness" (1 Jn. 1:9).

The remedy for shame is in Christ Jesus as well, but in a different way. For guilt's healing, He covers us with His righteousness (justification); for shame's healing, He wraps us in His holiness (sanctification). Shame is the experience of being degraded and hurt by the sinful words and actions of other people. In those situations, we're innocent of guilt; we've committed no sins that need forgiveness. What we do need quite desperately, though, is cleansing for our defilement, healing for our wounds, and restoration from the lingering effects of the sins committed against us. And that's exactly what Jesus provides in His sure word. "Come unto me," He invites, "and I will give you rest" (Matt. 11:28).

Resting securely in Jesus we find cleansing from defilement, healing from hurt, and renewal. And such healing and restoration happens—no surprise here—by the gospel—that is, the good news that God in Christ was reconciling the whole world unto Himself, not counting their sins against them (2 Cor. 5:19) and instead bestowing on them not just His perfect righteousness but also His absolute *holiness* (1 Cor. 1:30). Sanctification—that is, first being cleansed of defilement—then wrapped and clothed in the very holiness of God through faith in Jesus, is the remedy for shame.

So the very same gospel that forgives our guilt also cleanses us from shame. Another—a bit more vintage—word for forgiveness is *remission.* The New Testament word behind both of these English words has overtones of "release," "loose," and "discharge." In other words, by the forgiveness of our sins, Jesus Christ frees and liberates us from sin's bondage—in the case of guilt, by erasing our guilt and bestowing His own righteousness instead. In the case of shame, Christ Jesus heals our wounds by His redeeming love, cleanses us from the defilement of sins committed against us, and sanctifies us with His own holiness, thus claiming us as His very own and restoring us to full status as beloved children of our loving Father in heaven.

So you could put it this way: in Jesus Christ and His saving work, God puts all the effects of sin in full remission. The deadly disease of sin is conclusively set aside by Christ. All the sins we've committed against Him He removes from us as far as the east is from the west, and all the sins committed against us and the hurt they've caused He sets aside as well, healing our wounds and bestowing on us His loving favor instead. Guilt and shame find their common remedy in the gospel of Christ our Lord.

That's what Jesus teaches in the prayer He gave us: "And forgive us our trespasses as we forgive those who trespass against us." In the two halves of this petition, He deals first with our guilt and then with our shame. By teaching us to pray for forgiveness for the sins we have committed, He directs us to contrition and faith, confessing that we have sinned against God and deserve nothing but His wrath and punishment, seeking and imploring His grace for the sake of Christ His Son in full confidence that all sins have indeed been fully paid for by His suffering, death, and resurrection. Then having forgiven our sins, Jesus teaches us that we can deal openly and forthrightly with those who have sinned against us by also releasing the hurt and injury they've caused us: "as we [right here and now] forgive [release, loose] those who have sinned against us." By forgiving those who have sinned against us, the underlying cause of our shame is dealt with conclusively, and the ongoing power of shame to defile us is placed in remission. Because Jesus is the perfect *redemption* (payment) for our sin, He is not only our perfect *righteousness* erasing all our guilt but also our perfect *holiness* covering all our shame—thus healing our hurt as well (1 Cor. 1:30). In Christ Jesus, we are restored to wholeness before our Father in heaven, having the full rights of sonship to call on God as our beloved Father and to receive abundant blessings as His beloved children (Gal. 4:4–6).

God's Distribution System

But again, how do these magnificent realities become ours? Where and how can we take possession of forgiveness for the sins we've committed and healing for the sins committed against us? Are these things just ideas—nice ideas, godly ideas, biblical ideas—but, in the final analysis, just abstract concepts?

That's where the means of grace come in. They are God's way of distributing and conveying to us all the blessings and benefits of Christ. Christ Jesus is not into virtual realities. Everything He earned so long ago in terms of forgiveness, life, and salvation He brings and conveys to us here and now in vivid authentic actuality. In the Word of the gospel He bridges the gap between time and eternity. And by attaching that powerful, efficacious Word to earthly elements, God brings Christ's forgiveness, life, and salvation to us not virtually but concretely and sacramentally. In Augustine's terms, they are "a kind of visible word": tangible links to eternity.

The Watered Word—Holy Baptism

The place to begin is with Holy Baptism. Baptism is the sacrament of initiation . . . The Lord's mandate stipulates that it is foundational to making disciples: "And Jesus came and said to them, 'All authority in heaven and on earth has been given to me. Go therefore and make disciples of all nations, baptizing them in the name of the Father and of the Son and of the Holy Spirit, teaching them to observe all that I have commanded you. And behold, I am with you always, to the end of the age'" (Matt. 28:18–20). The authority given to Jesus by His Father in heaven is authorization to forgive sins on earth (Matt. 9:6). Here Jesus commissions His disciples to continue carrying on His work in His name and stead. He authorizes them to do what He had been authorized to do: to forgive sins on earth, thus discipling all nations by baptizing them and by teaching them.

To "baptize" means to wash. There has been a lot of controversy over the quantity of water to be used and the manner in which the washing takes place. The fact is, there's wide discretion possible in the mode of baptism, provided that water is applied "in the name of the Father and of the Son and of the Holy Spirit." In other words, baptism is not man's work but God's. Though people commonly say things like "I was baptized by Pastor _____ at _____ church" or "Brother _____ baptized me in the Jordan," the truth is that God Himself does the baptizing; to baptize in the name of the Father, Son, and Spirit means that God the Holy Trinity is the active agent in Holy Baptism. The great power of baptism is not in the water but in the Word of God contained in the water. If the sacraments are "a kind of visible word," then baptism is, you might say, a "watered Word." Baptismal water is not merely water but water included in God's command and combined with His promise: "Repent and be baptized every one of you in the name of Jesus Christ for the forgiveness of your sins, and you will receive the gift of the Holy Spirit. For the promise is for you and for your children and for all who are far off, everyone whom the Lord our God calls to himself" (Acts 2:38–39).

Baptism does something. Lutherans teach that baptism "works forgiveness of sins, rescues from death and the devil, and gives eternal salvation to all who believe."[13] Some Protestants teach that baptism is primarily a ritual or symbol signifying personal commitment to Jesus. The Bible, however, does not. The Scriptures are clear that "Baptism . . . now saves you" (1 Pet. 3:21). That's what Lutherans teach, too, for that's the Lutheran way: whatever Scripture teaches, we teach, even if it seems to conflict with human reasoning. That's the very nature of mystery/sacrament, after all. As Augustine puts it, "When the Word is added to the element, it becomes a sacrament." There's more here than meets the eye. There's more to baptism than just water; this is God's Word joined to the water. In baptism we are bathed in the Word of God. Holy Baptism is therefore no mere water bath but a "washing of regeneration and renewal of the Holy Spirit" (Titus 3:5).

What's more, in baptism God by His Word does exactly what He says. We are actually baptized not by a human being, but by God Himself: "in the Name of the *Father* and of the *Son* and of the *Holy*

Spirit." And so the water is just the outer setting for the real jewel contained in Holy Baptism: the Spirit's power through the Word of God. Thus Lutherans teach that Holy Baptism is the connecting link between Jesus and the believing Christian. Baptism is God's work, not ours. It is not you giving your heart to Jesus but His pledge to you, giving you a clean conscience before God by His saving work (1 Pet. 3:21). Baptism is not the Christian's work of obedience but Christ's work of inauguration into His death and resurrection.

By baptism into Jesus, every Christian is joined with Him in intimate union; in that water they die with Him in the death He died to sin, then rise with Him in newness of life. "Do you not know that all of us who have been baptized into Christ Jesus were baptized into His death? We were buried therefore with Him by baptism into death, in order that, just as Christ was raised from the dead by the glory of the Father, we too might walk in newness of life" (Rom. 6:3–4).

As Jesus carried all our sins with Him in His death, thus erasing forever the penalty that stood against us by His blood, He also rose triumphantly from the grave as victor over death, bestowing on all baptized believers His own perfect righteousness. Christ's salvation is a two-sided coin; first, by dying in our place, He pays the penalty for our sins ("delivered up for our offenses"). Then by rising from the dead, He actively bestows His perfect righteousness ("raised for our justification" [Rom. 4:25b]). Both benefits God Himself signs, seals, and delivers in Holy Baptism for every Christian to take hold of by faith. In this bath of regeneration, the Christian is plunged down deep into the death of Jesus for the remission of their sins and then raised up again triumphantly in His resurrection to live the risen life of Jesus from that day on.

So dramatic is the death and resurrection experienced in Holy Baptism that St. Paul exults, "I have been crucified with Christ. It is no longer I who live, but Christ who lives in me. And the life I now live in the flesh I live by faith in the Son of God, who loved me and gave himself for me" (Gal. 2:20). Notice that Paul doesn't talk about giving Jesus his heart; he rejoices rather that in baptism Jesus has given Himself to Paul. When the apostle writes, "Christ . . . lives in me," he's not talking in pictures. He means exactly what he says—namely, that every Christian from the day of his baptism on is no longer alone. He's inseparably linked with Jesus so intimately and personally that he lives in Christ, and Christ lives in him. "For as many of you as were baptized into Christ have put on Christ" (Gal. 3:27). Christ Jesus Himself is therefore the driving force and power of the Christian life each day.

Not Magic but Mystery

How can water do such great things, you ask? Again, I don't know. That's why baptism is a sacrament—a mystery, in other words. Yet I do know this: it's not the water that rescues from sin, delivers from death and the devil, and gives eternal salvation to all who believe. Not the water but the Word of God in and with the water does these things. Baptism is not magic; it's not like pulling a rabbit out of a hat or waving a wand to make something out of thin air. No, baptism is not magic but mystery—that is, God's Word combined with an earthly element. Take the Word of God away from the water and you have simple water only. But when His Word is combined with the water you have a baptism: a real "aqua vitae," or water of life—a water that brings and bestows the very life of God to all who believe His promise.

Faith is essential for salvation. Jesus puts it clearly: "Whoever believes and is baptized shall be saved" (Mark 16:16a). Though, as we have seen, faith itself is always a God-given miracle, the promises of God in Christ are received only by those who believe them. "Whoever does not believe will be condemned" (Mark 16:16b).

Here is how Luther in the *Small Catechism* answers the question: "How can water do such great things?": "Certainly not just water, but the word of God in and with the water does these things, along with the faith which trusts this word of God in the water."[14] Faith believes the gospel, including the gospel given in baptism.

You and Your Children

If not just baptism but also faith is required for salvation, why do Lutherans baptize babies? It would appear that only adults can believe; infants can't confess a living faith in Jesus, after all. Yet remember what I said about going not by what we see but by God's own Word and decree. Jesus Himself calls babes in arms "these little ones who believe in me" (Matt. 18:6). Faith is far more than intellectual knowledge or a decision of the will; it's trust in the heart worked by the Holy Spirit. Babies trust and love their earthly parents, why not their Father in heaven—especially when that love and trust is given by God Himself?

And the Holy Spirit always works by means of the Word. It shouldn't surprise us, then, that just as God called the universe out of nothingness by means of His powerful word and made Adam from lifeless clay by the breath of His mouth, so He can bring the spiritual rebirth also to infant children by means of His "watered word."

> Now there was a man of the Pharisees named Nicodemus, a ruler of the Jews. This man came to Jesus by night and said to him, "Rabbi, we know that you are a teacher come from God, for no one can do these signs that you do unless God is with him." Jesus answered him, "Truly, truly, I say to you, unless one is born again he cannot see the kingdom of God." Nicodemus said to him, "How can a man be born when he is old? Can he enter a second time into his mother's womb and be born?" Jesus answered, "Truly, truly, I say to you, unless one is born of water and the Spirit, he cannot enter the kingdom of God. That which is born of the flesh is flesh, and that which is born of the Spirit is spirit." (Jn. 3:1–6)

In this remarkable dialog with Nicodemus, a member of the Jewish intelligentsia of his day, Jesus tells him he must be born all over again spiritually if he is to belong to God's kingdom. Nicodemus is no fool; he responds that it's quite impossible for a grown man to enter back into his mother's womb to be reborn. Not so, Jesus responds. When you're born of human parents, you inherit their fallen spiritual nature ("flesh"), marking you, like the rest of mankind, as one of the "children of wrath" (Eph. 2:3).

Ever since Eden, every human being comes into this world in the same condition: blind, dead, and an enemy of God spiritually speaking. No matter how cute and innocent babies may appear, they come into this world under God's judgment, "dead in trespasses and sins" (Eph. 2:1), subject to illness and death like the rest of us, and—were it not for the one-way love of God in Christ—also doomed to eternal destruction in hell. No wonder, then, that Jesus insists that entrance into the kingdom of God is impossible apart from His remarkably astonishing quickening power: "that which is born of the flesh is flesh," sadly (Jn. 3:6). That's why you must be born all over again in order to see God's kingdom. And so it is; everyone born again by water and the Spirit has a new and spiritual nature: "that which is born of the Spirit is spirit" (Jn. 3:6).

Someone has observed that Lutherans baptize babies as though they are adults and adults as though they are babies. And they're right. Because we take God's Word seriously, Lutherans recognize that adult and infant faith alike is always a miraculous work of God by His Spirit through His Word, whether that word comes as oral preaching and instruction or applied by means of water.

The New Testament evidence makes it clear that wherever the Word of God was received in faith, whole households[15] were baptized in accordance with Jesus's command and promise: "Go therefore and make disciples of all nations, baptizing them in the name of the Father and of the Son and of the Holy Spirit, teaching them to observe all that I have commanded you. And behold, I am with you always, to the end of the age" (Matt. 28:19–20). Note that the commission to make disciples by baptizing and teaching is not limited to adult converts; it includes "all nations." Accordingly, when St. Peter on Pentecost Day urged his sin-stricken hearers to "repent and be baptized" for the forgiveness of their sins, he also included their families: "For the promise is for you *and for your children* and for all who are far off, everyone whom the Lord our God calls to himself" (Acts 2:39).

How wonderful that God doesn't discriminate; He offers His grace and mercy in Christ Jesus to adults and children alike by means of the power of His Spirit working through His watered word as well as His oral word. And a Christian's baptismal day is just the first day of the rest of His life.

Wanted: Dead and Alive

In baptism, a death and resurrection occurs for each and every Christian. This is not symbol or playacting; it's the real thing and the genuine article. Having been buried with Jesus by baptism into His death and raised up with Him in His resurrection, the Christian is now "dead to sin and alive to God in Christ Jesus" (Rom. 6:11).

Accordingly, Lutherans teach that baptism has significance far beyond the Christian's baptismal day. In fact, you could say that each Christian leads a baptismal life every day. He or she returns daily by contrition and repentance to the death and resurrection of Jesus. As mentioned, the baptized Christian always lives "in Christ." The baptismal pattern of dying and rising again is repeated each day of the Christian's life. Again and again he or she puts off the former way of life of the sinful nature and puts on instead the new nature bestowed in Holy Baptism, the very life of Jesus "created after the likeness of God in true righteousness and holiness" (Eph. 4:24).

Thus baptism becomes the key to daily Christian living. In Lutheran teaching, Holy Baptism is the secret to the vitality of the Christian life. There is a cyclical pattern to each Christian's life revolving around Holy Baptism, where every Christian is linked to the death and resurrection of Jesus. From that moment on, the Christian goes on dying and rising, putting off sin and putting on Jesus throughout his or her life.

And this, mind you, is not something the Christian does. Though Christian faith is a living, busy, active thing, its activity and action flows from Christ Jesus Himself. The baptized Christian confesses along with St. Paul, "It is no longer I who live, but Christ who lives in me" (Gal. 2:20).

Mystery, you say? Absolutely right; this is a great mystery—that a water washing could join us to Jesus and His saving work in such an intimate way that we can say we live in Jesus and He in us. But then, remember, it's not the water that does these great things; it's the Word of God in and with the water and faith that trusts the Word of God in the water. That's baptism for you: it's one of Augustine's "visible words"—a watered word, you can call it. But there are other mysteries too.

The Audible Word—Holy Absolution

Lutherans practice individual confession and absolution not because they want to hang on to obscure medieval tradition but because they believe the promise and institution of Jesus: "If you forgive the sins of anyone, they are forgiven; if you withhold forgiveness from anyone, it is withheld" (Jn. 20:23). Clearly Jesus intends that the forgiveness

He earned would continue to be announced in His name and stead to sorrowing sinners until He comes again in glory. So while we offer this great gift to penitent hearts, we never impose it on anyone. It would be horribly wrong to demand that people confess their sins and receive absolution. Why turn a gift into a burden and obligation? Yet it remains wonderfully true that by hearing forgiveness announced by one of Christ's authorized servants, this is valid and certain, even in heaven, as if Christ Jesus Himself were speaking to us.

There is some debate whether confession and absolution is a sacrament. That depends on your definition. If you go by a strict interpretation of Augustine's maxim—"When the Word is added to the element or the natural substance, it becomes a sacrament"— there's room for argument. No visible element is involved, after all, in the oral pronouncement: "I forgive you all your sins in the name of the Father and of the Son and of the Holy Spirit." It's only speech, after all. Yet what powerful speech it is! For when God's Word is applied in accordance with His will and intent, things happen. Remember, God's Word and Spirit can never be divided. Thus His Word is an efficacious word; by the power of the Spirit the Word does what it says. Just as at the initial creation, God said, "Let there be light," and light sprang out of darkness, so also when sins are absolved in the powerful name and authority of God—Father, Son, and Holy Spirit—then they are truly forgiven, removed from the sinner as far as the east is from the west.

I can almost hear you now: "Is this man suggesting that I'm not really forgiven unless I confess my sins to a pastor?" Of course not. Remember what I said: it's horribly wrong to turn a gift into an obligation. And God is surpassingly rich in His grace. He puts sin into remission, forgives sins, heals the wounds of shame, and bestows all the gift of salvation in more than one way. As Luther explains in the Smalcald Articles, one of the Lutheran Confessions of faith, "God is superabundantly rich [and liberal] in His grace [and goodness]. First through the spoken Word by which the forgiveness of sins is preached [He commands to be preached] in the whole world; which is the peculiar office of the Gospel. Secondly, through Baptism. Thirdly, through the holy Sacrament of the Altar, Fourthly, through the power of the keys, and also through the mutual conversation and consolation of brethren."[16] Notice here that the Lutheran confession enumerates

God's way of dealing with mankind—the means of Grace, in other words—in a way that includes not only the Word, Baptism, and the Sacrament of the Altar but also two additional categories: "the power of the keys" and "the mutual conversation and consolation of brethren." The power of the keys is a reference to confession and absolution, building from Jesus's words to Peter after he confessed Jesus to be "the Christ, the Son of the Living God": "I will give you the keys of the kingdom of heaven, and whatever you bind on earth shall be bound in heaven, and whatever you loose on earth shall be loosed in heaven" (Matt. 16:19). Notice here the authorization Jesus gives to Peter—and later all the disciples (Matt. 18:18)—to loose or free people from their sins, which is always the way forgiveness is described in the New Testament. It is, if you will, a kind of "power of attorney," in which the Son of God authorizes pastors to announce His forgiveness in His name and stead, thus actually forgiving sins in His place.

But there's more; in "mutual conversation and consolation," each and every Christian brings God's gracious word of forgiveness and healing to hurting hearts personally. Thus, though no human being has ever met God face to face, people can be certain that they have felt His love and received His compassion through their interaction with other Christians. "No one has ever seen God; if we love one another, God abides in us and his love is perfected in us" (1 Jn. 4:12). When God's love is "perfected," that means it's carried out, or brought to completion, in us; that is, there's a direct link between our love and God's. We love because God first loved us; thus, in our love, people meet up with His love. We are God's not-so-secret agents.

The Edible Word: Holy Supper

I mentioned earlier that all Christian churches practice baptism, though they disagree widely regarding its nature, power, and use. The same is true regarding the Lord's Supper[17]—it's also called Holy Communion[18] and the Eucharist.[19] First, what do they agree about? Well, all Christians are agreed that the night before His execution on the cross, Jesus gathered with His disciples to observe a last commemorative meal. It was His last opportunity to dine with them, as He said, "before I suffer" (Luke 22:15). They were observing the Passover Seder, the solemn yet joyful annual ritual meal in which faithful

Jews celebrated the deliverance of their ancestors from slavery in Egypt. During that dreadful night, the angel of death passed through the whole land and slaughtered all the firstborn in every household except where the blood of a sacrificed lamb marked the doorway (Exod. 12:27).

All Christians agree that Jesus ate this meal with His disciples and that during the meal, He instituted a sacred meal of His own to be observed with regularity by His followers ever after. Unfortunately, they disagree as to the nature and purpose of that meal. Some view it as primarily a memorial meal, a way of remembering Jesus and His profound love that led Him to the cross and death for sinners. True, Jesus did instruct His disciples to "do this in remembrance of me" (Luke 22:19). But there's far more going on in this meal than just remembering Jesus and His love; St. Paul calls this eating and drinking of bread and cup an actual participation in the body and blood Jesus gave at Calvary for the forgiveness of our sins (1 Cor. 10:16).

Real or Imaginary?

Remember, I told you that Lutherans are comfortable with paradox. That is, Lutherans prefer to let Scripture stand on its own, even when it may appear to conflict with human reason. So, for example, in this instance certain Protestant Christians interpret the words of Jesus in connection with this meal symbolically. "This is my body—This is my blood" for them means "This *represents/symbolizes* my body, my blood." Other Christians of Reformed or Calvinist affiliation believe that Christ is truly present in this meal, but only spiritually. In this supper, they believe, He invites the faithful to spiritually ascend to heaven, there to feed on Him by faith. Their reasoning is sound. After all, Jesus is no longer visibly present in this world; He has taken His body and His blood to heaven, where He sits in exalted glory. How then could He possibly be present in this world among us with that body and blood? This makes perfect sense humanly speaking. Yet remember that Jesus is God, and God is present everywhere, and uniquely so in this sacrament. Since Jesus's bodily ascension fills the whole universe also according to His human nature, Christians can and do eat and drink His body and blood along with the bread and wine they receive in this sacramental meal.

Other Christians, such as Roman Catholics, hold a still different view: they believe that since Jesus is our great high priest, in this meal He offers Himself repeatedly as the atoning sacrifice for our sin. By His word and decree, He transforms the bread and wine into His body and blood. Sins are remitted because Christians eat from the sacrifice being offered again and again on the altar during Mass. In this view, though the outer appearance of bread and wine remain, they are actually and substantially changed into the body and blood of Jesus.

Again, Lutherans appear to occupy the mediating position between these extremes. We hold to none of the extremes; in this sacrament Jesus is present neither symbolically nor spiritually nor substantively but bodily and sacramentally. That is, Jesus means what He says. Taking the elements of the Passover meal in His hands, He blessed and distributed the bread and cup to His disciples, telling them to eat and drink "my body, which is given for you" (1 Cor. 11:24) and "my blood of the new testament, which is shed for many for the remission of sins" (Matt. 26:26, KJV). Though His body and blood were offered only once as a sacrifice for sin (1 Pet. 3:18), He gives them repeatedly to Christians to eat and to drink in this holy supper as the sign and seal of sins forgiven and lives restored.

The bread is Christ's body; the wine is His blood. A mystery? You bet it is; a wondrous mystery indeed! How can it be that ordinary bread and wine could be at the same time the flesh and blood of Jesus, born of Mary, with which He purchased our salvation? I don't know. But then, as I told you earlier, I also don't know how the creator of the universe could be born of a young virgin and suckled at her breast. These are mysteries beyond human reasoning, to be sure. But they are also mysteries in the classic sense of tangible, natural elements containing glorious, profound supernatural realities. So we're back to our old friend Augustine's definition again: "When the Word is added to the element or the natural substance, it becomes a sacrament."

What's the Use?

So what's the use of the Sacrament of the Altar? Well, for starters, let's go with what Jesus said: the Sacrament of the Altar is "for you . . . for the remission of sins." Just as the flesh and blood of Jesus was the onetime payment for the sins of all the world when He died on the cross at Calvary, so now, repeatedly in this Sacrament, Jesus gives us the evidence that our sins are paid for: "My body given for you . . . my blood shed for you." Just as a receipt marked "paid in full" is evidence that a debt has been paid, so also in this Sacrament, we have the sign and seal of our redemption. Jesus hands us under cover of bread and wine the very flesh and blood with which the penalty of our sins has been removed (Col. 2:14). So then, believing this pledge and promise, every sorrowing heart burdened under the guilt of sin can find in this Sacrament sin's remission—a conscience free from guilt and a soul unstained by sin.

But there's more. In John 6, Jesus explains that He came to this earth not merely to forgive sins but to bestow life—the very life that He had with His Father in heaven before the world began. In the Sinai wilderness, God had miraculously fed His people with the heavenly manna. Jesus makes the remarkable claim that the manna in the wilderness was a dress rehearsal for the real thing: He Himself is the bread that came down from heaven to bring life to the world: "I am the living bread that came down from heaven. If anyone eats of this bread, he will live forever. And the bread that I will give for the life of the world is my flesh. . . . As the living Father sent me, and I live because of the Father, so whoever feeds on me, he also will live because of me" (Jn. 6:51, 57).

We said earlier that sin impacts people in two ways: they suffer from guilt because they have sinned and they suffer from shame because they have been sinned against. Jesus provides the antidote and healing for both. In His bodily suffering and dying and rising to life again, He abolishes guilt and bestows His perfect righteousness instead. Likewise, by the same fleshly suffering, death, and dramatic resurrection, He covers shame and defilement, heals wounded hearts, and wraps the broken in His perfect holiness.

When Jesus says, "Whoever feeds on me . . . will live because of me," He isn't just talking in picture language. He carefully defines the life that was in Him as the life He received from the *living* Father. He is the *living* bread, far different from the heavenly manna that the people of Israel ate for a time and then died. The flesh and blood of Jesus are life giving and death destroying because He Himself is full of life—the same never-ending life that He had with His Father from all eternity. When faithful Christians eat His body and drink His blood, they receive not merely forgiveness but God's very own life and salvation. Thus shattered hearts are mended, wounded souls are healed, and though in this fallen world we are headed for death and the grave, in the Sacrament of the Altar, we have access to the one who for our sakes died and was raised again. By eating and drinking His living flesh and blood, we already now have a share in His own risen life.

In a world quite literally dying to live, this sacred meal brings us life in all its fullness. In fact, in this eating and drinking, Jesus gives Himself to us—and He is life personified. All those things you've done that leave you with a boatload of guilt, remorse, and regret have been removed from you by His bitter suffering and death, and thus in this sacred meal He lifts that ugly load from you. But more than that, all the hurtful, shameful things that others have done to you Jesus Himself suffered in His own sacred body when He was tortured, mocked, defiled, and debased in His death—and so this meal is also the antidote for your hurt and pain. His blood not only erases the guilt of the sins you've done but also heals and cleanses you from the pollution and defilement of the sins you've suffered.

And here's the point: you don't have to ascend to heaven spiritually to get this healing and forgiveness. In this meal Jesus comes to you, and not just in some ethereal or spiritual way but in a most material—even earthy—manner to forgive you and heal you. Jesus meant exactly what He said to the crowds in Galilee: "He who eats me will live because of me" (Jn. 6:57; RSV). Under the old covenant, the consumption of blood was strictly prohibited: "You shall not eat the blood of any creature, for the life of every creature is its blood" (Lev. 17:14). Yet in His supper Jesus expressly commands us to drink His blood, thereby cleansing us of not only all our sins but also everything that defiles and contaminates us spiritually—from the inside out.

In the bread and wine of His supper, Jesus gives Himself personally and intimately to all the faithful. He places His holy body and most precious blood into the mouths of sinners and makes them saints. He gives Himself bodily to wounded, broken souls and makes them whole again. And since He burst the bonds of death itself and no grave could hold Him, in the living flesh and blood of Christ received in this sacramental eating and drinking, we have the promise of resurrection day: "Whoever feeds on my flesh and drinks my blood has eternal life, and I will raise him up on the last day" (Jn. 6:54). In this earthly meal we already rejoice with those loved ones who've gone ahead into heaven and now enjoy the eternal marriage feast of the Lamb in His kingdom (Rev. 19:9).

All this Jesus promises in His supper by means of His powerful Words: "for you." Here is Christ's love in action, strong to loose and free, powerful to cleanse and heal. There is liberation and healing in Jesus, and you don't have to go up to heaven to get it. In this sacrament Jesus comes down to earth to embrace you with His love, to make you whole, and give you hope to live again.

You just can't get closer to Jesus in this world than this. He meets you in this supper where, just as He did with the disciples the night of His betrayal, He hands you His own body and blood and says once again, "for you." Holy Communion, indeed! Here we are one with Him who laid down His life for us, who once was dead but now is alive forevermore. Here in the shadowlands of this fallen world we have a foretaste of the bright eternal joys ahead. Here, despite our fear and distress, we taste and see that the Lord is good (Psalm 34:8).

Channels of God's Grace

Word and *Sacrament* have a nicely sounding ring to them, don't you think? We Lutherans are always talking about God's Word and Sacrament. These means of God's grace are, as we have seen, the means and channels of God's own Spirit. As I said, you could actually call the means of grace the means of the Spirit, for God's Word is always the vehicle and instrument of God's Spirit. And whether this Word is spoken orally or joined to the visible elements of water, bread, and wine, God's powerful Word and Spirit do exactly what He sends them forth to do: to awake and strengthen faith, to raise from spiritual death and blindness to life and sight, to forgive and absolve sins, and to burst the bonds of sin and death and lift the burden of shame and hurt.

Above all, this Word and these powerful Sacraments are never perfunctory routine or empty ritual. They throb with the vitality and presence of the Son of God Himself. Jesus Christ, God's eternal Son, is not some departed hero whom we fondly remember and whose fortitude we hope to emulate. Jesus meant exactly what He said. Though unseen, He is with us still. Through these sacred means, God's eternal Son remains intimately present with His church until He returns visibly at the end of time.

In the last chapter of Matthew, we find Jesus connecting His earthly ministry with the ministry that continues to this day in His Church by means of His Word ("all that I have commanded you") and His sacrament ("baptizing them"; Matt. 28:19). Through these means, Jesus promises His ongoing presence. In the moments just before He vanished from the sight of His disciples to ascend to His Father's glorious throne, Jesus left this promise ringing in their ears: "I am with you." Notice carefully: there's no spiritual doubletalk here, no vague hope, no pious wish or future potentiality. He speaks in the vividly powerful present tense: "I *am* with you"—impressing on them His solemn intent to maintain ongoing intimate connection with His beloved church in every era by means of His gospel preached and sacraments administered: "And behold, I am with you always, to the end of the age" (Matt. 28:20).

Notes, Chapter 6

1. Unless otherwise noted, quotations from the Bible are taken from the *English Standard Version* (Wheaton, IL: Crossway, 2001).

2. "Although he is God and a human being, nevertheless he is not two but one Christ. However, he is one not by the changing of the divinity in the flesh but by the taking up of the humanity in God. Indeed, he is one not by a confusion of substance but by a unity of person. For, as the rational soul and the flesh are one human being, so God and the human being are one Christ." The Athanasian Creed, in Robert Kolb and Timothy J. Wengert, ed., *The Book of Concord* (Minneapolis, MN: Fortress Press, 2000), 25.

3. The Augsburg Confession, Article III(2), in Kolb and Wengert, *The Book of Concord*, 38.

4. The Large Catechism IV (18), in ibid., 458.

5. Augustine of Hippo, *Tractate 50* (John 15:1–3), par. 3, http://www.newadvent.org/fathers/1701080.htm.

6. "Then the LORD God formed the man of dust from the ground and breathed into his nostrils the breath of life, and the man became a living creature" (Gen. 2:7).

7. Preface in Kolb and Wengert, *The Book of Concord*, 5.

8. The Augsburg Confession IV, Concerning Justification, in Kolb and Wengert, *The Book of Concord*, 39–40.

9. "I believe that I cannot *by my own reason or strength* believe in Jesus Christ my Lord, or come to Him; but the Holy Spirit has called me by the Gospel, enlightened me with His gifts, sanctified and kept me in the true faith." *Luther's Small Catechism with Explanation* (St. Louis, MO: Concordia Publishing House, 1986), 15.

10. Charlotte Elliott, "Just as I Am, without One Plea," stanza 6, *Lutheran Service Book* (St. Louis, MO: Concordia Publishing House, 2006), 570.

11. Tullian Tchividjian powerfully captures God's divine monergism in human salvation in his provocative book, *One Way Love* (Colorado Springs, CO: David C. Cook, 2013). See also his clear defense of God's grace in contrast to what he has labeled "performancism" in much of contemporary evangelicalism with its "do more, try harder" sermons: "The Missing Message in Today's Churches," *Washington Post*, October 17, 2013.

12. *Luther's Small Catechism*, 15.

13. Ibid., 22.

14. Ibid., 22.

15. For example, in Phillipi, Lydia's and the jailer's households were all baptized. Acts 16:15, 33, respectively.

16. Smalcald Articles, Part 3, Article 4, in *The Book of Concord*, ed. F. Bente and W. H. T. Dau (St. Louis, MO: Concordia Publishing House, 1922), 213. The confession was written in both German and Latin. The brackets give the translation of what the Latin adds to the text.

17. "Lord's Supper"—this meal was instituted during the evening meal at Passover. Cf. "the cup after supper" (Luke 22:20).

18. "Holy Communion"—a translation of the "koinonia," or "participation" between the bread/body and wine/blood as well as the unity created by all who consume the body and blood together. "The cup of blessing that we bless, is it not a participation in the blood of Christ? The bread that we break, is it not a participation in the body of Christ?" (1 Cor. 10:16).

19. "Eucharist"—Greek for "thanksgiving," the prayer of thanks which Jesus prayed before the institution of this meal (1 Cor. 11:24), and the thanksgiving with which Christians participate in this sacred meal.

CHAPTER 7

God's Two Kingdoms

Todd Wilken

*Baptism constitutes a boundary between the Kingdom
of God and the kingdom of this world.*
> —William Weedon, director of worship for
> the Lutheran Church–Missouri Synod

At the conclusion of Handel's *Messiah*, there is a traffic jam of Alleluias celebrating the reign of "the Lord God omnipotent." Listening
to a live performance recently, I noticed that every line is repeated,
some many times, except one—a quotation of Revelation 11:15, set
as a brief chorale:

> The kingdom of this world
> is become
> the kingdom of our Lord,
> and of His Christ.

It is stunning to hear this short interlude in the middle of the heavenly chorus. Listening, I realized that this one line, set apart musi-
cally, states the reason for all those Alleluias. The line explains what
it means that "the Lord God omnipotent reigneth." Jesus Christ—by
his incarnation, life, suffering, death, resurrection, and ascension—
has assumed his rightful place as the king over all things, in heaven,
on earth, and under the earth. As Paul tells the Philippians, "God has

highly exalted him and bestowed on him the name that is above every name, so that at the name of Jesus every knee should bow, in heaven and on earth and under the earth, and every tongue confess that Jesus Christ is Lord, to the glory of God the Father" (Phil. 2:9–11).[1] Let the Alleluias begin.

But this final disposition of the universe where Jesus reigns over all things raises questions for us here and now: Hasn't he always reigned over all things? Doesn't he reign over all things even now? What is the difference between the end when "he shall reign forever and ever" and now?

The same question is raised by Luke's account of Jesus's temptation in the wilderness at the beginning of his public ministry: "And the devil took him up and showed him all the kingdoms of the world in a moment of time, and said to him, 'To you I will give all this authority and their glory, for it has been delivered to me, and I give it to whom I will. If you, then, will worship me, it will all be yours'" (Luke 4:5–7).

Is Satan lying? Does he actually possess authority over the kingdoms of the world? Is such authority really Satan's to give? Jesus's response doesn't directly refute Satan's claim. He doesn't say, "No, that authority is really mine." Nor does he say, as he later answers Pontius Pilate's claim of authority, "You would have no authority over me at all unless it had been given you from above" (Jn. 19:11). No, he simply says, "It is written, 'You shall worship the Lord your God, and him only shall you serve'" (Luke 4:8).

By definition, God is the highest authority. At the end, this will be completely manifest when "he shall reign forever and ever" and when "he [Christ] delivers the kingdom to God the Father after destroying every rule and every authority and power. For he must reign until he has put all his enemies under his feet" (1 Cor. 15:24–25). However, in the meantime, "we do not yet see everything in subjection to him" (Heb. 2:8). In the meantime, even those enemies, including Satan, appear to rule this world. It is an appearance we must reject if we are to understand our place in this world.

God's Two Kingdoms

Theologically, the monk kneeling in his cell and the average American Christian kneeling in his or her prayer closet have more in common than you would think. In their own way, both are attempting to do the impossible. Both are attempting to leave the world behind—a world in which they believe they no longer belong. Both are a bit confused.

Granted, the average American Christian is more spiritually conflicted about this than the ascetic. If the ascetic has divorced himself or herself from the world, the average American Christian is attempting a trial separation. The ascetic, both literally and figuratively, has turned his or her back on the world and shut the door. The average American Christian would like to, but can't, and he or she feels guilty about it every day. He or she sings, "I am but a stranger here, heaven is my home." Yet that person is trying to figure out why he or she is still in the world.

It is true, Satan claims sovereignty over this world; he is even called "the ruler of this world" and "the god of this age" (Jn. 12:31; 14:30; 16:11; 2 Cor. 4:4). But Satan is certainly not the sovereign of this world. Satan is sovereign nowhere, not even in Hell. His kingdom is not a true kingdom, since he is not king. He can never be anything more than what he is: a rebellious servant. His proper realm is that no man's land of "outer darkness" (Matt. 8:12; 22:13; 25:30) where he and all who serve him will eventually be prisoners. It is into this kingdom of darkness that we are all born, to which we all naturally belong, in which we first hold citizenship, and from which God must rescue us if we are to be naturalized into His kingdom of light.

> He has delivered us from the domain of darkness and transferred us to the kingdom of his beloved Son, in whom we have redemption, the forgiveness of sins. (Col. 1:13–14)

> But you are a chosen race, a royal priesthood, a holy nation, a people for his own possession, that you may proclaim the excellencies of him who called you out of darkness into his marvelous light. Once you were not a people, but now you are God's people; once you had not received mercy, but now you have received mercy. (1 Pet. 2:9–10)

Being rescued from Satan's kingdom removes the Christian from Satan's dominion but not from this world. This is the confusion that the ascetic and the average American Christian share. They both think that Satan rules this world; both want to renounce their citizenship in it, to emigrate from it, and to leave it behind. But they are confused.

Both fail to observe the simple, Biblical distinction between God's two kingdoms: His spiritual kingdom of the Church and his earthly kingdom of human authority and government. God rules both of these kingdoms, through different means, toward different ends. In His spiritual kingdom, God rules through his Word and Sacraments, toward the forgiveness of sins, salvation, and eternal life for its citizens. In his earthly kingdom, God rules through human reason, law, and force, toward civil order, peace, and protection for its citizens. In God's spiritual kingdom, the Church, the only authority is the Word of God, whereby God "calls, gathers, enlightens, and sanctifies the whole Christian Church on earth, and keeps it with Jesus Christ in the one true faith; in which Christian Church he forgives daily and richly all sins."[2] In God's earthly kingdom, he uses reason, law, and force, mediated by human authorities to punish wrongdoers and reward those that do good (Rom. 13:1–7; 1 Pet. 2:13–14).

The Christian's Dual Citizenship

The Christian is a citizen of both God's spiritual kingdom of the Church and God's earthly kingdom of human authority and government. Someone holding dual citizenship in the United States and Canada can only physically reside in one country at a time. While in the United States, he or she is subject to the laws of the United States; while in Canada, he or she is subject to Canada's laws. But the Christian resides in both God's spiritual and temporal kingdoms simultaneously. He or she does not cross the border from one into the other but is a citizen and resident of both, at the same time, all the time.

These two kingdoms are not of equal caliber. One serves the purpose of the other. One is ultimate, the other penultimate. One is permanent, the other is temporary. Although the two kingdoms should never be conflated or confused, the earthly kingdom finally exists for the sake of the spiritual kingdom (1 Tim. 2:1–4). Through his rule over both of his kingdoms, God sees to it that his one will is done, "on earth as it is in heaven" (Matt. 6:10).

In God's earthly kingdom, the Christian recognizes that God hides his rule behind human authorities and earthly government. Those authorities and governments may require many things; the Christian is bound to obey because those authorities have been instituted by God. Those authorities and governments may also require something contrary to God's Word. In that case, the Christian is bound to disobey. The Christian's allegiance to these two kingdoms is not equal. While he is in the world, he is not of the world. While he is called by God to "be subject to the governing authorities" (Rom. 13:1), he "must obey God rather than men" (Acts 5:29). Also, God's earthly kingdom is not simply the authorities found in "the government"—it has to do with families, how societies work, and with God's providential care of the natural order (his "first article" gifts, referring to Luther's explanation in the Catechism of what the Apostle's Creed says about God as creator).

God rules in both of these kingdoms. The Christian lives in both. Rescued from Satan's kingdom, the Christian is made a citizen of God's spiritual kingdom yet remains a full-fledged citizen of this world, God's world. It is true; Baptism is "a boundary between the Kingdom of God and the kingdoms of this world." But the Baptized live in both, all the time. Baptism calls us out of and back into the world at the same time. Baptism simultaneously separates us from the world and leaves us in the world. The Christian is a stranger here but also, strangely, a citizen here. Of course, his or her dual citizenship puts the Christian in an uncomfortable position.

Reason and Faith

The Christian's life as a citizen in both kingdoms also requires that he or she distinguish reason from faith as well as understand their proper relationship. Reason encompasses the Christian's natural faculties to observe, understand, and interpret the world around him or her. Faith encompasses faculties that are not natural to him or her: the ability to observe, understand, interpret, and believe the Word of God. Both reason and faith are given by God—reason by God's act of creation and faith by God's act of revelation.

Reason is not in and of itself contrary to faith. Jesus Christ possesses perfect human reason that completely agrees with God's Word in every respect. In the life to come, our reason will likewise conform perfectly to faith. However, reason—and especially fallen reason—can never result in or produce saving faith. Luther explains,

> Neither you nor I could ever know anything of Christ, or believe on Him, and obtain Him for our Lord, unless it were offered to us and granted to our hearts by the Holy Ghost through the preaching of the Gospel. The work is done and accomplished; for Christ has acquired and gained the treasure for us by His suffering, death, resurrection, etc. But if the work remained concealed so that no one knew of it, then it would be in vain and lost. That this treasure, therefore, might not lie buried, but be appropriated and enjoyed, God has caused the Word to go forth and be proclaimed, in which He gives the Holy Ghost to bring this treasure home and appropriate it to us.[3]

As with man's will, reason must know its limits.

In addition to this, understanding the proper relationship between reason and faith is crucial for the Christian living in both kingdoms. The coin of the realm in God's earthly kingdom is reason; in God's spiritual kingdom, it is faith. But the Christian remains a Christian at all times; his ultimate fealty is to faith and God's Word. Therefore, reason must always remain a servant of faith in both spiritual and earthly matters. If required to submit to reason in either earthly or spiritual affairs, faith is undermined and destroyed.

On the other hand, reason in service of faith is both necessary and useful to the Christian in both of God's kingdoms. While reason can never produce faith, it serves faith in many ways. Among the primary gifts of God, Luther includes "my reason, and all my senses."[4] Indeed, Luther's own writings and scholarship demonstrate that he possessed and employed those gifts at a very high level in service of God's Word. In earthly affairs, reason in service of faith produces what Harry Blamires called "the Christian mind": "the religious view of life, the view which sets all earthly issues within the context of the eternal, the view which relates all human problems—social, political, cultural—to the doctrinal foundations of the Christian faith, the view which sees all things here below in terms of God's supremacy and earth's transitoriness, in terms of heaven and hell."[5] This "Christian mind" integrates the eternal truths of God's spiritual kingdom into the temporal affairs of God's earthly kingdom, giving the Christian an "orientation towards the supernatural"[6] even while living in the natural world.

The Fourth Commandment

For Martin Luther, the commandment "Honor your father and mother" is spoken to the Christian living in God's two kingdoms, subject to two kinds of authority: earthly and spiritual. In explaining this commandment, he says first that it requires not only obedience to parents but also "all kinds of obedience to persons in authority who have to command and to govern."[7] He writes, "We have two kinds of fathers presented in this commandment, fathers in blood and fathers in office, or those to whom belongs the care of the family, and those to whom belongs the care of the country. Besides these there are yet spiritual fathers . . . who govern and guide us by the Word of God."[8]

God exercises authority in his earthly kingdom through earthly "fathers," including all earthly authorities from our parents to the highest reaches of earthly government. These earthly fathers rule in God's stead, exercising the authority of their various positions or offices. Their tools are reason and force. Reason is expressed in the rules and laws they make and administer. The enforcement of those rules and laws entails force of varying degrees, from a father sending a disobedient child to his room to a jury or judge imposing capital punishment and everything in between. God's purpose when he acts through earthly authorities is civil order and peace.

God also exercises authority in his spiritual kingdom through spiritual fathers. These are those who are called to the Office of the Ministry in the Church. These spiritual fathers also act in God's stead, preaching God's Word and administering the Sacraments. The Word and Sacraments are the only tools of these spiritual fathers. They use no force or coercion, only proclamation of the Word of God. God's purpose when he acts through spiritual authorities is the proclamation of repentance and the forgiveness of sins in Christ's name.

The fourth commandment requires of the Christian obedience to God in both the earthly and spiritual kingdoms, subject to both earthly and spiritual authority, administered through both earthly and spiritual fathers.

Vocation and the Neighbor

We return to the monk and the average American Christian. The answer they seek is not found by withdrawing from the world. They are trying to figure out why in the world they are still in the world. As Christians, they have been called out of the world and back into it at the same time. They have been called back into the world to serve their neighbor. They will never find him or her in a monk's cell or a prayer closet. Where will they find him?

The Christian finds his or her neighbor in the world, in his or her God-given vocations, not in his or her self-imposed isolation from the world. "In his earthly kingdom, just as in his spiritual kingdom, God bestows his gifts through means. God ordained that human beings be bound together in love, in relationships and communities existing in a state of interdependence. In this context, God is providentially at work caring for his people, each of whom contributes according to his or her God-given talents, gifts, opportunities, and stations."[9] The Christian is never without a vocation. In fact, every Christian has several: wife, husband, mother, father, child, friend, employee, citizen. This is precisely how the Christian lives under God's rule in both the earthly and spiritual kingdoms. This is where the Christian finds neighbors to serve. This is why the Christian is still in the world.

The Church has been called a colony or outpost from the future. It is true. Here, Christians are the "boots on the ground" from the age to come. The Christian lives as a citizen of God's spiritual kingdom in God's earthly kingdom. The Christian lives in faith toward God and in love toward his or her neighbor.

"Baptism constitutes a boundary between the Kingdom of God and the kingdom of this world." The Christian lives uncomfortably with a foot on both sides of that boundary. He or she lives in both of God's kingdoms. He or she trusts that, even now, Christ reigns, even though it looks like it is the enemies of Christ and even Satan who are in charge. The Christian wrestles his or her reason into submission to the Word of God and turns it loose to serve his or her neighbor. The Christian answers to two authorities, trusting that God governs through both. He or she looks forward to the day when "the kingdom of the world has become the kingdom of our Lord and of his Christ, and he shall reign forever and ever."

Notes

1. Quotations from the Bible are taken from the *English Standard Version* (Wheaton, IL: Crossway, 2001).

2. The Apostles' Creed, the Third Article, *Luther's Small Catechism with Explanation* (St. Louis, MO: Concordia Publishing House, 1991), 17.

3. The Apostles' Creed, Large Catechism, paragraph 38, in *The Book of Concord*, ed. F. Bente and W. H. T. Dau (St. Louis, MO: Concordia Publishing House, 1922), 300. See also Matthew 16:17; Romans 11:33–34; 1 Corinthians 1:18–21; 2:14.

4. The Apostles' Creed, the First Article, *Small Catechism*, 15.

5. Harry Blamires, *The Christian Mind: How Should a Christian Think?* (London: SPCK, 1963), 4.

6. Ibid., 3.

7. The Ten Commandments, *Large Catechism*, 141, in Bente and Dau, *The Book of Concord*, 277.

8. Ibid., 158, in Bente and Dau, *The Book of Concord*, 278.

9. Gene Edward Veith, "The Doctrine of Vocation: How God Hides Himself in Human Work," *Modern Reformation* 8, no. 3 (May/June 1999).

CHAPTER 8

Vocation versus Narcissus

Uwe Siemon-Netto

The mounting narcissist mind-set is an acute threat to the survival of ordered society in North America and Western Europe, for it focuses man's attention entirely on the "me." This chapter presents the specifically Lutheran doctrine of vocation as the most effective antidote against this destructive Zeitgeist because it directs the individual to the "you," the other person, and therefore away from the "me." The doctrine of vocation stresses the priesthood of all believers in the temporal world, where all have a call from God to serve their neighbor in all their everyday endeavors. By doing this in a spirit of love, Christians render the highest possible service to God.

This concept differs starkly from Roman Catholicism's sacramental view that vocation is limited to the ordained ministry or monastic life. It is also in variance with the pietistic and evangelical position that the Christian is to avoid the sinful world altogether or be "sanctified" by working as a missionary abroad or other kinds of church work. Luther, by contrast, has a much more down-to-earth message: he teaches that Christians, being assured of their salvation by grace through faith in Christ's redemptive work for them on the cross, are to roll up their sleeves and get involved in the secular realm without succumbing to its ways. In their secular vocations they become God's partners in the maintenance of the world and in the ongoing process of creation (*creation continua*).

The Empty Vessel Spirituality

Today's "narcissism epidemic"[1] can be thought of as a popular faith movement the practitioners of which endeavor to sit on their own altars and worship themselves. Over a century ago, the pioneering sociologist Max Weber exposed the link between the fixation on the self, the consumer economy, and internalized religious doctrines. He argued that the spirit of American capitalism was rooted in the post-Calvinist doctrine of double predestination, notably in Article 3 of the *Westminster Confession of Faith* of 1647, which states, "By the decree of God, for the manifestation of his glory, some men and angels are predestined unto everlasting life, and others foreordained to everlasting death."[2] Weber argued that this statement of faith resulted in Protestants scrutinizing themselves for signs of their election and measuring their state of grace by their success in accumulating assets to the glory of God. According to Weber, this led to the "Protestant work ethic" and to the emergence of capitalism.

Thus both in the spiritual realm and in the realm of work, the "me" mattered first and foremost, not the "you," not the neighbor on whom both the Old and the New Testaments focus the believer (q.v., Lev 19:18 and Matt. 22:29).

More recently, the "me" mind-set has evolved as a belief system of at least three generations: first the baby boomers, then generation X, and now the millennials, whom Joel Stein describes most eloquently in a *Time* cover story titled "The Me Me Me Generation." Stein calls the present time an "era of the quantified self."[3] He goes on to say, "Millennials are a generation mostly of teens and 20-somethings known for constantly holding up cameras, taking pictures of themselves and posting them online. They are narcissistic, overconfident, entitled and lazy. Their self-centeredness could bring about the end of civilization as we know it."[4] Referring to the Torrance Tests of Creative Thinking (TTCT), Stein recounts an unsettling result for the millennial generation: "Scores on tests of empathy . . . fell sharply, likely because of both the lack of face-to-face time and higher degrees of narcissism. Not only do Millennials lack the kind of empathy that allows them to feel concerned for others, but they have trouble even intellectually understanding others' point of view."[5]

This dearth of empathy among young Americans uncannily brings to mind a troubling historical detail: it was a similar personal deficiency that motivated Heinrich Himmler, the founder and leader of the Nazi SS, to make the destruction of Christianity his ultimate goal. Among the aspects Himmler hated most about Christianity, according to his biographer Peter Longerich,[6] was its principle of mercy, and mercy is surely a standard presupposing an individual's sense of empathy.

This lack of empathy and mercy is evident in the frightening statistic that 98 percent of the 1.2 million abortions in the United States every year are perpetrated for selfish reasons of "personal choice" and not even on medical or psychological grounds such as rape, incest, or a diagnosed danger to the mother's life or health.[7] This means that by the "personal choice" of one or more individuals (mother, father, physicians), other individuals (babies) can be legally liquidated even though their DNA shows that they are complete human beings no different from others except that they are not fully grown. Thus in a free and democratic society, a person can decide that another person's life is *lebensunwert* (not worth living), to use a term coined by the Nazis; moreover, such a personal decision rests on two conditions that in the healthier societies of the past might have fallen under the rubric of malice and aforethought, the criteria of murder in the first degree. They are the following: (1) Is the other person's continued existence convenient or inconvenient to his or her parents? (2) Is he or she young enough to be disposed of?

Other stark results of the narcissism epidemic are the alarming erosion of ethics in politics, finance, jurisprudence, and the media and the normalization of sexual immorality. This includes the glorification of homosexual behavior, a practice deemed *para physin* (against nature) since Plato's days, culminating in the acceptance of the legalization of same-sex marriage by a majority of Americans and Western Europeans, a trend Kirill I, the patriarch of Moscow and all Russia, chastised as an "apocalyptic symptom."[8]

It is the mark of the me me me generation that it eschews structure and therefore authority. "Millennials aren't trying to take over the establishment; they are growing up without one," Joel Stein writes. This corresponds to what Thomas Klie, a professor of

practical theology at Rostock University, has found in a study of
the burgeoning esotericism among young Germans. He reports
that while esotericists do affirm the existence of a "creative principle" larger than the individual, this doesn't mean much: "While
the Christian believes in a Creator God to whom he owes his life,
esotericists cannot bear the thought of any aspect of their existence being beyond their control. . . . In esotericism the believer
is his own creator."[9] Thus while in their minds the divine might be
greater than the "me," the "me" nevertheless trumps the divine.
Klie defines this worldview as "container spirituality" in the sense
that spirituality merely provides an empty vessel ready to be filled
by the believer according to his or her whim. It is hard to think of
a more accurate definition of the narcissism epidemic in the West,
a plague against which a backlash seems to be emerging on both
sides of the Atlantic.

My successor as director of the Center for Lutheran Theology
and Public Life in Capistrano Beach, California, Professor Jeffrey
Mallinson of Concordia University, Irvine, reports that today's
student generation is haunted by "a sense of abandonment." The
same applies to their contemporaries in Europe. The hundreds of
thousands of young Frenchmen demonstrating in the summer
of 2013 against their country's legalization of homosexual "marriages" angrily charged their parents' generation, the European
equivalent of the US baby boomers, "You have left us without any
values." Matching this, German philosopher Peter Sloterdijk told
the editors of Neue Zürcher Zeitung in Switzerland, "We are living
in a state of permanent improvisation."[10] He said this in a video
interview appropriately titled Zerbricht unsere Gesellschaft? (Is our
society falling apart?). To put my personal spin to this: A "me"-
centered society devoid of a sense of empathy living in a state of
permanent improvisation, not passing on values, and abandoning its young has only one place to go: Tohuwabohu, the Hebrew
word for the chaos that preceded Creation. Hence one of Dietrich Bonhoeffer's most evocative observations in his Letters and
Papers from Prison seems as timely today as it was under the Hitler regime in Germany seventy years ago: "One may ask whether
there have ever before in human history been people with so little
ground under their feet."[11]

"Do as Thou Wilt"—Do Your Own Thing

It might seem far-fetched, but the point could be made that today's narcissism epidemic with its lack of empathy is to some extent the fruit of (or influenced by) the New Age religion founded by the British occultist Aleister Crowley (1875–1947), who took pride in calling himself "the wickedest man in the world." Crowley was the author of *The Book of the Law*, which he claimed had been revealed to him by Aiwass, a communicator of Horus, the Egyptian God of war, in a hotel room in Cairo in April 1904. The message Crowley received sounds straight out of Himmler's textbook. According to Crowley, Aiwass told him, "We are not for the poor and sad. Beauty and strength, leaping laughter and delicious languor, force and fire are of us . . . We have nothing to do with the outcast and the unfit . . . Let them die in their misery . . . stamp down the wretched and the weak. . . . Pity not the fallen! . . . I console not, I hate the consoled and the consoler. . . . I want blasphemy, murder, rape, revolution, anything, bad or good, but strong."[12] The book's central proclamation is "Do as thou wilt. This is the whole of the law."

Timothy Leary, the drug guru of the 1960s, told television interviewers before his death in 1996, "I have been an admirer of Aleister Crowley. I think that I'm carrying on much of the work that he started over a hundred years ago. . . . He was in favor of finding yourself, and [proclaimed], 'Do what thou wilt shall be the whole of the law.' . . . It was a very powerful statement. I'm sorry he isn't around now to appreciate the glories he started."[13] Leary reminded his audiences that the maxim of the 1960s—"Do your own thing"—was merely a modern rendering of "Do as thou wilt, this is the whole of the law" (a slogan L. Ron Hubbard, founder of the Church of Scientology, also adopted). "Do your own thing" has of course remained a rallying cry of the "me" and the me me me generation; it is the creed of the narcissists and contrary to Jewish and Christian doctrines admonishing the believer to focus on the neighbor rather than himself or herself.

Switching from "Me" to "You"

In this eon of extreme self-centeredness, where even the most basic civilities such as using one's blinker before changing lanes on a freeway or returning telephone calls when such a courtesy does not seem to promise personal gain, are falling by the wayside, Christ's commandment, "Thou shalt love thy neighbor as thyself" (Matt. 22:39, KJV), appears curiously countercultural. Yet this admonition, which is related to Jesus's words, "Thou shalt love the Lord thy God with all thy heart, and with all thy soul, and with all thy mind" (Matt. 22:37), provides the very foundation for the most forceful antidote against the "me" epidemic: Martin Luther's doctrine of vocation, which says that in all their earthly endeavors, Christians are called to serve their neighbors out of love. In so doing, the Christian renders the highest possible service to God and becomes a member of the universal priesthood of all believers. It is one of the most attractive features of Lutheran theology in that the priesthood is thus not limited to the ordained ministry, as in Roman Catholicism, and that it encourages the believer to become active in the world without succumbing to its sinful ways.

In his commentary on Genesis 29:1–3, Luther writes,

> Because we dwell and live in the flesh, for this reason the flesh must be cared for, but without sin. The state and domestic affairs must be administered, since we are not yet in Paradise. Nor are we like the angels; but we live in the flesh in a natural life which has need for food, drink, clothing, house, offspring and agriculture. There is also a need of political government and of protection against evil men. Therefore it is necessary to retain those two parts of his life. They are support and protection. The home supports and cherishes children and the household. The state defends and protects all these.[14]

"Glorious works He does through us," Luther exults, explaining in detail man's divine assignment, all "completely secular and heathenish works," such as milking cows, serving in the military, working as a household servant, parenting, and also enjoying himself or herself:

> If the person believes and adheres to the Word and does not persecute the Word but gives thanks to it, then you should do nothing else than what Solomon says (Eccles. 9:7–9): "Go eat your bread with enjoyment, drink your wine with a merry heart; for God has approved

what you do. Let your garments be always white; let not oil be lacking on your head. Enjoy the life with the wife whom you love, all the days in your vain life which He has given you under the sun." What more could be said more pleasantly, more delightfully, and more clearly?[15]

Like other down-to-earth verities, Luther's liberating doctrine of vocation is often badly understood. I have even heard leaders of faithful Lutheran congregations in the American Midwest ask me, "Is this actually Christian?" Luther himself was exasperated by this widespread lack of appreciation of the importance of work in every-day life: "Not all men are able to understand this. Not even Erasmus saw it."[16] Strangely, the most incomprehensible aspect of Luther's message seems to be the most comforting: man does not even have to make any special effort to serve God by serving his neighbor. In Lutheran theology, vocation is understood as a state and not as a work. This means that the Christian does not serve his or her neighbor *per vocationem* (through the exercise of his vocation), thus perhaps earning brownie points in heaven or collecting proof of being one of the elect in the sense of the *Westminster Confession of Faith*. To the contrary, it is *in vocatione*—in the ordinary performance of his or her function as plumber, husband, wife, child, cook, soldier, student, politician, prince, or subject—that the believer serves God by serving his or her neighbor lovingly.[17]

The German word for one's vocation or professional occupation is *Beruf*, or "calling." Luther coined this term after translating a verse from the book Wisdom of Sirach, or *Ecclesiasticus*, which is accepted as canonical by the Roman Catholics and Orthodox but not the Protestants. This text says, "Stand by your agreement and attend to it, and grow old in your work. Do not wonder at the works of a sinner, but trust in the Lord and keep at your job; for it is easy in the sight of the Lord to make the poor rich suddenly, in an instant."[18] Sociologists of religion have long attributed the excellence of products from Lutheran regions to the fact that through the generations, their citizens have internalized the *Berufungslehre*, or doctrine of vocation. Mercedes-Benz, Audi, Volkswagen, Porsche, Saab, Volvo, and Peugeot are among the best-known brand names testifying to this Lutheran ethic; in a newspaper interview the 1980s, Roland Peugeot, the former CEO of the automobile manufacturing company bearing his name, explained the high quality of its cars with his family's Lutheran ethic. The Peugeots hail from Montbéliard in Eastern France that used to be part of the German duchy of Württemberg, the official religion of which was Lutheran.

The Christian as a Dual Citizen

All this is perhaps best understood if positioned within the larger framework of the aspect of Lutheran theology that pertains to the interface between the spiritual and secular aspects of human existence. This theology is often referred to as the two kingdoms doctrine, or the law-and-gospel dialectic, or in the words of the late US theologian William Lazareth, God's twofold rule in the world. This concept is central to Luther's teachings and is spelled out in Article 28 of the Augsburg Confession. In World War II and its aftermath, some Reformed theologians and high-church Anglicans misinterpreted the two kingdoms doctrine as some form of latter-day Gnostic dualism or, worse, the source of Lutheran quietism that conditioned German Protestants to cowardice in the face of Nazi tyranny. These charges were inaccurate, for this doctrine is entirely grounded in Scripture.

Based on Christ's words to Pontius Pilate—"My kingdom is not of this world" (Jn. 18:36)—Luther distinguished between two realms, both belonging to the same God but governed in two different ways. On the one hand, there is the spiritual realm, which Luther named *das Reich zur Rechten* (the kingdom to the right) because it is in this realm where Christ "sat down at the right hand of the Majesty on high" (Heb. 1:3). Here God has revealed himself in Christ (*Deus revelatus*). This realm is infinite. It will ultimately be completed in the *eschaton* when there will be no more sin and therefore no need for forgiveness.

The temporal realm is called *Reich zur Linken* (kingdom to the left). It will eventually disappear. Though sinful, it is nonetheless a reality God will not allow to slip from his ultimate control. Here He plays, in Luther's words, *Mummenschanz* (a masquerade). God remains hidden (*Deus absonditus*). He reigns indirectly through his "masks" (*larvae Dei*), meaning creation in general but human beings in particular. The non-Christian is a citizen only of the worldly kingdom, while the Christian holds dual citizenship in both realms, which, though distinct from each other, are not separated by some kind of spiritual Berlin Wall. Both realms interconnect and serve each other: the right-hand kingdom serves the secular world by supporting and protecting it in the Gospel, whereas the temporal world is a bastion enabling the Gospel to be preached.

The two realities mirror each other in fascinating paradoxes:

- *Man*: In the right-hand kingdom, only the believer is a member of Christ's body. In the left-hand realm, man is God's mask and cooperator, whether he is a believer or not; he is God's partner in the *creatio continua*, or ongoing process of creation, by procreating, tilling the soil, inventing new tools or medicines, and perhaps ultimately colonizing other planets.
- *The church*: As the Body of Christ, she is an integral part of His right-hand kingdom, but she is also present as a corporate citizen in the secular world, where she maintains real estate, renders charitable and medical services, pays ministers and other employees, and occasionally must fight lawsuits.
- *Sinners and perpetrators*: In the right-hand realm, repentant sinners are forgiven. In the left-hand kingdom, perpetrators are punished, whether they are Christians or not.
- *Governing principle*: Right-hand kingdom: the Gospel. Left-hand kingdom: the Law of Moses and natural law (cf., Rom. 2:15: "What the law requires is written on their hearts").
- *Mode of government*: Right-hand kingdom: grace, love, and faith. Left-hand realm: natural reason, which, though under sin, is nevertheless a gift from God to help man in his task to maintain order in the world. Luther called reason "the heart and the empress of the laws; [it is] the fountain whence all laws come and flow."[19] "In temporal matters," Luther said, "man . . . needs no other light than reason. This is why God does not teach in Scripture how to build houses, make clothes, get married, conduct war and the like . . . [F]or all this the natural light is sufficient."[20]
- *Rulers*: Right-hand kingdom: Christ. Left-hand kingdom: emperors, kings, presidents, prime ministers, governors,

mayors, parliaments, and voters. Secular rulers need not be saints. "It is sufficient for the emperor to possess reason,"[21] Luther wrote. In his Genesis Lectures, he made one of history's most celebrated theological statements on the topic of God and temporal power. It has been quoted around the world for centuries, except in recent American presidential election campaigns, where it would have been most helpful. In the late 1530s, Luther told his students at Wittenberg University, "*Deus per bonos et malos principes gubernat orbem terrarum*" (Through good and bad princes God governs the whole earth).[22]

- *Social structure*: Right-hand kingdom: all are equal. Left-hand kingdom: all are unequal; there are superiors and subordinates.
- *Activity*: Right-hand kingdom: resting and feasting with God and praising Him. Left-hand kingdom: all secular vocations, beginning with the vocation of being a toddler and culminating in the vocation of a helpless person on his or her deathbed who lovingly allow caretakers to exercise their vocation in love.

Vocation: An Expression of Discipleship

Both Christians and non-Christians have their assignments, according to Luther. In the case of the Christians, however, their vocations in the temporal realm cannot be separated from the Gospel. Citing the example of Peter leaving his nets at the Sea of Galilee in response to Jesus's call, Dietrich Bonhoeffer wrote, "For Luther, on the contrary, a Christian's secular vocation is justified only in that one's protest against the world is thereby most sharply expressed. A Christian's secular vocation receives new recognition from the gospel only to the extent that it is carried on while following Jesus."[23]

These two sentences are an excellent example of the paradoxical relationship between Christ and culture: On the one hand, the Christian lives in this sinful world where he serves his neighbors in love in his vocation. On the other hand, he must never lose sight of the fact that he does so in the full awareness that he is a disciple.

Pseudo-Lutherans have a history of distorting many aspects of Luther's theology of God's twofold reign in an infuriating manner, as Bonhoeffer's legendary outburst in *Discipleship* about "cheap grace" shows:

> [In the minds of these people] Christian life consists of my living in the world and like the world, my not being permitted to be different from it—for the sake of grace—but my going occasionally from the sphere of the world to the sphere of the church, in order to be reassured there of the forgiveness of my sins. I am liberated from following Jesus—by cheap grace, which has to be the bitterest enemy of discipleship, which has to hate and despise true discipleship. Grace as presupposition is grace at its cheapest; grace as a conclusion is costly grace. It is appalling to see what is at stake in the way in which a gospel truth is expressed and used.[24]

Cheap grace comes of course under the rubric of the "me" culture in that it affirms the "do as thou wilt" approach to everyday life, compounding this abomination of doctrine by helping itself freely and selfishly to the grace displayed in the spiritual supermarket. There is no qualitative difference here between this false religiosity and the empty vessel spirituality Thomas Klie has found among German esotericists. Cheap grace is the rejection of the Lutheran doctrine of vocation, which is always linked to Luther's theology of the cross that states that in this world (the left-hand kingdom), the Christian picks up his cross and follows Jesus.

As the Swedish theologian Gustaf Wingren explained, "To understand what is meant by the cross of vocation we need to remember that vocation is ordained by God to benefit, not him who fulfills the vocation, but the neighbor who, standing alongside, bears his own cross for the sake of others."[25] The temporal realm being a stage for God's masquerade, it is the place where all social classes, professions, and trades must bear the cross of vocation. As Luther said,

> If I had the choice, I would select the most sordid and rustic work of a Christian peasant or maid in preference to all the victories of Alexander the Great, Julius Caesar, etc. Why? Because God is here and the devil is there. This is the essential difference. The material of the works

is the same, and the distinguishing characteristics and the difference are infinitely diverse. For as God says: "The works and domestic duties of this woman namely, that she sweeps the house and obeys the housewife, please me." For "He has regarded the humility of his handmaiden" (Luke 1:28), where there are no great and glorious works except that at home she humbly discharges the duties of a maid, whether they are in the kitchen or among the cattle.[26]

To the naïve onlooker, the cross of vocation is often hard to fathom, Luther allows. In his treatise, *Whether Soldiers, Too, Can Be Saved*, he wrote,

> Now slaying and robbing do not seem to be works of love. A simple man therefore does not think it is a Christian thing to do. In truth, however, even this is a work of love. For example, a good doctor sometimes finds so . . . terrible a sickness that he must amputate . . . a hand, foot, ear, eye, to save the body. Looking at it from the point of view of the organ that he amputates, he appears to be a cruel . . . man; but looking at it from the point of view of the body, which the doctor wants to save, he . . . does a good and Christian work. . . . In the same way, when I think of a soldier fulfilling his office by punishing the wicked, killing the wicked . . . it seems [a] . . . work completely contrary to Christian love. But when I think of how it protects the good and . . . preserves wife and child, house and farm, property, and honor and peace, then I see how precious and godly this work is. . . . If the sword were not on guard to preserve peace, everything in the world would be ruined because of lack of peace.[27]

Called to Bear the Cross of a Voter

What seems to make Luther's doctrine on vocation, for all its clarity, so hard to grasp is its universality, for it covers the total spectrum of a Christian's life on earth, including political life in a democracy. In election campaign after election campaign, the theological discourse about faith and society becomes increasingly befuddled and banal, with few churchmen and even fewer media commentators competent enough to speak about these issues with authority. Yet solid guidelines for this have existed ever since the Reformation almost five hundred years ago, and no branch of the Christian church is better equipped than the Lutheran to drive home the point that in a democracy, Romans 13:1 ("There is no authority except from God, and those that exist have been instituted by God") applies to the voter as much as to elected officials, perhaps even more so because the voters are the sovereigns of a democratic nation.

As Wingren would have said, the voter bears the cross of a vocation, and it is a heavy cross indeed. The voter has the assignment from God to appoint sheriffs, councilmen, and presidents. In the sense of Romans 13, this makes voters *leitourgoi gar theou* (Rom. 13:6), or God's servants in His temporal realm. The Greek word *leitourgoi* implies that they are his liturgists in the world, the secular counterparts of the liturgists serving God with prayer and hymns of praise in the right-hand kingdom of Christ. Being called to serve their neighbor, they must focus on the singular and plural "you" and not the "me" and "us" when casting their votes. This precludes any motivation that for selfish ideological reasons would exclude any segment of one's fellow human beings, notably the most vulnerable: the unborn. Ignoring their right to live amounts, from the perspective of Lutheran doctrine, to vocational malpractice on the part of an electorate considering itself Christian. Seen this way, in the case of *Roe v. Wade*, the 1973 decision of the US Supreme Court was, in Luther's inimitable imagery, "monkey business and tomfoolery." It is gratifying to know that it was a Lutheran, William Rehnquist, who wrote the dissenting opinion on this deadly ruling.

In a democracy, the Christian electorate does not have the option of saying, "It wasn't me," when things go wrong because of their choice. Germans who elected Hitler in 1933 didn't get away with this excuse. Granted, making the right choice presupposes that voters are comprehensively informed before going to the polls and making decisions affecting their communities and nations.

And yet, it is also an important aspect of the doctrine of vocation that where man errs in exercising his divine vocation in the world, God will ultimately put things right.

Vocation as a Tool for Apologetics

"You can judge the quality of their faith from the way they live," said Tertullian of Carthage (160–225 AD), an early Christian apologist.

This is perhaps the most basic argument in favor of the doctrine of vocation as a means of Christian apologetics: there is an intriguing aura about the mother, scientist, farmer, statesman, car mechanic, soldier, or reporter serving their neighbor while exercising their ordinary vocation, not in a narcissistic or greedy manner, but out of love. It triggers curiosity. It makes bystanders wonder, "What motivates you, makes you act that way?" This gives the believer an opportunity to talk about his or her faith.

It is, moreover, perfectly possible to discuss the superiority of a sense of vocation over narcissism in entirely secular settings without being accused of violating the taboos in contemporary America against "spreading religion." In the spring of 2011, the superintendent of schools of three adjoining counties in Missouri invited me to address more than five hundred students and their teachers in a public school auditorium. I asked a random group of four or five students to join me on the stage and said to them, "Suppose an elderly lady collapses in front of you on the sidewalk. What do you do: step over her and walk on? Ask her if you can help and then move on if she doesn't answer?"

"No!" said the kids in unison. Then they debated how to make that woman comfortable and whom to call: the police? A doctor? An ambulance? I asked, "Why not just move on?" They replied, "That wouldn't be right. She is a human being like the rest of us. She needs help." I pressed on: "Why do you feel that way?" One responded, "It's like helping a neighbor extinguish the fire when his house is burning." What followed was a lengthy discussion between teenagers about the normal person's innate drive to help a neighbor in need, innate like hunger and thirst. "You know what this is?" I told them. "It's a vocation." They understood instantly. Yet we still had not broached the subject of God, the one who is doing the calling.

Then I tried to find out what they wanted to be when they grew up. One wanted to be a journalist, one a doctor, one a farmer, one an electrician. When I probed why they were dreaming of these vocations, they all answered that they wanted to serve their fellow man in these careers. After that, we discussed these vocations. It turned out that these very average young people thought that being of service was joyful, as one of them said. Finally, I asked them, "Do you know what the word *vocation* means?" They answered, "Calling." So

I said, "If we have a calling, somebody must be doing the calling. I as a Lutheran Christian believe that we have this calling from God. Some of you might have different ideas. A secular school auditorium is not supposed to be the place to discuss this. But you may ask your pastor, your parents, your grandparents, or wait until class is over, and we'll talk about this outside this building." We met after school and talked at great length. Afterwards, the high school principal told me, "Come back anytime you want. This is good stuff."

These were not yet expressions of vocational thinking in the sense of discipleship, for these young people, generally badly or not at all catechized, were not aware what this meant. But the students' remarks showed that in a healthy environment, young people seem to have an innate wish to serve their neighbors. I posit that this desire is part of what Luther called the *lex inscripta*, the natural law written upon man's heart, according to the Apostle Paul (Rom. 2:15). And this is in keeping with the findings of the St. Louis-based French anthropologist Pascal Boyer, who wrote in a Christmas edition of the German weekly newspaper, *Die Zeit*, "Religious thinking is an integral part of our standard cognitive equipment."[28]

This is the solid theological foundation on which Lutherans must build when championing the doctrine of vocation as the most effective remedy against the narcissism epidemic, provided they ever rose from their slumber. In the doctrines of the two kingdoms and of vocation, they have by far the healthiest argument against me, me and me.

Notes

1. Cf. Jean M. Twenge and W. Keith Campbell, *The Narcissism Epidemic* (New York: Free Press, 2009).

2. Quoted from the Center for Reformed Theology and Apologetics, http://www.reformed.org/documents/wcf_with_proofs/index.html?body=/documents/wcf_with_proofs/ch_III.html; Max Weber, *The Protestant Ethic and the Spirit of Capitalism*, trans. Talcott Parsons (New York: Scribner's, 1958), 104.

3. Joel Stein, "The Me Me Me Generation," *Time*, May 20, 2013, 28–36.

4. Ibid.

5. Ibid.

6. Peter Longerich, *Heinrich Himmler: A Life* (New York: Oxford University Press, 2012), 265.

7. William R. Johnson, "Reasons Given for Having Abortions in the United States," *Johnston's Archive*, October 9, 2008.

8. "Zeichen der Endzeit im Western," *idea.de*, July 25, 2013.

9. Cf. Evelyn Finger, "Die Renaissance der Unvernunft: Sehnsucht nach dem Selbst," *Zeit Online*, June 6, 2013.

10. Peter Sloterdijk, "Zerbricht unsere Gesellschaft?," *Standpunkte*, Neue Zürcher Zeitung, May 5, 2013.

11. Dietrich Bonhoeffer, *Letters and Papers from Prison* (New York: Macmillan, 1972), 3.

12. Aleister Crowley, *Liber Legis: The Book of the Law* (Cape Neddick, ME: Samuel Weiser, 1976), 2:17–21.

13. "Aleister Crowley's Influence in Music," http://www.jesus-is-savior.com/Evils%20in%20America/Rock-n-Roll/crowley_influence.htm.

14. Jaroslav Pelikan and Helmut T. Lehmann, eds., *Luther's Works*, American Edition (St. Louis, MO: Concordia Publishing House, 1955), 5:266ff.

15. Ibid.

16. Ibid.

17. Karl Eger, *Die Anschauung Luthers vom Beruf* (Giessen: A. Töpelmann, 1900), 117.

18. Sirach, 11:20–21.

19. Martin Luther, *D. Martin Luther's Werke, Kritische Gesamtausgabe* (Weimar: Hermann Böhlau, 1883–1929), hereafter abbreviated as WA, Tr VI, no. 6955.

20. WA 10 I 1:531, 6–16.

21. WA 27:417–18.

22. Martin Luther, *D. Martini Lutheri Exegetica Latina*, vol. 7, ed. Christoph Stephan Gottlieb Elsperger (Erlangen: Carl Heyer, 1831), 67.

23. Dietrich Bonhoeffer, *Discipleship, Dietrich Bonhoeffer Works* (Minneapolis, MN: Fortress Press, 2001), 4:49.

24. Ibid., 50–41.

25. Gustaf Wingren, *Luther on Vocation*, trans. Carl Rasmussen (Philadelphia: Muhlenberg, 1957), 29.

26. Luther, *Works*, 5:266ff.

27. Ibid., 46:96.

28. Pascal Boyer, "Das Hirn, Dein Gott," *Zeit Online*, December 23, 2008.

CHAPTER 9

Christian Liberty, the Arts, and J. S. Bach

Craig A. Parton

A Preface of Contrasts

What thou, My Lord, has suffered, was all for sinners' gain;
Mine, mine was the transgression, but Thine the deadly pain.
Lo, here I fall my Savior! Tis I deserve Thy place.
Look on me with Thy favor, vouchsafe to me Thy grace.

> —"O Sacred Head, Now Wounded," the chorale
> foundation for J. S. Bach's St. Matthew's Passion

He is jealous for me,
Loves like a hurricane, I am a tree,
Bending beneath the weight of his wind and mercy,
When all of a sudden,
I am unaware of these afflictions eclipsed by glory,
And I realize just how beautiful You are,
And how great Your affections are for me.
Chorus:
And oh, how He loves us so,
Oh how He loves us,
How He loves us all
Yeah, He loves us,
Whoa, how He loves us,
Whoa, how He loves us,
Yeah, He loves us. . . .

> —"How He Loves," by David Crowder

Mainstream American Christianity has responded to a rising secularism in the arts in general[1] and in music in particular by engaging in a fascinating kind of bipolar heresy: utter rejection of the art forms of "the world" (seen in rigid Calvinism and in strict fundamentalism, restricting the musical arts to what can be supported directly from Scripture—no more and no less) or rabid absorption of contemporary cultural forms fueled by a distrust of anything "stodgy, old, denominational, or liturgical" (as seen in evangelical megachurch worship styles, the consumer-driven contemporary music industry, and the rise of the agonizing "Christian Artist" and the equally agonizing "worship band"[2]).

How, pray tell, can serious Christian musicians avoid the two-headed Cyclops of legalism and license and yet pursue their craft with a dedication to artistic excellence? The answer, we suggest, is to go back before going forward. Back to Bach, J. S. Bach to be specific, who saw music as the outflow of gratitude to a holy God for saving him in Christ—creating music that was pedagogical in nature (pointing to a God of order and internal harmony) and often explicitly Christological in focus. The Christian musician should operate *sub cruces*, whether as a professional church musician or in any other musical vocation, displaying dedication to excellence above all and being serious about the theology they are conveying in their craft, regardless of the audience.

Musicians who are Christian theologians first have a rare opportunity through their art to serve both God and neighbor because of their liberty in Christ, which shows Christians how to avoid death from thirst on the arid plains of legalism and death from the blind gluttony of license.

Legal Music: Calvinism and Fundamentalism

Calvin's personal rigidity and his theological philosophy of *via negativa* as to music and its role in the worship service ("Neither is this Thou" formalized in the "Regulative Principle" of Reformed worship) stymied the musical arts and led to the segregated categories of "secular-worldly" versus "sacred-eternal" art forms. This is a division that the Lutheran Reformation explicitly rejected.[3] Ultimately, orthodox Calvinism concluded that only sacred and therefore largely noninstrumental musical forms (singing or chanting portions of the Old Testament and the almost exclusive use of the Psalter instead of hymns, frowning on instrumental interludes during the service where there was no biblical text and discouraging counterpoint and polyphonic music as promoting the flesh) were appropriate in the worship service.[4]

To be sure, some operating in Calvinist circles wrote hymn "tunes" (Louis Bourgeoise comes to mind for his work on the Psalter—though he fled Geneva for France after the less-than-endearing treatment he received in Calvin's Geneva; others like the poet Clement Marot and composer Claude Goudimel were also productive). However, all were largely constricted to putting the Psalms to metrical notation[5] because the philosophical and hermeneutical support for composing more liberated "spiritual songs" (Eph. 5:19) in worship petered out early in Calvinism. There is no question that the output, quality, and diversity of Calvinist "hymnody" never approached that of the musicians operating within the uniquely Lutheran frame of reference.

Mark Noll frames the issue with Calvin and music this way:

> These Reformed leaders (Calvin and Zwingli) defined a biblical reform of worship as hewing as closely as possible to specific scriptural guidelines. Thus, since the Bible said nothing specific about polyphonic music (the complex singing of multiple lines of tunes and texts), the use of the organ, or the free composition of new hymns, their churches would use only biblical materials (usually paraphrased Psalms) as their church music. Some results of this practice, like the tunes and texts of Calvin's *Geneva Psalter*, made a memorable musical contribution, but it was a limited contribution.[6]

Licensed Music: Evangelicalism

American evangelicalism grew up alongside secularism beginning in the eighteenth and nineteenth centuries.[7] Genetically democratic and utilitarian to the core, evangelicalism believes it can baptize *any* artistic or musical form found in popular culture since all such forms are "neutral" and high culture is for suspiciously educated elitists.[8] King David, evangelicals remind us, initiated liturgical dance in worship and favored a drum set to praise God.

Hardwired to see musical forms as means to personal growth with an accepting God who apparently has few musical standards, evangelicalism sees things like pipe organs, complex music, and thick liturgy as hiding the essence of worship and creating distance from God. God, rather, is a friend who likes us just the way we are and with no pretension. Evangelicalism also tends to be highly suspicious of actual professional musical qualifications. God wants us "up close and personal"; simple praise chorus music fulfills the American democratic ideal of fast and accessible, since anyone (with a synthesizer and a microphone) can be a Christian Artist, and "talent" is ultimately best decided by the marketplace and the numbers in attendance.[9]

Evangelicalism has sold out to the musical philosophy of *via affirmata* ("Even in this is Thou") but with no boundaries or discretion—it is freedom on steroids and popular culture is the pusher. Popular culture is largely built on selling exciting distractions. Thus the evangelical church brokers fun now. Rock 'n' roll can easily be put to Christian lyrics to make happy those reliving their high school days who now happen to be the deacons in the church, and gangsta rap can be sung with vaguely spiritual words with little hesitation or concern for the cultural baggage that might be coming along for the ride.

Liberated Music: The Lutheran Reformation

Contrary to the musical still birth resulting from strict Calvinism or prepubescent evangelicalism, one cannot study Luther and the sixteenth-century Reformation without being immediately impressed by Luther's affirmation of the arts and music in particular and their role in the life of the church and in the life of the individual Christian as well as the central importance of the arts in the furtherance of the Reformation itself. The innovative visual artist Lucas Cranach was Luther's close friend and collaborator, and his mass-produced woodcuts—as well as those of his imitators—played an important role in popularizing the Reformation.[10] Luther himself was an exacting and well-trained musician who had the highest regard for the masters of counterpoint and polyphonic music that had operated up to that point in the decidedly Roman Catholic ecclesiastical context (e.g., Josquin des Pres, Giovanni da Palestrina, the entire cantus firmus and plainchant tradition).[11]

Finding fertile ground in the incarnational theology of Luther, music in particular flourished from the very outset of the Reformation. Emphatically Lutheran hymnbooks multiplied like insurance salesmen in sixteenth- and seventeenth-century Germany, fueled by the brilliance of orthodox Lutheran composers and hymn writers like Johann Walter, Georg Rhau, Dietrich Buxtehude, Johann Hermann Schein, Paul Speratus, Michael Praetorius, Samuel Scheidt, Heinrich Schuetz, Philipp Nicolai, Hans Leo Hassler, Johann Crueger, Paul Gerhardt, and Hans Sachs. As Lutheran theology and teaching took root, it bore remarkable fruit in the arts and especially in music, culminating with J. S. Bach.[12] It is established that Luther had surely introduced congregational singing to his Wittenberg Church as early as 1523 and that, between 1525 and 1575, more than two hundred collections of hymns were circulating within the Lutheran churches of Germany.[13]

Music had an intensely personal place in the life of Luther. It not only reflects the harmony in the cosmos that exists in the Trinity from all eternity and has theological grounding in the Old Testament where the Temple had dedicated musicians for the service of the Lord but also "chases away the Devil" and was highly prized by Luther for its personal devotional power and its use in the Christian home. Luther puts it this way:

> We know that music is hateful and intolerable to devils. I firmly believe, nor am I ashamed to assert, that next to theology no art is equal to music. . . . [T]he devil . . . flees from the sound of music as he does from the sound of theology. . . . Christian musicians should let their singing and playing to the praise of the Father of all grace sound forth with joy from their organs and whatever other beloved musical instruments there are (recently invented and given by God), of which neither David nor Solomon, neither Persia, Greece nor Rome, knew anything. . . . He [Our Lord] loves to hear joyful song and stringed instruments.[14]

Luther to Bach and Beyond

Compare the thin musical swatch of Calvinism and that of praise chorus-driven American evangelicalism with the staggering canon produced by the "zealously Lutheran" J. S. Bach.[15] Bach's artistic palette covered numerous settings of the worship service (or "Mass"), including what is universally considered the greatest Mass ever composed (the Mass in B Minor, which Bach never heard performed in its entirety during his life and which commentators believe was written purely as an artist working in freedom to create a composition to be enjoyed only in heaven[16]). But he also wrote the hilarious so-called Coffee Cantata and purely instrumental music designed to fulfill the longings of the human spirit for transcendence.[17] He used Italian operatic structures in his sacred vocal music and employed admittedly emotive French dance forms in more than two hundred of his works. (Among the dance steps set to music repeatedly are gigues, sarabandes, courantes, polonaises, chaconnes, minuets, passepieds, gavottes, and bourees.)[18] In addition, who could overlook his more than two hundred existing cantatas[19] or "musical sermons," which alone are said to have done more for evangelism in Japan than all the efforts of missionaries combined over the centuries?[20]

The entire output of Bach comprises, at last count, 172 CDs, though musical historians are certain much was lost over the century between Bach's death in 1750 to his "rediscovery" by the Lutheran convert Felix Mendelssohn in 1827. Bach's "universality" (i.e., he understands the human condition and the answer to that condition and thus has staggering cross-cultural appeal) makes him the great icon of high culture, widely considered the greatest musician who ever lived.

One example will suffice to show Bach's rejection of the *via negativa*, his universality, and his mastery of many forms for the advancement of the Gospel: Cantata BWV 78 (*Jesu, der du meine Seele*, "Jesus, by Whom My Soul"). This work was composed in "three or four days" for a Sunday service in 1724. Robert L. Marshall describes it as follows:

> In sum, *Jesu, der du meine Seele* is one of Bach's most complex creations—a compositional *tour de force* that simultaneously observes or fulfills no fewer than five distinct principles of organization, some of which, one would have thought, were mutually exclusive. . . . At one and the same time . . . [this cantata] is a modern Italian concerto—based on a ritornello in the style of a sarabande from a modern French dance suite; it is a seventeenth-century passacaglia, that is, a

set of variations; but it is also a polyphonic motet constructed both on "points of imitation" reminiscent of Renaissance church music of the sixteenth century as well as on a *cantus firmus* according to compositional principles extending back to the Middle Ages; on yet another level the movement is a German Lutheran chorale in Bar-form: AAB—writ very large indeed.[21]

It is our contention that Bach's biblical understanding of "Christian freedom" allowed him to execute a vision for the musical arts that also prevented him from falling into either a rigid legalism or an unrestrained or naïve licentiousness. Though never absolutizing any one musical form as "sacred" (he composed for about every musical form and instrument, including seven works for the lute, the eighteenth-century precursor to the guitar), Bach never naïvely followed popular demands so as to merely titillate the listener, nor did he require the listener to endure a musical form unable to deliver the depth and context of the biblical content at issue.

Because Bach was *first* and foremost a serious orthodox Lutheran theologian and *then* a musician, he had a thoroughly biblical understanding of how the Christian life is worked out in freedom to pursue one's vocation at the very highest level of skill. This flowed inexorably from the Lutheran Reformation's *conserving* posture as to liturgics and the use of the arts in worship and its central focus on the proclaiming of the Gospel as the center of the Christian life and the understanding that we live in the freedom that comes from sin remitted for Christ's sake.

We will first examine the unique insights of the Lutheran Reformation that led to the flowering of the arts. Then we will briefly look at the twin temptations to Christian freedom posed by legalism and license and their devastating effect on the arts and music in particular. Finally, we will see how Christian freedom was understood and lived by Johann Sebastian Bach.[22]

Free to *Not* Be Me but Christ's Alone

The Lutheran Reformation led to a flowering of the arts in general and certainly in music in particular.[23] Why was this *necessarily* the case? The answer, Luther's biblical and thus incarnational theology[24] provided a most solid foundation for living in the assurance of sin forgiven on account of Christ. Creation itself is "hallowed" and while man remains a sinner, he is free now to explore all God's creation and to pursue his vocation (no matter how seemingly "lowly") while also reveling in the arts for the gift they were. As the Gospel came to have its rightful place in the Church, individual Christians were once again free to explore the ramifications of this newfound freedom in Christ as it might impact their vocations, whether as pastor, prince, painter, cook, constable, or cantor. After all, Christ Himself labored in the very human and secular profession of carpentry (Mark 6:3).

Artists in particular at the time of the Lutheran Reformation were set free to work not only for the glory of God reflected most clearly in the grace of God found at the cross of Jesus but also for the edification of their neighbor and, yes, even to pursue unique and innovative artistic expression and vision in their vocation. Artistic works reflecting biblical motifs were still of critical importance of course (especially as they focused on Christ's finished work and its implications), but so were works of raw nature and fallen humanity. Reformation musicians were free to not only put the liturgy or "Mass" to music (following their musical ancestors' abundant example on that score) but also to write music set to French dance forms and Italian operatic traditions (such as the arias found in Lutheran church cantatas of the seventeenth and eighteenth centuries).[25] So, yes, Bach would do the Mass in B Minor scored for double chorus, which exceeds maybe any work in musical history for its profundity and scope—as well as the stunning Passacaglia and Fugue in D Minor—but he would also do the Coffee Cantata and seven works scored for the lute. Similarly, Lucas Cranach the Elder would do his colossal Weimar altarpiece, Luther's death mask, and "polemical woodcuts" supporting Luther's theological points and yet would do his nudes and portraits of Venus—as well as trying his hand at boutique wallpaper![26]

In short, the Lutheran Reformation saw Christianity as bigger than any one style.[27] The Christian artist operating within the Lutheran Reformation tradition *conserved* the past and honored the existing high cultural tradition in the Church but did not idealize it as the only forms by which to please God and serve one's neighbor. Felix Mendelssohn is a particularly attractive example of this balance: he rediscovered the largely forgotten works of Bach and singlehandedly resurrected the St. Matthew Passion as an orchestral and choir work of staggering profundity.[28] But Mendelssohn was also a product of the nineteenth century, and his Reformation Symphony is distinctly—and properly—a product of Romantic influences.[29] It is decidedly "Romantic" and yet with an ancient face as it centers on Luther's sixteenth-century hymn *Ein' feste Burg* for its central melodic line.[30] Mendelssohn too is a most wonderful example of pursuing artistic excellence and freedom within his vocation as a professional musician. He stood on the conserving shoulders of Reformation giants yet expressed himself in a contemporary cultural form (nineteenth-century romanticism) to bring the Gospel of freedom in Christ to his own generation.

Whence came this newfound freedom that allowed an honoring of the best of the past (*conservative* in the best sense while clearly rejecting the salvation-by-works orientation of the medieval Roman Catholic Church) but also permitted serious exploration into other styles and forms (and thus decidedly *liberal* in outlook)? How were the Lutheran Reformers and Lutheran artists following in their wake able to enjoy artistic freedom and explosive creative expression that did not wander into license or legalism? The answer? By returning to Scriptural teaching on the nature of Christian freedom.

Paul and Luther: A Galatianal Theology

Luther's rediscovery of the gospel of grace in Christ freely given to the sinner based on Christ's fully sufficient work on Calvary's cross (the Copernican revolution in theology that changed the focus from man's efforts to merit heaven to Christ's work on man's behalf) might suggest that the Christian was now "free to sin." In fact, at one point in correspondence with his Wittenburg colleague Phillip Melanchthon, Luther advised the pensive Melanchthon (who was prone to introspection and wondering if he had fully repented of his sins) to "be a sinner and sin boldly, but believe and rejoice in Christ even more boldly, for He is victorious over sin, death and the world."[31] So is Luther counseling license?

But Luther countenanced no such thing and regularly referred to Paul in his lectures on Galatians (1535)[32] and Romans that the

Christian is now free from the law of sin and death to serve one's neighbor, not because God needs the good works but because the neighbor does (Gal. 5:13). That said, however, Luther also understood well the Pauline teaching about the power of the sinful nature inherited from Adam and honed and girded daily through acts of sin and rebellion. Man remains *simul justus et peccator* (simultaneously righteous and a sinner), and the law of God is always appropriate this side of heaven to curb the sinful passions and to state clearly God's standards even for the saved Christian.

Luther, following Paul, distinguished but never separated sanctification and Christian living from justification. Indeed, sanctification is simply the flipside of justification and is truly "Christ in us," while justification is always "Christ for us." Both sanctification and justification, however, are about Christ and not about the individual Christian. As Luther puts it, "As I am in Christ, so Christ, in turn, is in me. I have assumed Him and have entered into Him, have stepped out of sin, death, and the power of the devil. So He now manifests Himself in me and says: Go your way, preach, comfort, baptize, serve your neighbor, be obedient, patient, etc. I will be in you and will do everything."[33]

Contrast this with modern-day evangelicalism's utter confusion over sanctification. While justification is central to salvation and "closing the deal," it is assumed that the real purpose of the Church, and in particular Christian preaching, is to talk about sanctification ("Christian Living"), which really ends up talking very little about Christ and very much about the Christian. Sermons major in "application" (the "write this in your notebook" moment during most evangelical sermons). Instead of seeing the Christian life and thus Christian freedom as the life lived out of gratitude for what has been done for the Christian entirely *extra nos* at the Cross (remembering, as Romans teaches, that God justifies the *ungodly*; Romans 4:5), Christian freedom devolves into pitting sanctification *over* justification and leads easily to a Pelagian stew of works righteousness. Suddenly the dog has returned to its law-belched vomit.

The Lutheran Reformation reclaimed the biblical teaching that Christ has freed us from the law of sin and death not to do as we please but to please and serve our neighbor. In Christ, we have died to sin (Romans 6:2). That is our new identity—we are new creatures in Christ (2 Cor. 5:17). The Christian artist, therefore, is now free from the law of sin and death and is to no longer serve his own passions and unrestrained artistic urges (e.g., shocking the audience for the sole purpose of getting media attention or selling seats). While now truly "free" from sin's penalty, the artist too remains this side of death a sinner, and the law rightly must continue to be preached to constantly drive him back to the cross where his salvation is secure. The teaching of the Lutheran Reformation, contra modern evangelicalism or even the approach of *theosis* in eastern orthodoxy, has a low view of the ability to improve Old Adam or to "absorb" or laminate the old flesh onto union with the new Christ—that old nature must daily be drowned in baptism and in daily repentance and faith in Christ's merits. The new man comes alive from the dead, up from the watery depths of baptism and bright red now with the cleansing flow that comes from the Savior's pierced side and that is still nourished today by His very body and blood.

This teaching would free up artists within the Lutheran Reformation tradition to not absolutize prior art forms or to think that "new must be better." Instead each art form (both high and folk cultural forms existing in that "prepopular" culture era) presented possibilities to show gratitude for Christ's work on their behalf, to serve one's neighbor, and to express one's talent. Thus the Lutheran Reformation was a *conservative* Reformation[34] and did not assume that everything that had gone on in the church before 1517 was heresy.

Adiaphora, Anybody?

Any discussion of the Lutheran understanding of Christian freedom must consider the related concept of *adiaphora* ("things neither required nor forbidden by Scripture," as discussed in Article X of the Formula of Concord, one of the Lutheran Reformation's confessional documents). While *adiaphora* in the Lutheran Confessions is mainly concerned with how liturgical matters and ceremonies were to be approached in the Christian worship service so as not to obscure or contradict the Gospel, it has wider applications.

As important as it is to speak where God has spoken, it is also critical to not speak where God has not spoken. This is the domain of *adiaphora*—things neither required nor forbidden but permitted for free men and women in Christ.

The concept of *adiaphora* allows, for example, the Christian artist to work in a variety of cultural "types" or "expressions" without demanding that one type be baptized as the only true scriptural approach. Some Christian fundamentalists tend to absolutize, for example, certain musical genres (revivalist hymnody of the nineteenth century) as the sole legitimate expressions of biblical truth to the culture at large. Evangelicals can give the impression that the only music forbidden is that sung from a hymnal. Similarly, the Regulative Principle in Calvinism, which requires certain actions in a worship service and proscribes those not specifically mentioned in the New Testament, has this effect in the Calvinist liturgy. Lutheran worship, instructed by the principle of *adiaphora*, never went down this road. The result were cantatas, masses, passions, and instrumental music as part of the worship service, since none were forbidden by Scripture and all advanced or adorned the preaching of the Word and the administration of the Sacraments.

The Lutheran concept of *adiaphora* allows the Christian artist to operate in a wide range of cultural forms: high culture, folk culture, and even popular culture. No one cultural expression is baptized as biblically required (say, Gregorian or Byzantine Chant as the only approved vocal forms for worship, as the latter is in Eastern Orthodoxy)[35] or biblically prohibited (say, jazz, blues, or even rock). Similarly, personal practices that Scripture leaves to the individual conscience—such as drinking alcohol and smoking, which many Christians demonize—are neither prohibited nor required. They are to be exercised by the Christian with prudence and according to the context. (While a conscience may have no problem with the consumption of alcohol, the Christian living in Saudi Arabia might think twice about exercising that freedom. Smoking may be *adiaphora*, for example, but not prudent depending on one's circumstances—for example, in a confined space with small children present.)

While affirming the freedom of Christian artists, Lutheranism has historically operated, at least artistically, most comfortably and naturally in the realm of high culture. Lutheran Christians (like Bach, as we shall see) were recipients of a rich cultural and musical tradition handed down to them by a long line of extraordinary musicians operating at the highest levels of competency in their fields. Thus Lutheran hymnody, for example, boasts the likes of Schuetz,

Praetorius, Rhau, Schein, Hassler, Crueger, Walter, Speratus, Nicolai, and Sachs—all masters of polyphony and well versed in both composition and performance technique. In the fine arts, Reformation painters such as Albrecht Dürer, Lucas Cranach the Elder, and Hans Holbein operated at the most refined cultural levels within their society. Contrast this with many of today's so-called Christian artists whose "skill" centers on creating simplistic mantra-type music of an elementary and manipulative level but who nonetheless are teachers of the wider body of Christ through their music.

The Lutheran Reformation's teachings on Christian freedom can be summarized as follows:

1. Christian freedom derives directly from the freedom from sin and death won for us at the cross and freely announced and given to us in the Gospel and in the sacraments (Rom. 4 and 5).

2. The exercise of Christian freedom is in service to our neighbor and in gratitude for what God in Christ has done at the cross for the sinner. (Luther: "A Christian is a free lord of all and subject to no one. A Christian is a ministering servant of all and subject to everyone."[36])

3. While called to exercise our gifts as redeemed and free sinners "in Christ," we must always be aware that our fallen, sinful condition will seek to push us to exercise our calling in distorted and self-glorifying ways (Rom. 1–3).

4. Scripture baptizes no cultural form as normative (just as it baptizes no form of secular or ecclesiastical government) but allows Christians to exercise their gifts with wisdom and discretion in the cultural milieu and vocation in which they find themselves, whether that be high culture, folk culture, or popular culture. (Soldiers, for example, were not directed to become monks but to approach their vocation honestly as those operating in the kingdom of the left hand; Luke 3:14.)

5. While cultural forms (like rock music) may be "neutral," the Christian believer is not to be naïve about cultural associations that make effective Gospel preaching or artistic excellence unlikely within that form. Thus gangsta

rap is hardly "neutral" as a form for conveying Christian truth, especially if one is performing before a group of law enforcement officers.

Luther sums the practical application of all this for Christian freedom: "We must have discipline and honor respected . . . yet we do not want good fun, dancing, and drinking prohibited."[37]

Sanctification instead of justification and justification instead of sanctification are opposite ends of the same heresy. Christian freedom does not pit these doctrines against one another but sees them as complementary—to be distinguished for sure but never to be torn apart and separated from one another.

Lawyering up the Music

Legalism adds to Scripture with its "*Thou shalt not!*" Nothing ever quite measures up to what Scripture demands, according to this mind-set, and if we add just a wee bit here and a smidge there, it would be a much better guidebook for sanctified Christian living. What we need are more man-generated rules. Scripture is seen as speaking to daily issues of dress length, types of food to eat, schools to attend, business investments to make, who to date and marry, the weekend of Christ's return, and what movies can be watched. Scripture is supposedly silent about the condition of baptized infants but is crystal clear about the Lord's view of rock music.

The sixteenth century had its legalism in the arts, as seen in Ulrich Zwingli's denuding of the interior of the Grossmunster Cathedral in Zurich, which today looks like a homeless shelter, complete with a wooden table and chairs in the altar space as the only vestige of anything decorative. More contemporary illustrations abound. Bob Jones University (BJU) recently released a "music policy" that in essence anathematizes rock music. While not absolutizing a musical form as the one, true biblically sanctioned medium for church and society, one suspects that the altar call music of the nineteenth and twentieth centuries is high up on the honor list at BJU. No mention is made in the policy of any musical tradition earlier than the nineteenth century, but it is noted that there is a "range of music acceptability that is separate from the world."[38]

As earlier noted, Calvinism distrusted any music in the worship service. If not directly sanctioned by Scripture, it was suspect. So, metrical settings of the Psalms? Yes, because King David was a composer and obviously the Psalms made the hit parade. Metrical settings of verses? Well, maybe ok because Ephesians 5:19 talks about spiritual songs. Hymns? We will get back to you on that. . . .

Calvinism's "Regulative Principle" tends to absolutize elements of the worship service that the Lutheran Reformation considered adiaphora. As a result, Calvinistic worship tends to be "minimalistic" and austere. If Scripture does not require the element in worship or it cannot be deduced as necessary from Scripture, it is prohibited. Add to this its ambiguity about what is going on in Calvin's doctrine of the Lord's Supper and his localizing of our Lord's human nature to the right hand of the Father up in Heaven, and you have a "real absence at the communion altar" theology (or purely "*spiritual* presence") that is unlikely to inspire intense musical composition. Compare this with Bach's St. Thomas Kirche and the centrality of the communion service focusing on Christ's real presence (present as fully man and fully God) in the sacrament of Holy Communion *for the forgiveness of sins*. Christ's real presence in the sacraments is the subject of a significant portion of Bach's works, with one communion hymn alone, for example, used in no less than six of his cantatas.[39]

One example shall suffice to illustrate that Bach's solid sacramental theology was fed by the Scriptures as opened by Reformation theology. This comes from Bach's arrangement of Luther's communion hymn, *Jesus Christus, Unser Heiland, Der von Uns* ("Christ, Who Freed Our Souls from Danger"):

Christ Jesus, Our Redeemer born,
Who from us did God's anger turn,
Through His sufferings sore and main,
Did help us all out of hell-pain.
That we never should forget it,
Gave He us His flesh, to eat it,
Hid in poor bread, gift divine,
And, to drink, His blood in the wine.
Who will draw near to that table
Must take heed, all he is able.
Who unworthy thither goes,

Thence death instead of life he knows.
God the Father praise thou duly,
That He thee would feed so truly,
And for ill deeds by thee done
Up unto death has given His Son.

(BWV 665)[40]

As for denuded churches as seen in the antisacramental Anabaptist movement and Zwingli, it so infuriated Luther that it provoked him to come out of hiding at the Wartburg to level both barrels at the Anabaptists and the so-called Zwickau Prophets for their destruction of artistic treasures in the name of cleaning up the House of the Lord from papal abuses. Similarly, as for the Lutheran worship service, Luther's principle was that all aspects of the Western Rite of the Roman Catholic Church were to be *retained* unless they violated Scripture. So side altars, prayers to the saints, promotion of human works as meritorious to save—all that was out. But kept was the sign of the cross, biblical art, stained glass, candles, incense, the processional cross, vestments, the centrality of the preached word and sacraments, the church calendar including celebration of feast days and days honoring the saints, and of course the retention of polyphonic music and counterpoint.

Licensed to Kill Music

The Christian church is not unfamiliar with the abuse of Christian freedom wrought by licentiousness. At certain points in church history, license got theological traction in the idea that Christ died to fulfill the requirements of the law and thus the law had been abrogated (antinomianism) and was of no further utility. A form of antinomianism was present in Corinth, which enraged the Apostle Paul to the point where he severely chastised the Corinthians for their licentious ways (1 Cor. 5 and 6). The Lutheran Confessions deal explicitly with an antinomianism that occurred shortly into the Reformation and continued until even after Luther's death. (Articles 5 and 6 of the Formula of Concord address the issue directly.)

License takes away from Scripture and is typified by a "thou shalt" attitude that does not care what anybody thinks of one's behavior. While the Lutheran Reformation spoke of *lex semper accusat* (the law always accuses), licentiousness yawns at the function of the law for the Christian. License absolutizes freedom and unhinges Christian conduct from God's word as both Gospel *and* Law. Instead of sensitivity to my neighbor because of what Christ has done for me, my neighbor be damned if he can't understand my newfound "freedom."

In the area of the secular arts, license is basically the *plat de jour* of the contemporary priesthood operating in high culture. It is John Cage and music by chance, it is Jackson Pollock's randomness in painting, it is crosses soaking in urine, and it is couples having sex as "live art" at museums.

Theological license tends to pit justification *against* sanctification. Any suggestion that one's conduct is harming the Gospel is met with the disdainful retort that one is a "legalist" or has a defective view of justification and total forgiveness in Christ and is seeking to return to the Law in the Christian life. License in the Christian life ultimately reflects a defective view of justification and of vocation. We are free in the forgiveness won by Christ and our freedom is to be employed to serve our neighbors in our vocations and not to serve our own passions.

License has no standards. It is like the bumper sticker "My child is an honor student at Precious Steps Nursery School." License is seeded in a culture that says everyone gets a trophy who participates and those with no talent get on national television if they can shock sensibilities. As license acts out in popular culture, so it is in the church, which has few filters when it comes to popular cultural norms. The result for music? Everyone with a guitar and a song in the church is a Christian Artist. The appropriateness of the medium to convey the message is irrelevant, as is mastery of the medium. What matters is that one is a Christian Artist. Blues, gangsta rap, disco, boy band, rock—it is all good all the time. Whatever . . . special music lets everyone's Christian Artist out for the church to see.

License unduly exalts man as man and does not take seriously the nature of sin in its infectious state in the individual and in society. With indomitable confidence in Adam's "gifts" and the ability to "sanctify" any artistic form, today's Christian Artist makes his golden calves since, after all, "God did not say we *couldn't*."

The Christian Artist as Free to Serve
God and Neighbor in His Vocation

Bach understood Christian freedom as rooted in the Gospel of free grace in Christ, which liberated the artist to pursue service of God and neighbor not based on merit or worthiness but solely based on gratitude.

Bach's personality has been the subject of numerous works. Suffice it to say that with twenty children (and no less than eight harpsichords in the home), he was accustomed to a fair degree of chaos. Unlike Calvin, he was no stuffed shirt.[41] He knew great joy (the Coffee Cantata was likely performed first as an opera in the Bach home) and deep personal sadness (seven of his children predeceased him as well as his first wife). Laughter, however, was a regular staple in the Bach home, though Bach once spent a month in jail for whacking a member of a church ensemble for poor playing on the bassoon. He enjoyed drinking and smoking as well as dancing the French court dances of the day—of which he was a complete master. His marriages were happy and productive. His second wife, Anna Magdelena (an accomplished vocalist in her own right), greatly assisted his composition process by copying scores of the cantatas on Wednesday and Thursday of each week, after Bach had composed them on Monday and Tuesday.[42]

A home filled with laughter, love, smoking, drinking, dancing,[43] and, of course, music, flowed naturally from being a student of Luther and his advice that music was only next to theology as the highest of all the arts. All this arose directly out of Bach's serious Lutheran theology of which he remained a student throughout his life. It is that Lutheran theology that took sin seriously[44] and thus took Christ's all sufficient sacrifice as the foundation of all Christian freedom. Bach was free to serve—not his personal agenda or whims, but his God, his neighbor, and his unique artistic vision, neither constricted by pietistic and unscriptural rules and moral codes nor enflamed by some narcissistic demand to be "understood." That said, music was also to be "enjoyed" as he dedicated his Clavier-Ubung Parts I and II not to a prince or royal official or patron but to "lovers of music, for their spiritual enjoyment and for the refreshment of the mind."[45]

Freedom to Serve God

Bach's vocation was as a church musician, first at Arnstad and later at the St. Thomas Kirche in Leipzig where he functioned from 1723 to his death in 1750. Following the order of the Lutheran worship service of the day, he used his substantial abilities to accentuate elements of the Lutheran liturgy. This involved, primarily, composing musical interludes that adorned the sermon text for that Sunday. Only when he made the mistake of taking a position with a Calvinist prince in Cothen did his production stagnate, finally forcing him to find a way out by jumping to the post at Leipzig.[46]

Though he had composed some short masses and "secular" cantatas before Leipzig, it was at the St. Thomas Kirche that he was able to engage in a simply staggering output of sacred music. Included in the production is, of course, the full Mass in B Minor, more than two hundred cantatas (basically one a week for more than three years), various settings of the Lutheran Mass, motets, the Goldberg Variations, and his St. John's and St. Matthew's Passions (St. Mark's Passion has been lost). These include works of profound depth and sensitivity (the *De Profundis* of the Mass in B Minor has been called the most moving piece of music in the Western canon) as well as *Jesu, Joy of Man's Desiring* and his ebullient Christmas Oratorios.

We must say that without the vigorous Lutheranism of his day, it is doubtful we would see anything close to this production from even a Bach. He benefitted from a church structure and worship form (and philosophy of music) that allowed liberality in the expression of Christian freedom. When a communion service lasts three to four hours, officials are less likely to complain about elaborate organ fugues, scintillating orchestral pieces, or works for double choruses! Even if a Bach were alive today, there is neither the cultural/financial support nor vigorous theology in the Christian Church that would give him a platform to produce work on this scale as a professional church musician. Bach came in the fullness of time and when the church of the Lutheran Reformation was perfectly situated to encourage and foster his creative genius.

In addition, Lutheranism, not requiring a "Regulative Principle" in worship, had confessional documents warning against absolutizing any particular aspects of the worship service. Improvisation and embellishment were theologically permitted in the service as long as the Gospel and the sacraments were central and as long as they supported and adorned the written Word.

So while Bach had "freedom" to paint on a wide canvas in terms of his output of sacred music, Luther's Christocentric theology always brought him back to making "Christ and Him crucified" central to the Church's communal gatherings under the Word and sacraments.[47]

Freedom to Serve Our Neighbor

It is often forgotten that Bach also operated within a "secular" context, often serving a local Prince or wealthy patron as house musician. Even in that sphere, Bach understood his Christian freedom as always being *sub cruces* and therefore to be done to the glory of God in Christ and for the edification and service of his neighbor.

In understanding that his gifts can also serve the left hand of the kingdom, Bach served secular princes and patrons with all his substantial musical abilities. In fact, it can be argued that Bach would still be considered the greatest musician of all time even if he had never been given the post at Leipzig. By 1723 he had already composed the unaccompanied cello suites, the Brandenburg Concertos, countless works for solo instruments, many of his orchestral suites, and the monumental Passcaglia and Fugue in D Minor for organ. All these "secular" works are described by sensitive commentators as reaching transcendent or religious levels of profundity. To hear non-Christians like Glenn Gould, Pablo Casals, Albert Einstein, and Yo-Yo Ma talk about Bach's construction of purely instrumental music in adorational tones is to understand that Bach created excellence in every musical medium he touched, whether the music was intended for secular or for religious purposes. Operating on the Lutheran Reformation's teaching of the priesthood of all believers and benefitting from serious study of orthodox Lutheran theology, Bach is simply not understandable without appreciation of his serious application of Christian freedom resulting from his theology of the cross taken directly from Luther.

Even when operating for secular princes, Bach mastered his medium to such a level that today's high culture secularists want to identify with Bach as an "initiate" into a high priesthood of enlightened humanity. Even those with difficult cultural hurdles to overcome to appreciate a German, Baroque, Lutheran composer find the universality of the music impossible to resist.

Bach as Fifth Evangelist

What makes Bach so universally appealing?

First, he understood the depths of his personal sin and the fallenness of the world and experienced this in his own personal life. Having buried seven of his own children and his first wife, he was deeply acquainted with sorrow and suffering and did not trivialize sin, nor did he think highly of his own personal piety. Unlike so many modern Christian Artists, untrained in theology and quick to abandon the universal themes of Scripture for the latest pop culture quaalude to set a praise chorus to, Bach explored and never exhausted the universal and therefore always relevant themes of sin, redemption, and joy in the victory of God in Christ won at Calvary's cross and verified in the historical resurrection.

Second, Bach mastered whatever medium he attempted. An accomplished violinist and organist, he understood music theory and instrumentation on a level perhaps never seen since. This took tremendously hard work, as he himself commented, "I have had to work hard; anyone who works just as hard will get just as far."[48] Unlike other things, genius does not just "happen." It inevitably flows from rigorous discipline and total dedication.

Third, he saw all music as pedagogical or a vehicle for teaching truths (even uncomfortable truths about the wrath of God, judgment, human sin, and suffering as a Christian).[49] Christian musicians are fundamentally in the teaching vocation. Sadly, contemporary Christian musicians are often poor students of doctrine, seemingly unaware that they too will be held accountable as teachers of the Church.

Fourth and finally, Bach reveled in his freedom in Christ. He experienced personal and professional freedom that was neither legalistic nor licentious. Justification and sanctification worked themselves out in Christian freedom and the result is one that the world still flocks to hear.

A common though often unarticulated cultural concern about the Christian faith is that one becomes narrower if one becomes a

Christian. Bach stands as exhibit A to the falsity of that assertion. Christian belief opened up the windows of heaven so that the full skills and gifts of J. S. Bach could be exercised. No longer bound to satisfy the pride and adulation of his Old Adam, Bach was free to express his gifts with the full blessing of God Almighty.

While he began a number of his manuscripts with "SDG"—Soli Deo Gloria—he often ended simply with "JJ," which means Jesus Help. May that same eternal Savior help bring forth a generation of new Bachs, first as theologians of the cross (ensuring that their content is always universally relevant) and then as excelling all with their musical gifts bestowed on them by grace from on high and perfected by long hours of discipline and dedication to their holy calling to the art of music. Jesus, hear our prayer.

Appendix

Popular culture[50]	Traditional/high culture
Focuses on the new	Focuses on the timeless
Discourages reflection	Encourages reflection
Gives us what we want	Offers what we could not imagine
Pursued casually to "kill time"	Pursued with deliberation
Relies on instant accessibility	Requires training and patience
Celebrates fame	Celebrates ability
Emphasizes information and trivia	Emphasizes knowledge and wisdom
Formulas are the substance	Formulas are the tools
Tends toward relativism	Tends toward submission to standards
Incapable of deep or sustained attention	Capable of repeated, careful attention
Used	Received

Notes

1. Take, for example, the fun one would have had at one particular "performance" by Nam June Paik, the avant-garde South Korean "artist" who on one occasion "destroyed two pianos, cut off John Cage's tie with scissors, lathered Cage's head with shampoo, and eventually ran from the studio with a dead mouse clenched between his teeth. A few minutes later he called to say that the performance, *Etude for Pianoforte*, was over." Rob Haskins, *John Cage* (London: Reaktion Books, 2012), 92.

2. We note our indebtedness to Leonard Payton's hilarious "glossary" of contemporary evangelical music terms, where we learn that a "Christian Artist" is a "person who sings and whose recordings sell in large quantities," an "Accompaniment Track" is a "means of momentarily transforming ordinary folks into Christian Artists," and a "Worship Band" is "any collection of guitarists, drummers, synthesizer players, and persons holding microphones. All of them wish they were with a Christian Artist." Leonard Payton, "Is It a Prelude or a Quaalude?," *Modern Reformation Magazine* 4, no. 1 (January–February 1995): 12–13.

3. Russell Squire, *Church Music: Musical and Hymnological Development in Western Christianity* (St. Louis, MO: Bethany Press, 1976), 34, 114–15, 128. Squire puts it this way: "Actually, Calvin was not well disposed toward music. Thus in all the strongholds of Calvinism where it was not quickly modified by opposing forces, the development of the art of music was stifled. . . . Luther never followed the strictures of Calvin. . . . Luther never subscribed to the austere and severe phases of the unaccompanied community singing of the Calvinists and the Puritans." Ibid., 114–15, 128. See also George W. Forell, Harold J. Grimm, and Theodore Hoelty-Nickel, *Luther and Culture* (Decorah, IA: Luther College Press, 1960), 150 ("We know that both Calvin and Zwingli . . . are not only far removed from a medieval understanding of the cosmological-theological relevance of music, but positively reject that position").

4. Gunther Stiller, *Johann Sebastian Bach and Liturgical Life in Leipzig* (St. Louis, MO: Concordia Publishing House, 1984), 144 ("Calvin . . . consciously rejected the musical unity of sacred and secular song and instead demanded a separate ecclesiastical and sacred style" and made a conscious decision "against polyphonic singing and the use of instruments in worship").

5. Lewis Spitz, *The Renaissance and Reformation Movements*, 2 vols. (Chicago: Rand McNally, 1972), 2:580.

6. Mark Noll, "Singing the Word of God," *Christian History* 95 (Summer 2007): 16–17.

7. See John Warwick Montgomery, *The Shaping of America* (Minneapolis, MN: Bethany Books, 1976); Michael Scott Horton, *Made in America: The Shaping of Modern American Evangelicalism* (Grand Rapids, MI: Baker Book

House, 1991), nails the American evangelical personality with chapter titles like "Consumerism," "The 'How To' Gospel," and "Feeling's Believing."

8. For an excellent discussion of the rise of popular culture in the American church and its dominance today over every other form of culture, with disturbing analysis of why even high culture is looking to incorporate elements of popular culture in order to "sell the product" to the American music consumer, see Gene Edward Veith, *The State of the Arts: From Bezalel to Mapplethorpe* (Wheaton, IL: Crossways Books, 1991). See also, Kenneth A. Myers, *All God's Children in Blue Suede Shoes: Christians and Popular Culture* (Wheaton, IL: Crossways Books, 1989), esp. 72. See the appendix to this chapter for part of a chart done by Myers contrasting high culture with popular culture.

9. We note that while Bach signed his manuscripts with "SDG" (Soli Deo Gloria) and "JJ" (Jesus Help), contemporary Christian Artists sign their works with the litigious reminder that the rights holder is "CCLI, all rights reserved, copyright 2013, Little Steps for You Music, LLC, a subsidiary of Maranatha Music, Inc."

10. See Steven Ozment, *The Serpent and the Lamb: Cranach, Luther and the Making of the Reformation* (New Haven, CT: Yale University Press, 2011), 150 ("Throughout the 1520s, the chemistry between Cranach's art and Luther's theology succeeded beyond their fondest hopes").

11. "No one has questioned Luther's intense love of music, and no one has expressed any doubts as to his training and proficiency in music. His training was no doubt equal to, if not better than that received by candidates for the master's degree in music at most of our colleges and universities today"; Forell, Grimm, and Hoelty-Nickel, *Luther and Culture*, 146n3. "In addition to his interest in hymnody, both Latin and German, and his knowledge of the ancient plain song and the music of the liturgy, Luther was familiar with the vast literature of complicated, artistically interesting music found in motets and other polyphonic compositions"; Luther D. Reed, *The Lutheran Liturgy* (Philadelphia: Muhlenberg Press, 1947), 85.

12. That Bach was first and foremost a serious Lutheran theologian is abundantly evidenced through any number of means. For example, Pelikan has shown that all thirty-eight of Luther's hymns (both text and music) were used in some form by Bach as foundations for chorale preludes, cantatas, motets, hymn arrangements, or other works; Jaroslav Pelikan, *Bach among the Theologians* (Philadelphia: Fortress Press, 1986), 17–18. "The real native soil for the rise of Bach's cantatas was the Lutheran principal worship service [*Hauptgottesdienst*] in the first half of the 18th century," and Bach was "intimately acquainted" with the details of Lutheran theology; Stiller, *Johann Sebastian Bach and Liturgical Life in Leipzig*, 25, 175. Leaver notes that "the principal author in Bach's library is Luther, *whose influence is all pervasive*";

Robin A. Leaver, *Bach's Theological Library* (Stuttgart: Hanssler-Verlag, 1983), 25 (emphasis added).

13. Carl Schalk, *God's Song in a New Land* (St. Louis, MO: Concordia Publishing House, 1995), 23–25, catalogs the more important collections of hymnbooks in sixteenth-century Lutheran Germany.

14. Quoted in Ewald Plass, *What Luther Says: An Anthology* (St. Louis, MO: Concordia Publishing House, 1959), sections 3100, 3104, and 3105, 2:982–83.

15. Robin Leaver, *J. S. Bach and Scripture* (St. Louis, MO: Concordia Publishing House, 1985), 13: "Bach was his age's most powerful exponent of Martin Luther's theology and practice." See also Mark Noll, "Singing the Word of God," 19.

16. John Butt, *The Mass in B Minor* (Cambridge: Cambridge University Press, 2000), 20–21.

17. Of the Six Unaccompanied Cello Suites alone, Yo-Yo Ma (who had a film commissioned to correspond to each suite and who began playing them at age four) says they are "the most challenging music in the repertoire. . . . I have drawn inspiration throughout my life from their intellectual, emotional, and spiritual power." Yo-Yo Ma, "Inspired by Bach," in the 1997 Sony recording of the *Six Unaccompanied Suites by Bach Performed by Yo-Yo Ma*. Renowned cellist Mischa Maisky calls these suites his "personal Bible." Eric Siblin, *The Cello Suites: J. S. Bach, Pablo Casals, and the Search for a Baroque Masterpiece* (New York: Atlantic Monthly Press, 2009), 90.

18. Meredith Little and Natalie Jenne, *Dance and the Music of J. S. Bach* (Bloomington, IN: Indiana University Press, 2001), xi, xii, include a complete cataloging of the dance movements found in Bach's works, with forty titled dances alone in his Clavier-Ubung I and II. Bach was "full of rhythm in every part of his body"; ibid., xii (citing John Matthias Gesner).

19. As for how Bach managed to often write a cantata *each week* at Leipzig from 1723 to 1726, see the fascinating account of his compositional schedule while at St. Thomas Kirche, recounted at length in Stiller, *Johann Sebastian Bach and Liturgical Life in Leipzig*; see also Christoph Wolfe, *The World of the Bach Cantatas* (New York: W. W. Norton, 1996).

20. For this reason, Bach is often referred to simply as "the Fifth Evangelist." Bach Collegium Japan has sought to record all of the existing Bach cantatas in a dedicated chapel under the direction of Maestro Masaki Suzuki. For citations to Japanese authorities on the "tens of thousands" of recent Christian conversions due to Bach, see Uwe Siemon-Netto, "Why Nippon Is Nuts about J. S. Bach," *Atlantic Times*, 2006.

21. Robert L. Marshall, *The Music of Johann Sebastian Bach: The Sources, the Style, the Significance* (New York: MacMillan, 1989), 78–79.

22. The list of scholars who echo this is almost endless and includes Charles Sanford Terry, Philipp Spitta, Christoph Wolfe, Karl Geiringer, Gunther Stiller,

Robin Leaver, Albert Schweitzer, Robert Marshall, and Friedrich Blume. The proliferation of Bach festivals and the fact that his unaccompanied instrumental scores are almost universally required for auditions to serious orchestras support Schweitzer's comment that in Bach resided "perhaps, the highest among all creative artists." Schweitzer, *J. S. Bach*, 2 vols. (New York: MacMillan, 1958), 1:166.

23. Spitz, *The Renaissance and Reformation Movements*; Ozment, *The Serpent and the Lamb*; and Schalk, *God's Song in a New Land*, all make this point.

24. "Do not search what is too high for thee. But here it comes down before my eyes, so that I can see the babe there in His Mother's lap. There lies a human being who was born like any other child, and lives like any other child, and shows no other nature, manner, and work than any other human being, so that no heart could guess that the creature is the Creator." WA 37:42 (Christmas sermon, 1533), cited in *Day by Day We Magnify Thee: Readings in Luther* (Philadelphia: Fortress Press, 1982), 27.

25. Stiller, *Johann Sebastian Bach and Liturgical Life in Leipzig*, 24–25; and see the discussion by Marshall, *The Music of Johann Sebastian Bach*, 78–79.

26. Ozment, *The Serpent and the Lamb*, 150, 195, 216. Ozment calls Cranach the Elder the painter of the "the crude, the rude, and the nude."

27. Veith, *The State of the Arts*, 165.

28. Charles Sanford Terry calls St. Matthew's Passion the "deepest and most moving expression of devotional feeling in the whole of musical literature." C. S. Terry, *The Music of Bach* (New York: Dover Books, 1963), 77.

29. Heinrich Eduard Jacob, *Felix Mendelssohn and His Times* (London: Prentice Hall, 1963), 79–82.

30. See also BWV 80, Bach's cantata entirely built around this "Battle Hymn of the Reformation," as Pelikan calls it. Pelikan, *Bach among the Theologians*, 51.

31. Letter of August 1, 1521; Jaroslav Pelikan and Helmut T. Lehmann, eds., *Luther's Works*, American Edition (St. Louis, MO: Concordia Publishing House, 1955ff.), 48:281.

32. Luther, *Works*, 27:347. ("See, therefore, how foolish they are if they suppose that through the freedom by which we are freed from the Law and from sin, license is given for sinning. . . . For freedom consists in this, that we have no other obligation than to love our neighbor.")

33. Plass, *What Luther Says*, section 2253, 722.

34. "Simply stated, Luther's approach was to retain from the past whatever did not violate his understanding of the Gospel. . . . While certain new emphases did indeed characterize Luther's reforms—the importance of the sermon, communion in both kinds, the use of vernacular congregational song as an integral part of the liturgy—what is striking about Luther's approach is its basic conservatism." Carl Schalk, *Music in Early Lutheranism: Shaping the Tradition (1524–1672)* (St. Louis, MO: Concordia Academic Press, 2001), 18–19;

the magisterial tome on the subject of the conservative nature of the Lutheran Reformation is Charles Porterfield Krauth, *The Conservative Reformation and Its Theology* (Philadelphia: Lippincott, 1875).

35. Eastern orthodoxy argues that "the Fathers of the Church chose only eight modes or tones (ihoi) from the many which existed, for use in the Church. Others were rejected because they were seen to have a negative effect on the disposition of the soul for prayer and even encouraged the passions." N. Lungu, Gr. Costea, and Ion Croitoru, *A Guide to the Music of the Eastern Orthodox Church*, trans. Fr. Nicholas K. Apostola (Brookline, MA: Holy Cross Orthodox Press, 1984), 13.

36. Plass, *What Luther Says*, section 2409, 776.

37. Quoted in Forell, Grimm, and Hoelty-Nickel, *Luther and Culture*, 117 (citing Georg Buchwald's two-volume edited set of Luther's Sermons, vol. 2, 501). The contrast with Calvin could not be more stark. McNeill, the eminent Calvin scholar, puts it this way: "Calvin took himself very seriously." John T. McNeill, *The History and Character of Calvinism* (Oxford: Oxford University Press, 1970), 233.

38. See Bob Jones University Music Philosophy, http://www.bju.edu.

39. See Stiller, *Johann Sebastian Bach and Liturgical Life in Leipzig*, 137–38, which discusses the "considerable space" devoted to communion hymns in the various hymnals used by Bach at St. Thomas.

40. Johann Sebastian Bach and Charles Sanford Terry, *The Hymns and Hymn Melodies of the Organ Works*, vol. 3 of *Bach's Chorals* (Cambridge: Cambridge University Press, 1915–21). 3:231, http://oll.libertyfund.org/titles/2057. The words are by Martin Luther as translated into English by George MacDonald.

41. Schweitzer says of Calvin that he "laughed once." Schweitzer, *J. S. Bach*, 1:20.

42. See citations to Stiller, *Johann Sebastian Bach and Liturgical Life in Leipzig*; Wolfe, *The World of the Bach Cantatas*; and Marshall, *The Music of Johann Sebastian Bach*. We cannot resist noting the distinction between the happily married life of Luther and Katy von Bora, which was the foundation for the Protestant parsonage, with that of Calvin, who "looked upon marriage only as a convenient means of relieving oneself of domestic burdens." Francois Wendel, *Calvin: Origins and Development of His Religious Thought*, trans. Philip Mairet (Grand Rapids, MI: Baker Books, 1963), 65.

43. See Little and Jenne, *Dance and the Music of J. S. Bach*, where they state that Bach had "complete mastery of the technical and structural features of Baroque dance music"; for Bach's view of tobacco use, one need go no further than his comment, "I smoke my pipe and worship God" while wine is "a noble gift of God." Hans T. David and Arthur Mendel, eds., *The Bach Reader: A Life of Johann Sebastian Bach in Letters and Documents* (New York: W. W. Norton, 1945), 97–98 (this includes Bach's poem "Edifying Thoughts of a Tobacco Smoker").

44. Only one small example: Cantata BWV 179, titled "See to It That Your Fear of God Be Not Hypocrisy," which intones, "My sins sicken me / Like pus in my bones / Help me, Jesus, Lamb of God / For I am sinking in deepest slime."

45. Little and Jenne, *Dance and the Music of J. S. Bach*, xi.

46. Stiller, *Johann Sebastian Bach and Liturgical Life in Leipzig*, 143. ("Wherever Reformed and Pietistic activities became effective in the Lutheran Church, there were disastrous consequences for the practice of church music, as Bach's leaving his Muhlhausen position after barely 10 months alarmingly illustrates.")

47. This distinguishes Bach from say a Mozart, who never (even in his very Roman Catholic *Requiem Mass in D Minor, K. 626*) reaches to the depth and complexity of the human condition, nor for whom the totally finished work of Christ is central. The frivolity of Mozart, as compared to the rigor and seriousness of Bach, moved the eccentric piano genius Glenn Gould to write a television script on how Mozart had "become a bad composer." Gould surely goes over the top by saying that "Mozart died too late rather than too soon." Peter Ostwald, *Glenn Gould: The Ecstasy and Tragedy of Genius* (New York: W. W. Norton, 1997), 22; see also the Public Broadcasting Service transcript of television show aired April 28, 1968.

48. Marshall, *The Music of Johann Sebastian Bach*, 72.

49. For the way Bach envisioned his music as conveying truth and for his pedagogical emphasis, see James R. Gaines, *Evening in the Palace of Reason: Bach Meets Frederick the Great in the Age of Enlightenment* (New York: Harper Collins, 2005).

50. This is taken in part from a more comprehensive list done by Kenneth Myers, *All God's Children in Blue Suede Shoes*, 121ff.

CHAPTER 10

The Spiritual Life of the Christian

Cross and Glory

Steven A. Hein

The cross is our theology.

—Martin Luther

The cross comes before the crown and tomorrow is Monday morning.

—C. S. Lewis

Confessions of a Burned-Out Christian

Perhaps you have been one of those Christians who has secretly longed for a more fulfilling experience in your spiritual life. You have read the books and attended the seminars hoping for the right insight and advice that would bring improvement. But now time has passed. Many books, seminars, prayers, and commitments later, you have taken stock on the condition of your spiritual life in Christ. The victory over many sinful habits in your life has yet to occur. The surging power of the Spirit is still waiting to be felt. The *experience* of God's rich presence in your life seems as elusive as before. Indeed, few and far between are warm-hearted feelings from an inner experience of God's loving presence. And to top it all off, things just continue to go awry in your life.

Is this a picture of your efforts to improve your life in Christ and what they have accomplished? You worked hard to apply the bible-based principles that promised so much, only to be disappointed with the results. Discouraged and bewildered, you wonder where you have been going wrong. Have you missed the real power of prayer because of insufficient faith? Do you lack the level of obedience to be really *filled* with the Holy Spirit? Has your commitment faded from when you prayed to invite Jesus not only to be your Savior but also to take control as Lord of your life? Do you sense that you may be on the verge of spiritual burnout trying to feel like the rapture you see on the faces of the Gospel singers at the megachurch praise services? And in your darker moments, do you wonder if the troubling sins that stick in your life might be obstacles that are preventing you from receiving spiritual blessings that others say they have received?

If you have had some of these experiences and they are tempting you to toss in your spiritual towel and make your exit from a life of faith, the Lutheran tradition would like you to take another look. St. Paul commended the following perspective to the Corinthians: *We preach Christ crucified.* He insisted that he would know nothing among them *but Jesus Christ and Him crucified* (1 Cor. 1:23; 2:2).

The apostle's stance indicates that in this world the Christian lives only in the cross of Christ and he lives there with some crosses of his own (Matt. 16:24). Martin Luther began his movement of recovering the New Testament Gospel echoing St. Paul's resolve when he declared, "The CROSS is our theology."[1]

Searching the Scriptures, Luther discovered that Christian life in this world is lived in union with Christ the crucified. It is the cross that shapes the contours of the Christian's spiritual life for now. All the elements of glory are reserved for when Christians are taken out of this vale of tears to live in the full presence of God on that Better Day. Because the cross shapes life in Christ for now, the realities of sin from within and without impact the experience of the Christian in his daily walk. If you are an ordinary saint who trusts in the grace of Christ, who regularly feeds on the Gospel, and who has a keen sense of your sinfulness but a not-so-keen experience of how your life in Christ often feels, then Lutheranism believes *you are normal!* God is not waiting or requiring you to do anything first (during or after) to provide you with every blessing of the Gospel. However, because spiritual life with Christ is now lived in his cross, the crown of glory will only flood the Christian's experience of Christ in the life to come. Sounding so very much like a Lutheran, C. S. Lewis observed, "The cross comes before the crown and tomorrow is Monday morning."[2]

Spiritual Life as Fellowship with God in the Cross of Christ

The Lutheran way recognizes that many aspects of the cross life of the Christian reflect realities best understood by way of paradox. The Scriptures often present two seemingly opposite realities where both must be embraced and appreciated without the tension between them relaxed or resolved. The dual yet paradoxical realities of Law and Gospel, sin and grace, dying and rising, repentance and faith, sinner and saint, faith and experience, and now and not yet describe the ambiguous nature of how the experience of our spiritual life in Christ should be understood.

When Luther first proclaimed, "The CROSS is our theology," he implied that the cross is not simply the beginning of our spiritual journey—not simply the appropriation of a happy outcome of life with God for us dead sinners. It is also the means by which our spiritual journey continues in this life, and it is the experience of the journey itself. God apprehends us in our Baptism. There, we are splashed with grace and united to Christ the crucified, where a death to sin, our sin, is both beheld and experienced (Rom. 6: 3–11). The Word in the water joins us to Christ the crucified and brings simultaneously a death to sin and an emergent life now lived in the righteousness of Christ. It is not simply that we *were* baptized into Christ the crucified; we *are* baptized in the cross of Christ. The sinner's progress in his spiritual journey leads both to and from the experience and inheritance of Christian Baptism. The cross not only shapes our spiritual life; it also describes the kind of experience we will have as we both approach and arrive at the cross of Christ. This does not simply happen once, but rather it is the heartbeat of the Christian's spiritual life. Christian Baptism at its core is a uniting with Christ in his cross, dying to sin, and rising unto newness of life in His righteousness. In the Christian's life in Christ, this happens again and again. You do not *get saved* in the cross of Christ and then five minutes later move on from there. Dying to sin and rising in the crucified Christ becomes a daily regimen that revisits the death of the old sinful self and the renewal of the new creation.[3] The new life in Christ arises by the killing of the Law and the raising of a new life from the Gospel. For Luther, we make progress along the path to righteousness by always starting over again—dying and rising, repentance and faith worked by God in His Law and Gospel.[4] We mature as a new creation in Christ as we advance in the cross toward glory by returning again to our Baptism. This spiritual journey is attended also by the experience of the crosses we have been given, which can involve suffering, trials, and, at times, even feelings of abandonment. Luther insisted that these experiences are normal in the spiritual life of all Christians.[5]

Jesus has been raised from the dead and received His heavenly glory. He has had His Easter, but we have not. The experience of victory over sin, death, and the Devil is history for Christ, but it is faith and hope for us. The cross and tomb are only empty for Jesus. At Easter Lutherans celebrate a not-so-empty tomb of Jesus. All of us who are baptized into the death of Christ are still there, awaiting our glorious resurrected life. So the spiritual life of the Christian has two installments: cross and glory. It is cross life for us now, and glory in the better day that is coming.

Embracing Luther's cross theology recognizes that God's saving work and our experience of it involves a kind of *salvific worldliness* in His method.[6] He chooses to enlist worldly elements and structures of his fallen creation as instruments or means to accomplish His saving purposes. Consider the incarnation of His Son and the cross. God takes up and hides Himself in ordinary human flesh. He then enlists earthly family life, the carpentry trade, and the political and religious movements of the day into the service of His saving work. He works out but hides His righteousness and pardon for us in the grisly act of capital punishment by crucifixion. By ordinary perception, we see His chosen worldly instruments and events. However, it is only by the eyes of faith that we see the glory of God in the Suffering Servant and our righteousness that He acquired. That Lutherans understand God at work in the world through Christ requires us to hold on to both what we see and what is given to faith. Neither dimension is to be denied or omitted from the Church's faith and confession. In the Incarnation and the cross, God reveals the ultimate expression of salvific worldliness where the extraordinary work of God is hidden and revealed in ordinary events of this fallen world. As Luther observed, "Man hides his own things in order to conceal them; God hides his own things to reveal them."[7]

Salvific worldliness is much the same when God is having His way with us in our spiritual life. We are all familiar with Luther's championing of justification by faith apart from all works of the Law. This is the happy "faith alone." But Luther embraced another distinction about faith alone that oftentimes is not so happy. We are justified by grace through faith alone, *apart from our experience*. Pivotal for Luther and Lutherans is the insistence that faith is to be anchored completely in the external Word of promise, not in anything that we may experience in our life in Christ. Our spiritual experience in this life can often be punctuated by sinful wretchedness from within and without. Externally, trial and tribulation can visit us from the doings of God in this fallen world. He also hammers us with His Law internally as it has been inscribed on our hearts. Justification by faith alone renders a divine citizenship with all God's saving gifts and blessings of salvation *in, with, and under* our temporal citizenship and all that its still-fallen character can bring us. What flows from our temporal citizenship in the Devil's playground is fully given to our senses and openly experienced, but what flows from our divine citizenship is given to and apprehended by faith alone.

The tension between worldly experience with its trials and tribulations and the saving gifts given to faith are encountered in the daily living of the believer by moving back and forth between them. Neither the divine blessings nor the temporal trials and tribulations cancel the other out or call them into question. This tension between what we experience and what is given to faith may well intensify as we grow and mature in Christ, and it will not come to an end until the Day of Glory arrives. On that day, nothing more will be added to the saving gifts we have already received in our Baptism and what we receive in Holy Absolution and the Lord's Supper. But in glory, faith will be no more, and we will enjoy all the saving gifts and blessings by rich luxuriant experience (Rev. 7:13–17). What Luther called *theologies of glory*, though very attractive today, falsely promise some experiences of glory to supplement faith in this life, if you will just perfect some law-oriented, bible-based principles. With Luther, Lutherans champion a justification by faith alone apart from all experience in this life, confessing a cross life now and the experience of glory only when Christ comes to gather His Bride.

Holy Anguish: The Experience of the Cross of Christ

Luther reminded the Church in his *Large Catechism* that Satan assails and vexes all Christians through temptation. His explanation of the sixth petition in the Lord's Prayer ("and lead us not into temptation") promised the Christian no exemption from trials and temptations. Rather, Luther maintained, "No one can escape temptations and allurements as long as we live in the flesh and have the Devil prowling about us. We cannot help but suffer tribulation, and even be entangled in them, but we pray here that we may not fall into them and be overwhelmed by them."[8]

Heiko Oberman, in his magnificent treatment, *Luther: Man between God and the Devil*, captured the legacy of Luther, who taught the Church something startlingly new, something radical and perhaps unsettling. Spiritual distress is not simply the lot of marginal Christians and occasional crazy monks in monasteries. It is the common inheritance of all believers.[9] Luther's discovery that the just shall live by faith alone included the recognition that faith will not be left alone in the Christian life. Faith will be assaulted by attacks and temptations of the Unholy Spirit. Christian life is found in the cross of Christ and that means we shall also be living with a cross of our own. Cross life for the New Creation that emerges from Baptism not only has us contending with the Old Adam and a fallen world; it also brings us turmoil and affliction from the powers and principalities of the Prince of Darkness (Rom. 8:22; Gal. 5:17; Eph. 6:11–12). Peace with God brings conflict and adversity with the world, the flesh, and the Devil.[10]

This new evaluation of spiritual distress by Luther leads to twin conclusions, both of which can be rather unsettling and unpopular. First, as Oberman summarizes Luther, "tribulations are not a disease, so there is no cure for them." Second, "only firm faith in God's unalterable promise enables spiritual crises to be withstood—not overcome."[11] God's Law reveals with brutal lucidity what has become of all of us. Each one of us is exposed in our unworthiness and spiritual bankruptcy. The Devil is on a relentless campaign to replace the *joyous exchange*[12] of the cross with the demands of the Law for morality, godliness, and good works. God's holy Commandments are co-opted by the Devil to concoct a seeming airtight case that for us, there is no salvation! Only when we get to this point does it become clear that the mercy of God in the divine foolishness of the Gospel is our only refuge.

How does this play itself out for ordinary saints in everyday life? Perhaps something like this: We grow up in ordinary homes, reflecting the ethos of our time and place, and they make their mark on us. We become fully participating citizens of the here and now. We struggle with our sexuality and loneliness, and perhaps we marry. A new household is formed with babies' spilt milk and messy bedrooms. Our teenagers can walk out the door and we know that almost anything can happen to them, and often it does. We experience joys and sorrows with our spouse, our children, and our circle of friends. Quarrels and misunderstandings punctuate our relationships with loved ones as well as good times had by all. Our work life moves like the tide between excitement and boredom, success and failure. We can be hired, fired, promoted, and forgotten. People who matter to us suffer injury, addiction, and disease. So can we. They will get better or they will die. So will we. And more often than we would like, we sense compelling evidence that our government, our economy, and our church denomination are going to the dogs.[13]

We experience life as bittersweet: our cup is somewhere between half empty and half full. We long for much more than our daily living provides. For that reason, the voice within can hammer us with a painful conclusion: the life we are living falls woefully short of our longings for what it ought to be for would-be citizens of the Kingdom of God. But this is only half of it. We also experience our slice of life as it has passed through the *grim reaper* of the Law that is lodged in our hearts. And perhaps for many of us schooled in the Scriptures, the cutting edge of that Law is razor sharp. The voice of the Law is continually telling us that we are falling short of our vision. If we are called to a life of fear, love, and trust in God, if we are called to a faith that expresses itself in a life of service with reordered loves, then the Law cuts us with its bitter verdict: *we aren't, we don't, and we can't.*

Experiences such as these, while they are ordinary and should be expected, can drive us to a state of helplessness and hopelessness. It is just like taking in Christ on the cross with all our senses. There is the hammer of our fallen world that beats on our sense of membership in the family of God and the blade of the Law that assaults our righteousness through faith. Luther called this helplessness and hopelessness *Anfechtung. Anfechtung* is a profound anguish. It is an assault upon us by the world, the flesh, and the Devil that can often reduce us to a state of doubt about who and what we are in Christ. It tempts us to despair of God's promises, it challenges our confidence, and it puts our faith to the test.[14]

Yet as Luther also recognized, this is a *holy* anguish, an instrument of the gracious God, and part of living in the cross of Christ. God is the one behind our anguish, and He uses it to crucify our fleshly complacency and self-confidence. Then He uses it to send us running back the other way to the security and confidence of His Word of promise that is given to faith. From faith, we see the righteousness of Christ that is ours, and from faith, hope is renewed in the coming glory of the Kingdom. With faith's vision renewed in the Gospel promise repeatedly, faith is strengthened, the New Creation is renewed, and the call of the Christian's vocation is revitalized. Here is the central heartbeat of Christian living, the experience of life in the old world that produces a holy anguish coupled with the transforming power of faith fed by the Gospel. In tension, as we move back and forth between them, Luther believed this duality to be a common inheritance for all Christians baptized into the cross of Christ.

Beware of those who promise a sweet, calm tranquility in this life from God by perfecting your commitment to spiritual exercises. They did not work for Luther in the monastery and they will not work for us. Do not believe that we can reach a lofty level of sanctification where we can be free of the battles that rage in our minds and hearts in this life. We walk by faith and hope for the better day that is coming when eternity blesses us with the full fruits of Christ's victory at His Heavenly Banquet. For now, we join Christ in His battle against the powers of darkness within and without as very much a junior partner. This is His mission and ministry. His resources and work have come packaged to us in the form of the two ministries: Law and Gospel. Through these, our spiritual life in His cross is strengthened and matured. Moreover, His work of sanctification in us and the extension of His kingdom through us in the world are carried out.

The Spiritual Life of the Christian
Expresses Life in the Cross of Christ

When all was said and done concerning how the theology of the cross renders the believer living in the world, the saints of God end up looking very ordinary. In the Lutheran tradition, faith going to work in the world presents the Christian with a regimen for life that looks rather indistinguishable from would-be citizens of the Kingdom of the Devil. Following Luther, spiritual life is called to exercise a life of faithfulness that—compared to much of Western Christian thinking before the Reformation—is decidedly worldly and mundane in its appearance. Luther urged the Christian to leave behind the exercises of monastic life, pilgrimages, Eucharistic parades, and various acts of pious self-denial in a struggle for personal holiness. The righteousness of Christ shall be your holiness already accomplished and bestowed. You cannot get any more righteous or holy than you already are in your Baptism. Therefore, Lutherans understand that the Christian is directed to channel his or her efforts in faithful living toward meeting the ordinary temporal needs of his or her neighbors as they are encountered where they commonly live, work, and play. Such a life of faith renders the believer rather unidentifiable in general society. Indeed, the good pious Christian called to live in the cross of Christ is and remains in this life a bit of a phantom, a sociological uncertainty, indistinguishable from the average citizen of this world. The character of godliness and piety that Luther advocated involved the call to a life of faith and faithfulness with a decidedly worldly accent.

Christian life is lived as a *calling*, a vocation that flows from God's call and love for us in Christ. Through the Gospel, He has called us to be sons and daughters in His family. This call is first a summons to a life of faith—a call to trust in the saving work of Christ and who and what we are by His grace—forgiven and adopted children of His love. Christians have received their vocational call from God in Baptism. Baptism bestows on each of us God's gracious claim to be His child. His call brings full and secure membership in His Kingdom. The tasks that God has given to us act out our faith in His calling. They are the means of expressing our faithfulness to Him and His family. True Christian spirituality expresses or acts out our trust in who we are in God's call. Our works in vocation shape the expressions of true Christian spirituality where we live, work, and play.

For some people, the term *good works* conjures up images of extraordinary deeds one takes time out in life to perform. For others, the Boy Scout slogan "Do a good turn daily" comes to mind. Still others may think of some sort of compulsive *do-goodism*. The Lutheran tradition is not comfortable with any of these images. It understands good works as the fruit of faith. Good works and how they fit into the Christian life are conceptualized according to what some have called the *botanical model*. Jesus said He is the vine and we are the branches, and if we abide in Him we will bear much fruit (Jn. 15:1–5). Fruit, as we know, is simply the byproduct of a healthy growing fruit tree or vine. Fruit just appears on the branches spontaneously and effortlessly as a consequence of being alive, according to the type of branch that God created. It is just the nature of grape vines to produce grapes, apple trees to produce apples, and so on. It is as simple as that. Reflect on what this means for a moment. The vineyards are silent at night, are they not? There is no grunting or groaning as the fruit matures—and no whining questions: "Do we have to produce grapes? How many?" They just silently do it!

Lutherans believe there is insight here about good works in the Christian's life in Christ. To live in Christ is simply to bring forth the works of Christ. These are works that He produces simply by being who He is through each of us by virtue of who we are. As we live in Christ and His righteousness through faith, our faith is just naturally and spontaneously fruitful in works of loving service. It is what faith does. As an indicative statement, faith *is* active in love.[15] Moreover, God is love. He created and redeemed us from sin to love. It is not a matter of legal compulsion or coercion, as if works of love were something foreign to our recreated nature. The grace by which we live and grow in Christ is the grace that empowers and engenders a fruitful faith. Works of love are how faith expresses itself in daily living. They are spontaneous and seemingly effortless, without calculation or self-concern. As Jesus described the loving heart that gives, "The right hand does not know what the left hand is doing" (Matt. 6:3).[16]

Works of loving service just happen as we are grasped repeatedly by the astonishing reality that the grace and righteousness of Christ are the end of all legal requirements. We are free from the demanding works of the Law, and we are free to turn love outward, to focus on the needs of others as our love and trust in Christ liberates us from preoccupied self-concern. For Luther, the Gospel is the end of all calculated striving to please, to become acceptable, or to perform to become fit and worthy. We are finally and forever secure in His love to abandon self-concern and burst forth our bottled-up love outward to God and others. By sheer grace alone we have forever become secure as the children of God, citizens of the Kingdom of God, and the bride of Christ. This is the incredible power of the Gospel that energizes the sanctified life with the fruit of loving works. The pardon is powerful!

Lutherans understand that our works are ultimately to be of service to Christ (Jn. 13:13–17). There are some important qualifications in doing this, however, that are not very flattering. First, we do not have anything He needs. Second, all that we are and all that we have that is good, He made and gave to us. Anything of real worth, we call a blessing, and Lutherans praise God from whom *all* blessings flow. It is our neighbor who needs our gifts, skills, time, and blessings that the Lord has entrusted to us. Our spouse; our children; those who live next door; fellow employees; the customer; the client; those whom we encounter where we live, work, and play—these are the ones who need our goods and works of service. Jesus instructs us that, as He served the neighbor (and the servant is not above his Master; Jn. 13:16), so also must we. Thus the Lord makes this kind of arrangement. When we serve these, He will credit it as service rendered to Him (Matt. 25:35–40). The outward works of this worldly service are seen and perceived by all. But what drives these works; our inward faith in Christ; and fear, love, and trust in God are hidden. Spiritual life where faith expresses faithful service in the world (as with Christ and his saving work) is extraordinary as hidden and ordinary as revealed. Here is how Luther understood the economy of faith and works: Place your faith in God and give your works to your neighbor. The spiritual life of the Christian embraces simultaneously the freedom of God's grace and the bondage of the neighbor.[17]

On another level, Lutheranism recognizes that the Christian's spiritual life entails an eternal fellowship with Christ and all the saints that belong in His Church. This Church is the family of God that transcends our space and time reaching also into the heavenly mansions. On earth, this community of faith is scattered, but hidden, throughout the world. But through faith, we confess the presence and fellowship of this eternal Kingdom when we gather together around the proclaimed Gospel and the administered sacraments. The Kingdom of God and its fellowship in the world are both hidden and revealed. They are hidden in terms of *who* all the saints are but revealed in terms of *where* they are, as they gather around their Lord who reveals Himself in His Word, in Holy Absolution, and in His Holy Supper. The spiritual life of the Christian is refreshed continually by this Divine Service of the Lord.

The Cross Life of the Christian Anticipates the Life of Glory

Let's conclude our survey of the Christian's spiritual life by noting some very Lutheran understandings about life in eternity. Many a best-selling Christian author today tries to sell some bible-based principles with promises of a spirituality that mimics old beer commercials. They promise an experience of the Almighty that *just doesn't get any better than this*. They either intentionally lie or have been completely bewitched by some very poor theology. In Heaven, however, it really does get better! Since sin is not a something but rather a corruption or lack of what is good, Heaven and the glorious resurrected new life deliver us from the curse of a spoiled creation and existence. We do not grieve for a departed loved one who dies in the faith; we grieve for ourselves in our loss of that beloved person. Uncle Bob, who has departed this life in the faith, is doing just fine, thank you very much. He has finally arrived at the green pastures beside the still waters. We, however, have been left behind and must continue to struggle here in the valley of the shadow of death for a while longer.

The book of Revelation is especially rich with pictures of Heaven accentuating important things about death valley that are not there. In Heaven, it's what you no longer get that counts a great deal. Listen to the interlude between the sixth and seventh seal in the second vision of John:

Then one of the elders addressed me, saying, "Who are these, clothed in white robes, and from where have they come?" I said to him, "Sir you know." And he said to me, "These are the ones coming out of the great tribulation. They have washed their robes and made them white in the blood of the Lamb."

Therefore they are before the throne of God, and serve him day and night in his temple; and he who sits on the throne will shelter them with his presence. They shall hunger no more, neither thirst anymore; the sun shall not strike them nor any scorching heat. For the Lamb in the midst of the throne will be their shepherd and he will guide them to springs of living water and God will wipe away every tear from their eyes. (Rev. 7:13–17)

It has been a common notion among Christians that the difference between Heaven and Hell and the work of God is that in Heaven God rules with mercy, but Hell is the abode where His justice holds sway. You either eventually receive God's mercy and are saved, or you receive His justice and are damned. Actually, the true picture of Heaven and Hell are in many ways almost the opposite. Heaven is really the only place where the justice of God reigns supreme, while at the same time, ironically, it is the only eternal condition that is patently unfair. Yes! Unfairness is the name of the ethos of Heaven. It absolutely reeks with unfairness. Yet at the same time, Heaven is also where God's justice reigns supreme. Through the justice of God, you get mercy. That is, in God's justice as opposed to ours, everybody gets what they do not deserve. God's execution of justice for the sins of the whole world is found in the universal vicarious atonement of the cross of Christ. The innocent Jesus receives the punishment for all our sins, and we guilty ones get off, scot-free. Through the vicarious sacrifice of the Lamb of God, all bound for Heaven live by undeserved grace—but grace that is through the execution of God's justice, not in spite of it.

It is the will of God that reigns here. Heaven is where God's will is not simply to be done; it *is* done . . . it is all that there is. However, if you will have nothing to do with the bleeding charity of His justice where His will has been done but rather you insist on yours over against His, then Hell is God's consequential provision for you. It is a fiction that Hell is a place where God's justice is meted out against unrepentant sinners. He already executed his justice against all evil and evildoers with His Son on Calvary's cross. Jesus died for all, not simply the repentant (2 Cor. 5:19). Here Luther and Lutheranism part serious company with the Reformed who champion a limited atonement on the cross. All in Hell are both forgiven and justified. They just insist on living separated from these realities and the Author of them. Rather than say to the Lord God, "Thy will be done," the Lord God has said to them, "Thy will be done." In this sense, C. S. Lewis has observed, "The gates of Hell are locked on the inside."[18] Hell is populated with all who insist on their rights and what they deserve . . . and they are willing to die for it.

In Heaven, the corrupted things we suffer from being fallen in a world that is cursed will be no more. What you get is the Lamb Who was slain and in Whose blood you have been washed clean. In Heaven, the Church gets to be finally with her heavenly lover. As the beloved bride of the Heavenly Bridegroom, she is able to throw away the love letters that have been the stuff of her love relationship with Him as all in Christ are brought home and into His everlasting arms forever. What you get in Heaven, in a positive sense, is your new creation heart's desire. What you get in Heaven quite simply is God—your Creator and the Redeemer—and more richly than you have ever known Him or had Him in this life. Cross life has passed away. Spiritual life is now lived out in the glory story . . . forever.

Notes

1. *D. Martin Luthers Werke: Kritische Gesamtausgabe* (Weimar: Hermann Böhlau, 1883), 5.176.32–33 (hereafter cited as WA). The capitals are Luther's.

2. C. S. Lewis, *The Weight of Glory* (New York: Macmillan, 1980), 18.

3. "Thus a Christian life is nothing else than a daily Baptism, once begun and ever to be continued. For we must keep at it incessantly, always purging out what pertains to the old Adam, so that whatever belongs to the new man may come forth." Martin Luther, *The Large Catechism*, 4:65, *The Book of Concord*, trans. Theodore G. Tappert (Philadelphia: Fortress Press, 1959), 445.

4. We make progress by always starting over again in Luther's thinking because of the paradox that, in our Baptism, we have the complete righteousness of Christ yet we are always in need of more. See his discussion of this paradox in his Psalm 4:1, Jaroslav Pelikan and Helmut T. Lehmann, eds., *Luther's Works*, American Edition (Philadelphia: Fortress Press, 1958), 10:53. The American Edition hereafter is cited as AE. It was Luther who refreshed

Western Christian thinking by the rediscovery that God's Word is rightly understood and divided by distinguishing between two different words or ministries of God: Law and Gospel. The Law God uses to accuse and condemn us of our sin and work repentance. The Gospel is God's revelation and bestowal of the saving works and gifts of Christ.

5. Heiko Oberman, *Luther: Man between God and the Devil*, trans. Eileen Walliser-Schwarzbart (New York: Doubleday, Image Books, 1992), 184.

6. This term *salvific worldliness* was first used to describe the character of God's saving work in the world in my essay, "The Outer-Limits of a Lutheran Piety," *Logia* 3, no. 1 (1994): 6.

7. A sermon of Luther's delivered on February 24, 1517, WA 1.138.13–15.

8. M. Luther, *Large Catechism*, 3:106; *Book of Concord*, 434.

9. H. Oberman, *Luther: Man between God and the Devil*, 184.

10. These excellent observations about Luther by Oberman were set forth in Steven A. Hein, "*Tentatio*," *Logia* 10, no. 2 (2001): 2, 33.

11. H. Oberman, *Luther: Man between God and the Devil*, 178–79.

12. This was Luther's term describing what happens when the baptized sinner is united to the crucified Christ. In this union, each gives to the other what he or she has. The sinner gives his or her sin to Christ and Christ in return gives His righteousness to the sinner. This is the *joyous exchange*.

13. This depiction of the bitter/sweet experience of our spiritual life in Christ was first set forth in S. Hein, "*Tentatio*," 34.

14. Luther's best discussion of this tension and *Anfechtung* is found in his *Operationes in Psalmos* (WA 5) and *Luther's Commentary on the First Twenty-Two Psalms*, trans. John Nicholas Lenker (Sunbury, PA.: Lutherans in All Lands, 1903).

15. For a fine examination of the social dimension of Luther's ethics, see the reprinted edition of George Forell's classic work, *Faith Active in Love: An Investigation of the Principles Underlying Luther's Social Ethics* (Eugene, OR: Wipf & Stock, 1999).

16. Quotations from the Bible are taken from the *English Standard Version* (Wheaton, IL: Crossway, 2001).

17. This summarizes the paradoxical character of the Christian's life in one of Luther's early but most profound essays, his *Treatise on Christian Liberty*, better known as *The Freedom of the Christian* (1520). In this essay, Luther put it this way: "A Christian is a perfectly free lord of all, subject to none. A Christian is a perfectly dutiful servant of all, subject to all." AE 31:344. The characterization of Luther's duality as "the freedom of grace and the bondage of the neighbor" was used as the title of my essay, "The Freedom of Grace and the Bondage of the Neighbor," which appears in *A Handbook for Classical Lutheran Education* (Ft. Wayne, IN: Consortium for Classical and Lutheran Education, 2013), 151–57.

18. C. S. Lewis, *The Problem of Pain* (New York: MacMillan, 1962), 127.

CHAPTER 11

The Cultural and Aesthetic Impact of Lutheranism

Angus J. L. Menuge

At the core of Lutheran identity is a profound emphasis on the nature of man—both fallen man and the God-man Jesus Christ. In order to tell the truth about God, we must tell the truth about man. If we minimize our fallen condition, we encourage the delusion that we can do something to make ourselves right with God. But then Christ is no longer recognized as absolutely necessary and sufficient for our salvation (Rom. 3: 20; Eph. 2: 8–9; Heb. 9: 11–12). The fundamental truth that we are enemies of God (Rom. 8: 7), by nature turned in every direction but God's (Rom. 3: 11–12), is the crown of rebellious thorns that frames the pure gift of our beautiful savior.

On this understanding, art and science are not idolatrous attempts to reach up to God—to supplant him with the works of our hands and minds. They are responses to what God has already done in Christ to save us. In gratitude, believing artists and scientists seek to love and serve their neighbor. This is not man offering up his works to God, but God at work in man providing for His people.[1] The artist is set free to tell the truth about man, revealing our desperate and conflicted condition and pointing us to Christ as our only savior. The scientist is set free to tell the truth about nature. The cosmos, like man, is fallen. But the cosmos is not a mute accident: it is the creation of God who still speaks through it. And it is Christ in whom the cosmos, including the scientist, holds together (Col. 1: 17). By attending to Lutheranism's emphasis on realistic anthropology, Christology, and a developed doctrine of vocation, we will see why Lutherans make profound and distinctive contributions to the arts and sciences.

Christ and Culture

A helpful rubric for understanding why Lutheranism differs in its cultural impact from other branches of Christianity is provided by H. Richard Niebuhr's classic work, *Christ and Culture*.[2] Niebuhr distinguishes five types of Christian response to culture, and although his typology is idealized and does not do full justice to every position (including the Lutheran one, which Niebuhr rejects),[3] it does help to highlight the main contrast between a Lutheran response to culture and that typical among Anabaptists, liberal Protestants, Roman Catholics, and the Reformed.

The first two of Niebuhr's types demand an extreme response of rejection or affirmation of culture. Advocates of the "Christ against Culture" approach (such as the Anabaptists) see the works of culture as dangerous obstacles to our devotion to Christ. We must eschew especially the high culture of art and science as sources of idolatry. The result is bare churches and Christians who abandon the world of science to secularism. The idea of carving out a God-pleasing vocation of artist and scientist is rejected in a self-righteous quest of cultural renunciation. By contrast, proponents of the "Christ of Culture" approach (so-called cultural Christianity) recommend the Christian fully embrace the highest cultural achievements of humanity, as if there are no legitimate concerns about possible abuses. The result is that Christians are encouraged to follow ideological fads in the arts and sciences, even if artists suppress the truth about man (e.g., suggesting man is intrinsically good or merely an absurdity) and scientists suppress the truth about nature (e.g., by refusing to consider the evidence of design).

More sophisticated responses realize that both obedience to Christ and a concern for culture need to be taken into account. After all, the same God who saved us in Christ first called us to be stewards of the rest of creation (Gen. 1: 28), converting nature into culture to serve human purposes. This "cultural mandate" implies that our culture-making work in the world is, within lawful boundaries, an act of obedience to God, not an act of rebellion. Yet at the same time, God calls us to work in the world to preserve it as a trust for future generations and to serve our neighbor, so there must be right and wrong ways to transform culture. Thus the three other models Niebuhr discusses mainly disagree about the best way to balance our "horizontal" call to make culture (our call into the world) with our "vertical" call to place God above all things (our call out of the world).

The classical Catholic model of Thomas Aquinas ("Christ above Culture") suggests that the best answer is a grand synthesis of the highest achievements of culture with revealed truth. Aquinas maintained that the Fall had disrupted the supernatural ends of man (we are no longer God oriented), but not our natural ends (so it is still possible for us to serve our neighbor through culture making in this world). In the intellectual sphere, Aquinas thought this meant that the greatest pagan philosophy (especially Aristotle) included useful natural knowledge of man and the world that could be supplemented from above by Christian revelation. Thus to Aristotle's four "cardinal virtues" (prudence, justice, temperance, and courage) available to all men, believers or not, Aquinas added the three theological virtues (faith, hope, and charity), available only to Christians. In the arts, the approach of the Italian Renaissance was to take the highest achievements of classical art and use them to point to God. On this understanding, grace completes a basically sound nature, which promotes the optimistic ideal of the fully integrated "Renaissance man." In the sciences, there was an attempt to combine an Aristotelian metaphysical framework for biology, physics, and cosmology with the latest empirical findings.

Protestants rejected this synthesis model because it did not tell the truth about man or nature. The Fall did not simply disrupt our supernatural ends but marred all our faculties ("total depravity") so that we are liable to misuse even our greatest gifts of creativity and reason to serve ourselves and dishonor God. So our art might portray the Renaissance ideal of man achieving the Greek ideal of human flourishing, yet the reality is that all fall short of the glory of God (Rom. 3: 23) because of our inborn sin (Ps. 51: 5). And our metaphysical preconceptions about how God must govern the world reflect an arrogant and misplaced attempt to anticipate God's actions, when what we need is the humble attempt to find out what He has done. Still, in the approach of the Reformed ("Christ, the Trans-former of Culture"), it was hoped that just as Christ transforms us by the renewing of our mind (Rom. 12: 2), so one could expect Christians to transform culture for the better. One result is an emphasis on distinctly Christian approaches to art and science.

Lutherans share with the Reformed a belief in our total depravity and see as folly any attempt to synthesize the eternal Word of God with the temporal works of our hands. But they are less confident in our ability to "Christianize" a culture that is always falling away from God. Lutherans agree that art and science may, to some extent, reflect scriptural truths about man and nature, but such works are still the result of sinful people who seek to suppress the truth (Rom. 1: 18, 21–23). Christians are indeed transformed by grace, but in this fallen flesh, they are still plagued with sin. Thus in this "Christ and culture in paradox" approach, we are simultaneously saints (because of grace) and sinners (because of our fallen nature). To the extent that God is at work in us, we may produce great art and work that serves our neighbor by telling the truth about man and telling the truth about nature. But God's pure light of grace shines through a flawed prism, and even our best efforts are marred by our sin and limited by our finitude. We can expect some imperfect images of heavenly truth but not the final glories that are God's alone. Yet this paradoxical dynamic, emphasizing God's power and man's weakness, has been the crucible yielding some of the greatest art and science the world has ever seen. It is not the final truth, but it is perhaps as honest an attempt to approximate that goal as man can make with God's help, and so, by confessing its own limitations, it all the more succeeds in pointing to the one alone who is Good, the one alone who is the Way, the Truth and the Life.

Art: Telling the Truth about Man

Art suffers an injustice when we insist that it must tell the truth about God without first confessing the truth about ourselves. The Anabaptists of Luther's time are a prime example. They raged against religious art, seeing it as an idolatrous obstruction to God's pure revelation from above. They correctly pointed out that some people gave their veneration to saints and made superstitious idols of relics and other "holy" devotional artworks. But their response did not focus on the sinful inclinations of the human heart but merely on external objects that some people might abuse. They smashed religious art and denuded churches, but the sinful human heart is quite capable of finding its God-substitutes within the mind—in its own vain desires and imaginings—even without physical symbols. Telling the truth about man means admitting it is not the symbols themselves—physical or mental—that are the issue but our attitude toward God. If the attitude is one of faith in Christ, then a religious symbol is merely a pointer or vehicle for that faith and thus helps believers focus their devotion beyond the symbol itself. On the other hand, if the attitude of the heart is wrong, and a person has a misplaced trust in themselves (Rom. 1: 22) or temporal powers and authorities (Ps. 146: 3), then removing external religious symbols will do nothing to remedy their spiritual condition.

> Luther did not believe that images, whether painted on church walls or planted in human hearts and minds, possessed any intrinsic power to save or damn the human soul. He did believe that man was by nature an unrelenting image-maker, and to that extent religious images helped him to receive and keep his faith. Suppressing the physical images only slammed a door on human nature, which was the surest way to turn previously harmless images into ungodly idols. Taken simply for what they were, religious artworks greatly aided Christian piety wherever they were displayed, and for that reason decorative art remained plentiful and prominent in Protestant churches and Luther's publications.[4]

As it encroached on Wittenberg itself, Luther publicly rejected the Anabaptist ("Christ against Culture") approach: "When Luther's former ally Karlstadt broke images and glass at Wittenberg (1521), Luther came out from his hiding-place at the Wartburg to protest. Next year he preached openly against Karlstadt: we are free to possess images or not."[5]

Luther rejected the Anabaptists' actions because, in their self-righteous attempt to defend God's glory, they did not first examine the depth of their own depravity. Indeed, Luther accused the "iconoclasts of 'internalizing' idols in the heart by physically eradicating

them from the eyes, thereby promoting the truest form of idolatry."[6] After all, any physical image is somewhat resistant to our will,
whereas in our imagination, ideas can be manipulated virtually
without limit to serve our desires. As C. S. Lewis realized, only God
is an effective iconoclast: He will shatter our misconceptions of Him
to reveal Himself to us,[7] and if we attend closely to His Word, that is
where He will do it. Luther's example shows clearly that "the Reformation was not against art *as* art,"[8] and indeed he warmly embraced
the art of Lucas Cranach (1472–1553) as a means of conveying religious truth. Luther and Cranach were so close that they were god-
fathers of each other's children, and Cranach not only provided
woodcuts as illustrations of Lutheran themes but, for a time, published Luther's books and pamphlets, helping spread the message of
the Reformation.[9] Luther also corresponded with the great Albrecht
Dürer (1471–1528), a major admirer of Luther whose work Cranach
closely studied.

Does Luther's enthusiasm for art mean that he fits in the mold
of "Christ of Culture" or "Christ above Culture"? Is he indifferent to
the potential for abuse and deception that art provides? Not at all. In
fact, while accepting that there is no foolproof method for counter-
acting the depravity of the human heart, Luther argued that some
approaches were more beneficial than others, and this is reflected
in some of Cranach's greatest works. Precisely because the natural
man is an inveterate idolater, the Reformers took the view that the
best religious art would be carefully designed to point beyond itself
to God. As one may look through stained glass to the glorious sun
that illuminates it, their art drew the viewer through itself to the one
alone that brings light into the world. "Convinced that an imageless
faith was impossible, a mere 'self-effacing image' became the reformers' goal. By that was meant an image that repudiated both image
worship and iconoclasm by directing the viewer to a transcendent
reality no artwork could ever intrinsically be. What the eyes saw in
religious art was not the divine reality itself, but the engagement of
the viewer's heart and mind in visible, spiritual worship."[10]

In their theological-artistic collaboration, Luther and Cranach
developed what came to be known as the "Wittenberg style." Using
a minimalized, flattened image, the viewer cannot easily take the
earthly subjects portrayed as objects of our final confidence. Rather,

they appear as emblems, illustrations, or emanations of a deeper and higher reality that transcends them all. Thus the images should serve as icons, not idols, that help to raise our thoughts and affections to things above. As man's incompleteness reveals his need for Christ, so art that is self-effacing and intentionally incomplete reveals the greater Artist who stands above the artwork and both artist and audience. Like John the Baptist, the art points beyond itself to the true Lamb of God.

Following Augustine, Luther and Cranach both knew that the Greeks had been mistaken in supposing that man could flourish without God. The Greco-Roman ideal of the "wise man," in whom the virtues had been fully instilled, was revived during the Italian Renaissance, and its product was depictions of otherworldly heroes with anatomically perfect bodies and a nobility of which legends are made. But as St. Paul realized (1 Cor. 1:20–25), this ideal is an unattainable one: it does not tell the truth about what man can become in this life, and to the degree it encourages us to pursue that ideal without Christ, it does not tell the truth about God. Even before Luther developed an explicit, systematic theological understanding of the Christian as saint and sinner, Lucas Cranach had an instinctive grasp of this reality.[11] In his personal life, Cranach knew melancholy, even experiencing what we today call a "midlife" crisis,[12] and he deeply distrusted the idea that the aristocracy was exempt from the troubles that afflicted the commoner.

Cranach's depictions of people were unlike the hero figures of Renaissance art in a number of ways. For one thing, he realized that "ordinary people" were just as valuable as the aristocracy before God, as he fully accepted the Reformation's emphasis on the priesthood of all believers (1 Pet. 2: 9) and on the importance of family life, as monks and nuns were being called out of the cloisters and into marriage. But he also realized that the spiritual condition of man had universal dimensions, and so when he turned to aristocratic figures, his goal was to humanize them, to show that they too were flawed and frail reeds. In his portraits, there is "a sympathetic demythologizing of the educated and the privileged . . . of people like Cranach himself. Despite their learnings and earnings . . . the beautiful people, when closely observed, are no less vulnerable to the threats of nature and the whims of fates than are the needy, simple folk."[13]

Cranach, like Luther, saw that each human soul is the battleground of spiritual warfare and that discontent, melancholy, and depression can afflict even the cultured Christian. For Luther and Cranach, this portrait of man is true both because it is scriptural (Rom. 7) and because it captures life as we live it. For both men, theology is not merely a matter of learning and disputation but a lived dialectic, so that the mind that is opened to the scriptures discerns how true to life they are.

So in Cranach and Luther, we do not see a triumphalist emphasis on transforming the Christian (Christ the Transformer of Culture) but a more cautious depiction of the new life in Christ struggling with the Old Adam. From this, we can appreciate Cranach's portrait *Sibutus* (1511): "In the tormented face and the searching hands of the famous orator the viewer beholds only *Angst*. . . . Although a wondrous creature, man remains inconstant and unreliable, unsure of what he wants and stymied when he gets it, altogether his own worst enemy and by no means any prescient, Renaissance 'lord of all.'"[14]

Yet this apparent pessimism about the human condition is balanced by supreme confidence in the work of Christ. Just because we are powerless to save ourselves, and Christ has done it all, we no longer see our works as helping to save us but only as responses in gratitude to God that serve our neighbor. Thus in Cranach's masterpiece, *The Schleissheim Crucifixion* (1503), Christ dominates the foreground, "packaged and bound up with the most perfect bow-ribbon loincloth . . . a redemptive gift of salvation laid out appealingly for the viewer."[15]

Since it is our neighbor's need that drives vocation, Lutheran artists realize that their main concerns are to be competent in their techniques and faithful in their goals. It is sometimes claimed that Lucas Cranach does not qualify as an artist of the first rank because he so closely followed the work of his great contemporary, Albrecht Dürer. In fact, Cranach studied (and initially imitated) Dürer's work because, as an apprentice, he was humbling himself to learn the very best available techniques. Yet not only did Cranach strive to better his master; he also used his newfound skills in the service of different ends. "Cranach . . . seized upon Dürer artworks because they were the best of the time and Cranach never doubted he could make them better."[16]

Figure 1. Lucas Cranach the Elder, *The Schleissheim Crucifixion* (1503), http://commons.wikimedia.org/wiki/File:Lucas_Cranach_d.%C3%84._-_Klage_unter_dem_Kreuz_%28Alte_Pinakothek%29.jpg.

In particular, with his focus on the human predicament and on the importance of family life, Cranach's "own talents and personal interests were directed to the Reformation's *second* front, its moral-secular, domestic-social agenda rather than the theological-ecclesiastical battles."[17] For example, Cranach appropriated and redirected a popular image in Germany at the time, the holy kinship, which depicted the extended family of Jesus descending from Mary's mother, St. Anne. Cranach's first work on this topic (also known as

Figure 2.   Lucas Cranach the Elder, *The Holy Kinship with a Self-Portrait,* http://www .wga.hu/support/viewer/z.html.

The Torgau Altarpiece [1509]) innovates by making the human figures much larger than in his previous work, thereby elevating and ennobling the family. In a later version including a self-portrait (1510–12), he replaces the saints with a self-portrait and includes his wife and in-laws. This suggests the profound theological truth that through grace, we are all adopted sons and daughters of God (Gal. 4: 1–7). It is also a wonderful way of saying that God's Word is for us: it is to be realized in the here and now of our ordinary life on earth and not only in the eternal hereafter. Both versions notably include books, reinforcing the central Reformation insight that the church can be preserved from doctrinal corruption only if the laity can read the scripture for themselves. Indeed, even the first version of *The Holy Kinship* was offered in the form of a souvenir print with the clear goal of promoting the family as the center of religious education.[18]

Taking Cranach as its leading representative, the distinctively Lutheran contribution to art involves dedication to competence (learning the very best techniques of production) and service (using those techniques to meet our neighbors' need to know the full truth about themselves in relation to God). It builds up the family as the primary building block for both church and society, ennobles the vocations of ordinary life, and supports the church by revealing our need for the Gospel. Here one finds neither the triumphalism nor the nihilism of modern art, where artists lurch between narcissistic self-preoccupation and cynical debasement and transgression of all boundaries. The idea that honest self-expression is necessarily "authentic" and valuable is rejected, because it may only reflect our sinful self-deception: the blind leading the blind. Like Blaise Pascal (1623–62), the Lutheran artist reveals man as both much more wretched and yet much greater than modern and postmodern minds can comprehend: "What sort of freak then is man! How novel, how monstrous, how chaotic, how paradoxical, how prodigious! Judge of all things, feeble earthworm, repository of truth, sink of doubt and error, glory and refuse of the universe! . . . Know then, proud man, what a paradox you are to yourself."[19]

Pascal saw what Luther and Cranach had earlier seen. Man is wretched because, contrary to the Greco-Roman and Renaissance ideal, he inevitably falls short of the standards intended for him: he does not, and cannot, flourish as he was originally meant to do. Yet herein lies his greatness, for this enables man to see that he needs

Christ and that only in him can he find healing from sin and the wholeness and community for which he was made. Christ is the wise man we seek, for he is the wisdom of God (1 Cor. 1: 24). By telling the truth about man, the Lutheran approach to art also tells the truth about the God-man Jesus Christ.

Science: Telling the Truth about Nature

If we apply Niebuhr's fivefold typology to science, we see important parallels with Christian engagement with art. For the "Christ against Culture" school, science is viewed with suspicion because its theories and laws can so easily become idols of the mind, undermining allegiance to the scriptures and Christ's Lordship. We see expressions of this attitude today in some Bible colleges that would rather not explore ideas that might trouble some students, such as cosmology and neo-Darwinian evolution. At the other extreme, we find cultural Christians who adopt an uncritical "me too" attitude, according to which the scriptures and Christian doctrine can always be reinterpreted, modified, or even discarded, so that there is no tension between the faith and the latest scientific claims and discoveries.

Sadly lacking in all this is serious reflection on the distinctive nature of general and special revelation. Going back at least as far as Augustine,[20] theologians have made a distinction between God's two "books": the book of God's Word (Holy Scripture) and the book of God's world (the book of nature). The book of nature reveals to us the existence of God and some of His attributes (Rom. 1: 18–20; Psalm 19: 1–2), but it does not tell us who God is or how man can be saved from sin. God's plan of salvation is revealed only in the scriptural portrait of Christ. So God provides two complementary books, one that tells us *of* Him, another that introduces us *to* Him. Thus there can be no question of simply rejecting the study of nature in favor of scripture, for that is to close our eyes to one dimension of God's self-revelation. But it also does not make sense simply to embrace anything man says about nature without considering whether it coheres with special revelation. This is because God's twin revelations are not equals in authority or epistemic status. A scientific theory is a man-made construct that attempts to make sense of God's creation using finite, fallen reason. Such a theory is not only fallible, but it can at best provide a model of a contingent, temporal reality. It does not and cannot contain the ultimate and eternal truth of God. For as Jesus says, "Heaven and earth will pass away, but my words will not pass away" (Mt. 24: 35, ESV). God's Word contains final and ultimate truth about the nature of reality that science is incapable of providing.

The hard question, therefore, is, given God's dual revelation, and given the supreme status of scripture, how should the Christian scientist understand the proper relationship between the two revelations? It turns out that getting this wrong is bad for both theology and science, while getting it right develops a stimulating and productive partnership that benefits them both.

The classical Roman Catholic approach to this question is epitomized by Thomas Aquinas's grand synthesis of Aristotelian thought with scriptural doctrine. It is important to emphasize that historically, "philosophy" included not only the metaphysics, epistemology, and ethics still called philosophy today but also early examples of natural science, including physics, cosmology, and biology. Thus a consequence of the Thomistic synthesis was the assumption that the Aristotelian framework was a solid basis for investigating the natural world. But this synthesis is objectionable on both theological and scientific grounds, as became especially clear during the Reformation.

Theologically, synthesis is an inappropriate model because it means that fallible constructs of man with only temporal validity are implicitly given the same status as the infallible, eternally valid Word of God. As Niebuhr famously warned, such an approach tends to promote a dual error, "the absolutization of what is relative" and "the reduction of the infinite to a finite form."[21] On the one hand, scientific theory is confused with ultimate truth, and on the other hand, the ultimate truth of scripture is relativized to agree with accepted scientific thought. The trouble is that the history of science is largely the story of abandoning theories recognized as inadequate. Marrying theology to any given scientific paradigm thus creates reactionary pressure to retain the paradigm in the face of conflicting data and may frustrate or delay scientific progress. What is more, when that progress eventually occurs, the impression is given that since the church cannot be trusted in its scientific pronouncements, its theology is also suspect.

Two examples of such an inappropriate and ill-fated marriage between theology and science are provided by the overenthusiastic endorsement of Aristotelian cosmology and of contemporary evolutionary theory. For Aristotle, the Earth was a central, stationary platform,[22] surrounded by crystalline spheres of the planets and fixed stars. It was assumed that the heavens were a perfect realm of uniform circular motion while the sublunar realm of the Earth was the domain of corruption and decay. Then Nicolaus Copernicus (1473–1543) challenged the idea that the Earth was stationary by proposing a heliocentric system, in which the Earth is one of many planets orbiting the Sun. And Tycho Brahe (1546–1601), a Lutheran astronomer, realized that the Greeks had also been wrong in their claims about the heavens: comets have erratic paths (not uniform circular motion) and pass between the planets (so the crystalline spheres cannot exist). Galileo Galilei (1564–1642) provided further evidence to support the Copernican system, arguing that relative motion would explain why the Earth seems stationary and using his telescopes to discover the moons of Jupiter (which show that our solar system has more than one axis of rotation and that moons can travel with a planet) and the phases of Venus (which are easily explained if Venus orbits the Sun).

These discoveries created embarrassment for the Catholic Church because it had bought so heavily into the Aristotelian system. To be fair, the evidence available at the time did not decisively favor the Copernican system, since there was no convincing demonstration of the Earth's motion, and some of the best Catholic theologians were open to the new scientific ideas: they were aware that scriptural texts suggesting a stationary Earth might simply reflect an Earthbound perspective and that scientific theories can be useful models for making predictions even if their account of underlying realities is mistaken. But the fact remains that the Catholic church had found the Aristotelian system only too useful in propagating its views of hierarchical authority in church and state. This is because in Aristotle's system, the stars, planets, and the Earth know their place and follow a prescribed path, which was interpreted as an image of how each person should fulfill his or her function in both the ecclesial and civil spheres: "The reason some churchmen resisted giving up Aristotelian physics and cosmology was because these were intimately tied to an overall vision of moral and social life. If that tie were broken, they feared morality itself would be destroyed."[23]

While Galileo's house "arrest" sounds frankly pleasant to many time-strapped scholars and his *Dialogue Concerning the Two Chief World Systems* was indisputably tactless,[24] banning the book remains an embarrassment for scientifically minded Christians and a stumbling block for unbelievers that reflects the danger of tying Christian thought (in this case, sociopolitical and ethical ideas) too closely to a dominant scientific paradigm.

The same mistake has been repeated in the modern era by attempts to reconcile Christian doctrine with Darwinian evolution. The result of these misguided efforts has been versions of "theistic evolution," which either misrepresent what the scientific theories are saying or compromise important Christian doctrines (or both). The trouble with saying that God might guide the Darwinian process in order to create is that Darwinian natural selection is by definition an *unguided* causal process. Thus the renowned evolutionary biologist Ernst Mayr explains, "Darwinism rejects all supernatural phenomena and causations. The theory of evolution by natural selection explains the adaptedness and diversity of the world solely materialistically."[25]

But materialistic causes reduce either to chance or necessity, neither of which is guided. So appeal to guided evolution offers only the appearance of making peace with Darwin, not the reality. It also follows that if one fully embraces the Darwinian model, then God's providence is unreal (since even God cannot intentionally act through wholly unintended means) and there is no natural knowledge of God (since God cannot communicate to us through nature if nature is not a vehicle of His intentions). Sophisticated attempts to avoid these difficulties generally result either in a version of Darwinism that Darwinists reject or reinterpretations of providence and the natural knowledge of God that simply are not what biblical theologians have ever meant by these doctrines. The Darwinian circle cannot be squared by scripture.

Besides this, there is something mistaken in principle in supposing that the scientific method excludes the idea of design. If in fact, as Kepler believed, the cosmos is comprehensible only because it reflects God's providential design, then refusing to consider evidence that points to that conclusion will inevitably result in a universe that does not make sense. As the great Lutheran rocket scientist Wernher von Braun (1912–77) said in a famous letter to the California State Board of Education,

> To be forced to believe only one conclusion—that everything in the universe happened by chance—would violate the very objectivity of science itself. . . . What random process could produce the brains of a man or the system of the human eye? . . . What strange rationale makes some physicists accept the inconceivable electron as real while refusing to accept the reality of a Designer on the ground that they cannot conceive Him? . . . It is in scientific honesty that I endorse the presentation of alternative theories for the origin of the universe, life, and man in the science classroom. It would be an error to overlook the possibility that the universe was planned rather than happening by chance.[26]

If we are to take the supreme authority of scripture seriously and do not wish to marry it to any worldly scientific theory, would it be better to follow the Reformed path, to transform and "redeem" the science so that it reflects Christian truth? This sounds appealing until one realizes that this is the effort to finally clean up just one in a sequence of manmade constructs. It is a bit like waxing a car that will be on the scrapheap tomorrow: just what is the point of trying to mummify what by its nature is passing away? And the problem, too, is that the Christian is still infected by sin and attempts to "Christian-ize" science once and for all run the risk of falsifying the science or compromising theology to bring the two into a harmonious relation. Like the synthesis model, the transformation model is apt to absolu-tize the relative or to reduce the infinite to the finite. Thus in its worst abuses, the transformation approach tries to use science, not merely to support, but to *prove* Christian doctrines or bible passages, and in the process, the science often turns out to be suspect or outdated and the interpretation of doctrine or scripture to be wooden, ignoring a profound eternal truth in order to turn the bible into a science man-ual it does not claim to be.

As against all this, the Lutheran "paradox" model has clear advantages, as can be seen both theoretically and in its historical con-tribution to the rise of modern science. The Lutheran understanding of cultural engagement is by nature multidimensional, recognizing the claims of both the eternal and the temporal.

Even the Christian scientist can hope at best to find penultimate approximations to ultimate truth, models limited by their temporal validity and the limited understanding of our fallen, finite minds. We are saints on account of Christ's work and God's declaration of innocence, but that does not change the fact that sin infects all our efforts, including the effort to understand the natural world. So the Lutheran posture toward science encourages neither synthesis nor transformation. Instead, standing on God's eternal and infallible Word and with confidence only in Christ, the Lutheran engages in a critical dialogue with the world's scientific theories. Rather than viewing them as either sources of ultimate truth or satanic idolatry, the Lutheran posture is to sift these theories to discover ways in which they may glorify God and serve our neighbor. They may provide evidence, not proof, that God is at work, and they may help us to provide technologies and remedies for our neighbor, even if they also contain erroneous assumptions. Thus no theory, however controversial, is simply rejected or ignored without a careful consideration of its merits, and no theory, no matter how widely accepted, is simply embraced as the last word on the matter.

This approach is admirably displayed in the distinctively Lutheran approach to astronomy. It has often been claimed that Luther opposed scientific innovation, in large part because of a comment attributed to him in *Table Talk*[27] about a "certain new astrologer who wants to prove that the earth moves": Luther allegedly complains that in Joshua 10: 12–14, it is the Sun, not the Earth, that the Lord commands to stand still. However, as John Warwick Montgomery shows, there are multiple problems with this attempt to discredit Luther's attitude toward science.[28] Most telling are the facts that Luther's remarks were informal, do not name Copernicus, and precede the publication of Copernicus's work by four years and that, after its appearance, Luther never made a single critical comment about the theory. Like the best Catholic theologians, Luther was aware that scripture reports events as they appear from our perspective, a point reiterated by the great Lutheran astronomer Johannes Kepler (1571–1630): "Now the holy scriptures . . . when treating common things (concerning which it is not their purpose to instruct humanity), speak with humans in the human manner, in order to be understood by them. . . . Joshua meant that the sun should be held back in its place in the sky for an entire day with respect to the sense of his eyes, since for other people during the same interval of time it would remain beneath the earth. . . . For the gist of Joshua's petition comes to this, that it might appear so to him."[29]

In addition, a widely held view of the time was scientific instrumentalism—the view that the best way to view scientific theories was as mathematical instruments for calculating observed effects—allowing one to remain agnostic about these theories' apparent ontological implications.

Perhaps most telling are the facts that, with Luther's full approval, the Wittenberg astronomers were pivotal in the publication of Copernicus's *De Revolutionibus Orbium Coelestium* (*On the Revolutions of the Celestial Spheres*) and were allowed to study its implications and to teach it without interference or censure. It was Georg Joachim Rheticus (1514–74), the Wittenberg mathematics professor hired by Melanchthon, who visited Copernicus in 1539, summarized the work and eventually had it published under Copernicus's name just before Copernicus's death in 1543.[30] Andreas Osiander (1498–1552), the Lutheran theologian, was asked to supervise the actual printing of the volume and is often castigated for adding an unsigned letter as a preface, where, contrary to Copernicus's own view that his theory portrays objectively reality, Osiander claims that it is a mathematical model that does not aim to disclose the "true causes of these movements" but only to provide a "calculus which fits the observations."[31] However, Osiander is merely expressing the standard Wittenberg interpretation of the Copernican system—an attitude of scientific instrumentalism—which was held both by Rheticus and his Wittenberg colleague, Erasmus Reinhold (1511–53). Given the lack of convincing proof that the Copernican model was correct and its obvious mathematical value, this open-minded, cautious posture finds an admirable balance between uncritical acceptance and blank rejection of a controversial idea. If it seems overly cautious to us today, that may be because we read history with the benefit of later scientific advances and because we too easily think our current perspectives cannot be as erroneous as Aristotelian cosmology turned out to be.

Not only were Lutherans open to and supportive of the scientific innovations of others, they also made important contributions of their own. We already saw how the Lutheran astronomer Tycho Brahe discredited important planks of Aristotelian cosmology, and it was his meticulous tabulation of astronomical data that allowed Johannes Kepler to make further progress, showing that the planetary orbits are elliptical and that their velocity is inversely proportional to their distance from the Sun. Here it is vital to see that Kepler's scientific work was guided by his theological convictions. Kepler had trained for the ministry but due to some confessional reservations decided instead to apply his considerable mathematical gifts to the study of astronomy. At first, he was concerned that natural science was not a God-pleasing vocation, since at the time, the Catholic teaching of the estate of the clergy suggested that the only proper callings from God were out of the world and into the monastery or the church. However, the Reformers emphasized the priesthood of all believers (1 Pet. 2: 9), and this, combined with the idea that nature was God's other book, enabled Kepler to see himself as a priest in the book of nature.[32] With both books open, and realizing the supremacy of Scripture, Kepler's study of the book of nature was guided by his prior acceptance of the biblical teaching of providence.

Kepler believed that God provided for his creation through mathematical laws, a reflection of the divine logos, and that, as creatures made in the image of God, this same logos was reflected in the natural light of human rationality. Thus he expected nature to be governed by universal laws of nature and that our mind was attuned to the discovery of those laws. When Kepler derived his three laws of planetary motion from the data provided by Brahe, he confidently believed that "he had discovered the part of God's providential plan that embodies the pattern of the cosmos, and the divine laws by which God regulated its moving parts."[33] Elsewhere, Kepler says his hope is to disclose God's cause and plan for creating the world.[34]

To be sure, Kepler went too far in suggesting that the five Platonic solids could be used to determine the spacing of the six known planets. But while the conviction that God orders the cosmos in a rationally comprehensible way was insufficient to guarantee the accuracy of Kepler's model, it did inspire him to make significant improvements to the Copernican system. (Copernicus still believed in epicycles, equant points, and exclusively circular planetary motion.) The ideal Lutheran attitude to science, whether or not any scientist has ever achieved it, is a combination of confidence in the existence of coherent truth and modesty about our ability to discern it.[35] Scientists should be confident because they stand on Christ as foundation, and he is the same yesterday, today, and forever (Heb. 13: 8). Thus there is nothing scientists have to do to make themselves or the world secure, and so, realizing their finitude and sin, they can be modest about the significance of their work. They are set free to do *the best they can* to discern God's work in the world for His glory and the neighbor's service.

Kepler clearly understood what it meant to glorify God through science, describing his investigations as "true worship" in God's other "temple."[36] Indeed, Kepler was apt to adorn his scientific works with doxology, ending his work, *Harmony of the World*, as follows: "I thank Thee, O Lord, our Creator, that Thou hast permitted me to look at the beauty in Thy work of creation; I exult in the works of Thy hands." Kepler completes the same passage with a clear sense of his calling to serve others through science: "See, I have here completed the work to which I felt called. . . . I have proclaimed the glory of Thy works to the people who will read these demonstrations, to the extent that the limitations of my spirit would allow."[37]

Since scientists are called to serve their neighbor in the here and now, they do not need final answers that science is incapable of providing. All the more can they maintain a healthy critical distance, sifting ideas to find those that are the best currently available while accepting none as ultimate truth. Dreams of a final scientific theory are just that—dreams.[38] For the Christian scientist, these dreams are like Cranach's art: merely images of the beatific vision in which at last we have that complete knowledge that eludes us due to our incompleteness and sin: "For now we see in a mirror dimly, but then face to face. Now I know in part; then I shall know fully, even as I have been fully known" (1 Cor. 13: 12, ESV).

Lutheranism: Telling the Truth about Christ

So why does the Reformation matter? Mainly because it shows Christ alone as savior. It does this by telling the truth about man's sinful, conflicted condition, and this truth about man is a powerful impetus to great art. This art shocks not by the gratuitous transgression of modern art but by exposing the reality behind our self-righteous self-deception. But it gives hope not by calling attention to a prima donna artist but by a self-effacing style that draws the mind through the work to Christ as Lord. This same Christ is not only calling us beyond the world to God the Father; He is also actively present in the world. He is the *logos* running through and holding creation together, so that in studying the natural world, one can, without idolatry, worship the God who made it and even now sustains it. Why is the Lutheran contribution to art and science so great? Because it transcends both art and artist, both science and scientist, and it discloses Christ at work throughout reality: "For the whole Christ, body and spirit is present throughout the universe today. . . . [J]ust as God is everywhere, so the God-man Jesus Christ is everywhere, displaying his grace and love."[39]

Let us pray that the artists and scientists of today are drawn by the Holy Spirit to see their work as a worshipful vocation, telling the truth about man and the truth about nature in order to tell the truth about Christ.

Notes

1. See Gene Edward Veith, *God at Work: Your Christian Vocation in All of Life* (Wheaton, IL: Crossway Books, 2011).

2. H. Richard Niebuhr, *Christ and Culture* (New York: Harper and Row, 1951).

3. See critical essays by Angus Menuge, Robert Kolb, and Gene Edward Veith in Angus Menuge, ed., *Christ and Culture in Dialogue* (St. Louis, MO: Concordia Academic Press, 1999).

4. Steven Ozment, *The Serpent and the Lamb: Cranach, Luther, and the Making of the Reformation* (New Haven, CT: Yale University Press, 2011), 133.

5. G. G. Coulton, *Art and the Reformation* (Cambridge: Cambridge University Press, 1928), 411–12.

6. Ozment, *The Serpent and the Lamb*, 138.

7. C. S. Lewis, *A Grief Observed* (New York: Bantam, 1976).

8. Francis A. Schaeffer, *How Should We Then Live? The Rise and Decline of Western Thought and Culture* (Old Tappan, NJ: Fleming H. Revell, 1976), 89.

9. Ozment, *The Serpent and the Lamb*, 107–8.

10. Ibid., 134.

11. Ibid., 56.

12. Ibid., 79.

13. Ibid., 51.

14. Ibid., 83–84.

15. Ibid., 44.

16. Ibid., 66.

17. Ibid., 80.

18. Bonnie Noble, *Lucas Cranach the Elder: Art and Devotion of the German Reformation* (Lanham, MD: University Press of America, 2009), 170–73.

19. Blaise Pascal, *Pensées*, trans. A. J. Krailsheimer (New York: Penguin Books, 1966), no. 131, 64.

20. Rebutting the Manichaeans and arguing that nature is essentially good despite its fallen condition, Augustine said, "But had you begun with looking on the book of nature as the production of the Creator of all . . . you would not have been led into these impious follies and blasphemous fancies with which, in your ignorance of what evil really is, you heap all evils upon God" (St. Augustine, *Contra Faustum Manichaeum*, 32.20, in *Nicene and Post-Nicene Fathers*, ser. 1, vol. 4, ed. Philip Schaff [Grand Rapids, MI: Christian Classics Ethereal Library], http://www.ccel.org/ccel/schaff/npnf104.pdf, 583). Origen had anticipated this view by maintaining that the natural world is full of symbols, suggesting a text that might be read. See the eminent historian of science Peter Harrison's "The Bible and the Emergence of Modern Science," http://www.st-edmunds.cam.ac.uk/cis/harrison/Peter%20Harrison%20-%20lecture.htm.

21. Niebuhr, *Christ and Culture*, 145.

22. Contrary to urban legend, Aristotle did know that the Earth was round because he realized that it was the rounded shadow of the Earth that explained the crescent phases of the moon.

23. Nancy Pearcey and Charles B. Thaxton, *The Soul of Science: Christian Faith and Natural Philosophy* (Wheaton, IL: Crossway Books, 1994), 39.

24. Galileo invents the figure Simplicio, who defends the geocentric paradigm and who may easily be taken as a spokesman for the views of Pope Urban VIII.

25. Ernst Mayr, "Darwin's Influence on Modern Thought," *Scientific American*, July 2000, 82–83.

26. Wernher von Braun, "Letter to the California State Board of Education," September 14, 1972, http://www.sandiegoreader.com/news/2012/jul/18/excerpt-letter-california-state-board-education/#ixzz2gIzeLOUT.

27. Theodore G. Tappert, ed., *Luther's Works*, vol. 54, *Table Talk* (Minneapolis, MN: Augsburg Fortress, 1967), 4638.

28. John Warwick Montgomery, "Luther and Science," *In Defense of Martin Luther* (Milwaukee, WI: Northwestern Publishing House, 1970), 87–114.

29. William H. Donohue, ed., *Selections from Kepler's* Astronomia Nova (Santa Fe, NM: Green Lion Press, 2008), 19–20.

30. Peter Barker, "Astronomy, Providence, and the Lutheran Contribution to Science," in *Reading God's World: The Scientific Vocation*, ed. Angus Menuge (St. Louis, MO: Concordia Publishing House, 2004), 168–69.

31. Andreas Osiander, "The Unsigned Letter," in *Philosophy of Science: An Historical Introduction*, ed. Timothy McGrew, Marc Alspector Kelly, and Fritz Alhoff (Malden, MA: Wiley-Blackwell, 2009), 110.

32. See Peter Harrison, "Priests of the Most High God, with Respect to the Book of Nature," in *Reading God's World: The Scientific Vocation*, ed. Angus Menuge (St. Louis, MO: Concordia Publishing House, 2004), 59–84.

33. Peter Barker and Bernard Goldstein, "Theological Foundations of Kepler's Astronomy," *Osiris* 16 (2001): 113.

34. See Barker, "Astronomy, Providence, and the Lutheran Contribution to Science," 157–87.

35. For a development of this idea, see Nathan Jastram, "Scientists Called to Be Like God," and Kurt Marquart, "Science: Sacred Cow or Sacred Calling?," both in *Reading God's World: The Scientific Vocation*, ed. Angus Menuge (St. Louis, MO: Concordia Publishing House, 2004), 243–69, 271–94.

36. Harrison, "Priests of the Most High God, with Respect to the Book of Nature," 70.

37. Johannes Kepler, quoted in Montgomery, "Luther and Science," 99.

38. The atheist cosmologist Steven Weinberg explores the idea of a final physics in his *Dreams of a Final Theory* (New York: Vintage Books, 1994).

39. Montgomery, "Luther and Science," 93.

CHAPTER 12

Conclusion

Where Does One Go from Here?

John Warwick Montgomery

The chapters of this book have presented a churchmanship quite different from that with which the majority of readers will have been acquainted. The advantages of the Lutheran theology and worldview should now be quite plain. So what does one do about it?

If one is still troubled by particular Lutheran teachings, the obvious solution is to read more fully on the subject (see the recommended readings at the end of this book) or consult well-trained Lutheran pastors—or both. At very worst, one may gain by aligning one's existing theology and ecclesiastical style as far as possible with the solidity of the Lutheran approach.[1] But if one has become convinced of the value of the Lutheran option, one needs to act on it. Agnosticism—whether in general or on particular issues—must never be a resting place. If it is used as an excuse for not making a decision, agnosticism becomes a contradiction in terms—a decision not to make a decision![2]

Assuming that one now wishes to dive in at the deep end, the best plan is to attend services at local Lutheran churches. But here one must be careful. There are two major (and some minor) Lutheran denominations in the United States and in other countries where Lutherans worship. These may be described (fairly superficially, it is true) as "conservative" versus "liberal."

To be sure, since the Lutheran position is the most theologically serious of Protestant belief systems—centering as it does on
the Cross of Christ and salvation by grace alone, through faith
alone, and deriving from the Scriptures alone—a liberal Lutheran
is often the equivalent of a conservative Methodist or conservative
member of the United Church of Christ! That is to say, the spread
from conservative to liberal in Lutheranism is much narrower than
found in most mainline church bodies today. Lutherans, in general,
are conservative in their beliefs and church practices, following
Luther's concern to remove from church teaching and practice only
that which is prohibited by Scripture—as opposed to the Zwinglian
notion that one discards everything in church tradition that is not
expressly mandated in the Bible.

Having said this, however, it is important to recognize that the
"liberal" Lutheran denominations have made significant concessions
to the secular culture, and these color negatively the effectiveness of
their gospel preaching and activities. Thus the Evangelical Lutheran
Church in America (ELCA) has entered into pulpit and altar fellowship with the mainline Episcopal Church in the United States
of America (ECUSA), the Presbyterian Church (USA), the United
Church of Christ, and the United Methodists, thus aligning with the
most liberal of the mainline Protestants and gliding over important
theological differences. In addition, the ELCA now ordains women
to the pastoral ministry and allows for clergy who are practicing
homosexuals—in stark contrast with the classical Lutheran (and
Christian) tradition.[3]

Our strong advice is to do one's church hunting among the conservative Lutheran bodies—the Lutheran Church–Missouri Synod
(the largest and most influential of the conservative Lutheran denominations), the Wisconsin Synod, the Evangelical Lutheran Synod, or
the smaller Lutheran church bodies that, in recent years, have come
into existence through splits from the ELCA in disagreement over
what are regarded as unscriptural deviations from classic Lutheran
teaching and practice.

The problem with liberal Lutheranism is not unique; its difficulties are the same as are met with in all liberal denominations
and local (often designated "ecumenical") community churches. As
I have discussed in extenso elsewhere,[4] the heart of the problem is

the underlying liberal fallacy that to impact a secular society the church needs to secularize its beliefs to fit the ideological environment. Is the society moving to accept homosexual practices? Then one needs to twist Scripture to allow such in the church. Is women's liberation the flavor of the day? Then one must allow the ordination of women to the pastoral ministry. Does the culture buy Darwinian evolution? Then the church (regardless of Gen. 1–3) ought to modify its theology to accord with that philosophical orientation.

What one encounters here is the slippery slope. Secular culture believes in self-salvation and refuses to face the fact of sin—violation of the will of the righteous Creator of the universe. The secularist therefore has no reason to take seriously the redemptive work of Christ on the Cross (no sin, no need to be saved). When one begins modifying biblical teaching to fit a secular mold, there is no stopping the process. It will inevitably destroy the very gospel itself.

And, indeed, this has been the history of every mainline church body that has jumped on the liberal theological bandwagon. The Presbyterian Church (U.S.A.) was once a bastion of biblical orthodoxy; now it is but a pale reflection of what it once was, with no serious regard for the *Westminster Confession of Faith* or the other fundamental Calvinist creeds. The Methodist Church today would cause John Wesley to turn over in his grave: social action has swallowed up the evangelistic fervor that made that church one of the most powerful factors in the American Great Awakening.

When a church body no longer accepts the Bible as "inerrant"—as fully true and the sole means by which God's will can be discerned and His message to mankind set forth—theology becomes little more than a cultural phenomenon. Secular pressures are always present, so all of the denomination's beliefs become subject to the flux of human opinion. God's truth goes begging.

And the concrete results are not hard to perceive. The mainline liberal churches continually decline in membership, only seeming statistically to be thriving because of ecumenical unions among them. Why is this so? Because people seeking a meaningful religious home are offered nothing but the miseries of secularism dressed up as religion. A church that is little more than a Rotary or Elks Club with religious trappings is not an attractive option for those seeking religious answers in a lost, often tragic world. It is axiomatic that the more a denomination takes the Bible seriously, the more attractive it becomes to the seeker.

So our advice is not to begin one's search for a Lutheran church home in liberal Lutheran circles. But what about problems in the conservative Lutheran framework?

Sometimes one finds a local Lutheran church where, though the great Lutheran theological tradition is officially held, the atmosphere is such that the advantages seem outweighed by the disadvantages. Here are some examples: A church where, instead of the classical liturgy and great music, all has been cheapened by an effort to duplicate evangelical, gospel-song styles and "church growth" gimmicks. Or a church where conservative theology has somehow been transmuted into reactionary social policies (refusal to engage in any cooperative evangelistic outreach with biblically conservative but non-Lutheran churches or with evangelists such as Billy Graham who are not Lutherans themselves). Or a church where the ethnic has somehow overwhelmed the theological (old Germans or Scandinavians who see the local church as an extension of and a refuge for their family backgrounds and traditions).[5]

What then? There are only three possibilities if no better Lutheran parish can be found, since Scripture requires us to engage in regular, communal worship (Heb. 10:25): (1) Join the problematic congregation and help to change its perspective. However, *that* can be unrealistic, especially for a new member. (2) Ignore the negative aspects of the situation and focus on the positive—the preaching of the biblical gospel. Fine advice, but often psychologically or sociologically impractical. (3) Go to a non-Lutheran church that most closely approximates the Lutheran ideal in beliefs and practices.

A word about this third solution. Admittedly, such a recourse must be classed as a lesser of evils. But ours is a sinful world in which ecclesiastical perfection is not to be found anywhere. Moreover, the name attached to a church is not the most important thing. As the great Lutheran confessional standard, the Augsburg Confession, has it (Art. 7), the church exists wherever "the Gospel is preached in its purity and the holy sacraments are administered according to the Gospel." It may be that under certain messy social conditions, a church not having the Lutheran name may be more Lutheran (in the theological sense) than churches declaring themselves to be such.

But with the diversity in American culture (likewise in other Western nations today), it is rare if one cannot find a Lutheran church where the great advantages of that grand theological tradition are not present. As nineteenth-century Danish Lutheran pastor Nicolai Grundtvig put it,

> Built on the Rock the Church doth stand,
> Even when steeples are falling;
> Crumbled have spires in ev'ry land,
> Bells still are chiming and calling—
> Calling the young and old to rest,
> Calling the souls of those distressed,
> Longing for life everlasting.
> Here stands the font before our eyes
> Telling how God did receive us;
> Th' altar recalls Christ's sacrifice
> And what His table doth give us;
> Here sounds the Word that doth proclaim
> Christ yesterday, today, the same,
> Yea, and for aye our Redeemer.[6]

Notes

1. As mentioned in the introduction (chapter 1), Walter R. Martin, while remaining a Baptist, benefited from Lutheran belief in the sacramental character of the Lord's Supper and the Christocentric focus of Lutheran systematic theology. We have known many Anglicans who are de facto (though not de jure) Lutherans in their central theological beliefs.

2. Cf. John Warwick Montgomery, "Is Man His Own God?," in *Christianity for the Toughminded* (Minneapolis, MN: Bethany, 1973), 24–25.

3. In France, the confessional landscape is complicated by the recent (2013) union of Lutheran and Reformed bodies to create a national "Protestant Church"—and in the Alsace by the Lutheran and the Reformed churches having pulpit and altar fellowship with each other. But there still exists a small, French-speaking, confessional Lutheran body, the Eglise Evangélique Luthérienne-Synode de France et de Belgique, in doctrinal fellowship with the Lutheran Church–Missouri Synod in the United States.

4. See John Warwick Montgomery, *The Suicide of Christian Theology* (Minneapolis, MN: Bethany, 1970); Montgomery, *The Shaping of America* (Minneapolis, MN: Bethany, 1976); Montgomery, *Christians in the Public Square* (Calgary, Alberta: Canadian Institute for Law, Theology and Public Policy, 1996).

5. If you want real misery, consider a Norwegian Lutheran church where a *lutefisk* dinner is the great congregational event of the year. I kid you not, having had that culinary experience, which truly represents eating "the Piece of Cod that passeth all understanding."

6. Nicolai Grundtvig, *Kirken den er et gammelt Hus*, trans. Carl Döving (1909), alt. From *The Lutheran Hymnal* (St. Louis, MO: Concordia Publishing House, 1941), 437.

Select Bibliography
for Further Reading

Bainton, Roland. *Here I Stand: A Life of Martin Luther*. New York: Penguin, 1995.

Elert, Werner. *The Christian Ethos*. Eugene, OR: Wipf & Stock, 2004.

Forell, George W. *Faith Active in Love: An Investigation of the Principles Underlying Luther's Social Ethic*. Minneapolis, MN: Augsburg Publishing House, 1964.

Giertz, Bo. *The Hammer of God: A Novel about the Cure of Souls*. Minneapolis, MN: Augsburg Fortress Publishing House, 2005.

Kleinig, John. *Grace upon Grace: Spirituality for Today*. St. Louis, MO: Concordia Publishing House, 2008.

Lazareth, William H. *Luther on the Christian Home: An Application of the Social Ethics of the Reformation*. Whitefish, MT: Literary Licensing, 2011.

Luther, Martin. *What Luther Says*. Edited by Ewald M. Plass. St. Louis, MO: Concordia Publishing House, 2006.

Montgomery, John Warwick. *Crisis in Lutheran Theology*. Bloomington, MN: Bethany House Publishers, 1973.

———, trans. *A Defense of the Lutheran Faith on the Eve of Modern Times: Hector Gottfried Masius' "Défense de la Religion Luthérienne."* Milwaukee, MN: Northwestern Publishing House, forthcoming.

———. *In Defense of Martin Luther*. Milwaukee, MN: Northwestern Publishing House, 1970.

Pieper, Francis. *Christian Dogmatics*. 4 vols. St. Louis, MO: Concordia Publishing House, 2003.

Reed, Luther D. *The Lutheran Liturgy*. Minneapolis, MN: Fortress Press, 1975.

Saarnivaara, Uuras. *Scriptural Baptism: A Dialog between John Bapstead and Martin Childfont*. Eugene, OR: Wipf & Stock, 2003.

Sasse, Hermann. *Here We Stand: Nature and Character of the Lutheran Faith*. St. Louis, MO: Concordia Publishing House, 1988.

———. *This Is My Body: Luther's Contention for the Real Presence in the Sacrament of the Altar*. St. Louis, MO: Concordia Publishing House, 2003.

Senkbeil, Harold. *Dying to Live*. St. Louis, MO: Concordia Publishing House, 1994.

———. *Sanctification: Christ in Action*. Milwaukee, MN: Northwestern Publishing House, 1997.

Stiller, Gunther. *Johann Sebastian Bach and Liturgical Life in Leipzig*. St. Louis, MO: Concordia Publishing House, 1984.

Veith, Gene Edward. *God at Work: Your Christian Vocation in All of Life*. Wheaton, IL: Crossway, 2011.

———. *The Spirituality of the Cross: The Way of the First Evangelicals*. St. Louis, MO: Concordia Publishing House, 2010.

Wingren, Gustaf. *Luther on Vocation*. Eugene, OR: Wipf & Stock, 2004.

Contributors

Adam S. Francisco (Ph.D., Oxford) is associate professor of history and political thought at Concordia University, Irvine, California. He studied Arabic and Islamic theology at the Centre for Islamic Studies at Oxford. He served as Albin Salton Fellow at the University of London's Warburg Institute; assistant professor of history at Concordia College, Bronxville, New York; and visiting professor of historical theology at Concordia Theological Seminary, Fort Wayne, Indiana. He is the author of *Martin Luther and Islam* as well as numerous articles about Islam and Christianity.

Steven A. Hein (Ph.D., St. Louis) currently serves as director of Concordia Institute for Christian Studies, an organization that offers auxiliary educational services to Lutheran congregations and church gatherings across the country. He also serves as associate pastor at Shepherd of the Springs Lutheran Church in Colorado Springs and affiliate professor of theology and ethics at Colorado Christian University. He has previously served for over two decades as a professor of theology at Concordia University, River Forest. He has served on the board of directors of the Consortium for Classical and Lutheran Education and is a contributing editor to the theological journal *Logia: A Journal of Lutheran Theology*. He has published numerous scholarly articles and is a contributor to *A Handbook for Classical Lutheran Education* and *Lives in the Balance: Equipping God's People for the World's Fight and the Soul's Salvation*.

Cameron A. MacKenzie (M.A., Chicago; Ph.D., Notre Dame) is Forrest E. and Frances H. Ellis Professor of Historical Theology, Concordia Theological Seminary, Ft. Wayne, Indiana, and chairman of the department. He is also an ordained clergyman of the Lutheran

Church–Missouri Synod. At Concordia since 1983, he regularly teaches courses in the history of the Christian Church such as Reformation Era, Luther's theology, Calvin and Calvinism, Puritanism and the history of the English Bible. He has published many articles in the field of church history, lectures frequently, and is the author of *The Battle for the Bible in England, 1557–1582.*

Angus Menuge (Ph.D., Wisconsin) is professor of philosophy at Concordia University, Wisconsin. He currently serves as the president of the Evangelical Philosophical Society. His research interests include philosophy of mind, philosophy of science, apologetics, and C. S. Lewis. He earned his Ph.D. in philosophy from the University of Wisconsin–Madison and a diploma in Christian Apologetics from the International Academy of Apologetics, Evangelism and Human Rights, Strasbourg. He is editor of *C. S. Lewis: Lightbearer in the Shadowlands, Christ and Culture in Dialogue, Reading God's World,* and *Legitimizing Human Rights.* He is author of *Agents under Fire: Materialism and the Rationality of Science.*

John Warwick Montgomery (Ph.D., Chicago; D.Théol., Strasbourg; LL.D., Cardiff; D.U.J. [*h.c.*], Institute for Religion and Law, Moscow) is professor emeritus of law and humanities, University of Bedfordshire, England, and director, International Academy of Apologetics, Evangelism and Human Rights, Strasbourg, France (http://www.apologetics academy.eu). He is a US and UK citizen living in England and France. His biography is included in *Who's Who in America, Who's Who in France,* the *European Biographical Directory, Who's Who in the World,* and *Contemporary Authors.* His wife is the internationally renowned harpist Lanalee de Kant. Dr. Montgomery is an ordained Lutheran clergyman, is an English barrister, and is admitted to practice as a lawyer in four American jurisdictions and in the corresponding US federal courts; he is also an *avocat à la cour, Barreau de Paris.* For his success in defending religious liberties before the European Court of Human Rights, he was awarded the Patriarch's Medal of the Romanian Orthodox Church. Dr. Montgomery is the author of over one hundred scholarly journal articles and more than fifty books in English, French, Spanish, and German (http://www.1517legacy.com). He is internationally regarded both as a theologian and as a Christian apologist;

his debates with the late Bishop James Pike, death-of-God advocate Thomas Altizer, and situation-ethicist Joseph Fletcher are historic. His work has been the subject of several academic theses, one of which, by Prof. Dr. Ross Clifford of Australia, has been published as *John Warwick Montgomery's Legal Apologetic: An Apologetic for All Seasons* (Bonn, Germany: VKW). In 2008, he was honored by a 768-page Festschrift, *Tough-Minded Christianity*, edited by William Dembski and Thomas Schirrmacher (Broadman & Holman). Website: http://www.jwm.christendom.co.uk.

Craig Parton (M.A., Simon Greenleaf; J.D., California-Hastings) is a trial lawyer and partner with the oldest law firm in the Western United States (located in Santa Barbara, California). Upon graduation from college, he spent seven years on staff with Campus Crusade for Christ, the last four as national lecturer for Crusade. He traveled to over one hundred universities and colleges across the country defending the Christian faith through lectures and debates. He received his master's degree in Christian apologetics under Dr. John Warwick Montgomery at the Simon Greenleaf School of Law, an institution devoted to the integration of Christian faith and legal reasoning. Mr. Parton then took his juris doctorate at the University of California, Hastings Law School in San Francisco, where he served as executive editor of the law journal *COMM/ENT*. His current academic responsibilities include that of United States director of the International Academy of Apologetics, Evangelism and Human Rights in Strasbourg, France (http://www.apologeticsacademy.eu). He has published articles in both law reviews and numerous theological journals, including *Modern Reformation, Logia: A Journal of Lutheran Theology*, and the *Global Journal of Classical Theology*. Mr. Parton has contributed articles to Festschrifts for both Prof. Dr. John Warwick Montgomery and Prof. Dr. Rod Rosenbladt. He is the author of *The Defense Never Rests: A Lawyer's Quest for the Gospel, Richard Whately: A Man for All Seasons*, and *Religion on Trial*.

Rod Rosenbladt (M.A., Trinity; Ph.D., Strasbourg) is professor of systematic theology and Christian apologetics at Concordia University, Irvine. He is also the cohost of the nationally syndicated radio program *The White Horse Inn*. He has served in California as a staff member with InterVarsity Christian Fellowship and as a parish pastor. He has contributed to several books including *Christianity for the Tough Minded*, *The Agony of Deceit*, and *Christ the Lord*. Also noteworthy is his lecture that became a viral video, "The Gospel for Those Broken by the Church."

Harold L. Senkbeil (M.Div., S.T.M, Concordia Theological Seminary) is the executive director for spiritual care for DOXOLOGY (http://www.doxology.us) since 2008. He served as parish pastor for thirty-one years prior to joining the faculty of Concordia Theological Seminary, Fort Wayne, Indiana, as associate professor of pastoral ministry and missions from 2002 to 2008. Pastor Senkbeil is the author of several books, including *Dying to Live: The Power of Forgiveness* and *Sanctification: Christ in Action*. He has served the Lutheran Church–Missouri Synod in a number of capacities, including the LCMS Commission on Theology and Church Relations (1998–2002) and the Concordia Seminary, St. Louis Board of Regents (2011–present).

Uwe Siemon-Netto (Ph.D., Boston) is an international journalist from Germany. He has been a reporter with the Associated Press; a staff correspondent of Germany's Axel Springer publishing group in London, New York, Vietnam, and the Middle East; a North American correspondent of *Stern Magazine*; and religion editor of United Press International. He holds a Ph.D. in theology and sociology of religion from Boston University and an honorary D.Litt. from Concordia Seminary, St. Louis. He is the author of *The Fabricated Luther: Refuting Nazi Connections and Other Modern Myths*, *The Acquittal of God: A Theology for Vietnam Veterans*, and *Triumph of the Absurd: A Reporter's Love of the Abandoned People of Vietnam*.

Gene Edward Veith (Ph.D., Kansas) has been professor of literature, provost, and interim president at Patrick Henry College. He previously served as the culture editor of *World Magazine*. He was on the faculty for nineteen years as professor of English at Concordia University, Wisconsin, where he also served as the dean of the School of Arts and Sciences. He has also taught at Northeastern Oklahoma A&M College and has been a visiting professor at the Estonian

Institute of Humanities, Gordon-Conwell, Regent College (Vancouver), and Wheaton College. In addition, he also serves as the director of the Cranach Institute at Concordia Theological Seminary in Ft. Wayne, Indiana. He has been a fellow at the Capital Research Center and the Heritage Foundation. Dr. Veith received his B.A. in letters (literature, philosophy, history, and classics) from the University of Oklahoma and his M.A. and Ph.D. in English from the University of Kansas. He was awarded honorary doctorates from Concordia Theological Seminary and Concordia University, Irvine. He is the author of over twenty books on topics involving Christianity and culture, classical education, literature, theology, and the arts. They include *The Spirituality of the Cross, God at Work, Postmodern Times, The State of the Arts, Modern Fascism, Classical Education,* and *Loving God with All Your Mind.*

Todd Wilken (M.Div., Concordia) is the host of the national radio program *Issues, Etc.* He also serves as assistant pastor at Trinity Lutheran Church in Millstadt, Illinois. He has served as a guest instructor for Christ Academy at Concordia Theological Seminary, Fort Wayne, Indiana, and for the International Academy of Apologetics, Evangelism and Human Rights in Strasbourg, France. He has written articles for numerous publications, including *The Lutheran Witness, Modern Reformation,* and *Higher Things.* He is author of the booklet *Same-Sex Marriage: Facing the Question* and has served as editor for the *Doctrine and Practice* and *The Issues, Etc., Journal.*

CPSIA information can be obtained
at www.ICGtesting.com
Printed in the USA
LVOW01*0056200117
521607LV00007B/43/P